Class, Sports, and Social Development

Richard Gruneau, PhD
Simon Fraser University

Library of Congress Cataloging-in-Publication Data

Gruneau, Richard S., 1948-
    Class, sports, and social development / by Richard Gruneau.
        p. cm.
    Includes bibliographical references (p.   ) and index.
    ISBN 0-7360-0033-X
    1. Sports--Social aspects.   2. Sociology.   3. Sports--Social
aspects--Canada.   I. Title.
    GV706.5.G78   1999
    306.4'83--dc21   98-40543
                                                                              CIP

ISBN: 0-7360-0033-X

Permission notices for material reprinted in this book from other sources can be found on page 181.

Acquisitions Editor: Steve Pope; **Managing Editor**: Cynthia McEntire; **Assistant Editor**: Kim Thoren; **Graphic Designer**: Nancy Rasmus; **Graphic Artist**: Sandra Meier; **Cover Designer**: Buerkett Marketing; **Printer**: Versa Press

Printed in the United States of America

10   9   8   7   6   5   4   3   2   1

Human Kinetics
Web site: http://www.humankinetics.com/

United States: Human Kinetics
P.O. Box 5076, Champaign, IL 61825-5076
1-800-747-4457
e-mail: humank@hkusa.com

Canada: Human Kinetics
475 Devonshire Road Unit 100, Windsor, ON N8Y 2L5
1-800-465-7301 (in Canada only)
e-mail: humank@hkcanada.com

Europe: Human Kinetics
P.O. Box IW14, Leeds LS16 6TR, United Kingdom
(44) 1132 781708
e-mail: humank@hkeurope.com

Australia: Human Kinetics
57A Price Avenue, Lower Mitcham, South Australia 5062
(088) 277 1555
e-mail: humank@hkaustralia.com

New Zealand: Human Kinetics
P.O. Box 105-231, Auckland 1
(09) 523 3462
e-mail: humank@hknewz.com

For Shelley

contents

foreword to the 1999 edition

What leaps from the pages of this book, fifteen years after it was first published, is its confidence, its intellectual and political verve. The author obviously felt that he was tackling an issue of importance in providing a social analysis of sports. In this he had to overcome a rooted assumption—still present in much cultural analysis—that sport was a trivial matter, something on the sidelines of human existence, and hardly worth attention by serious intellectuals.

Gruneau set about the task with vigor, impatiently pushing aside obstacles, objections, diversions. The book tackles tremendous theoretical issues—it is a treatise on social theory almost as much as a treatise on sports. It does this not in a spirit of arrogance, but in the certainty that these problems should, and would, yield to persistent questioning.

The intellectual moment of the late 1970s and early 1980s certainly shaped the book. Its theoretical ideas rest on the "new left" critique of mainstream sociology, a critique which had revealed the thinness of survey-driven positivism and the hollowness of functionalist social theory. In conventional social science there was little to be found that would illuminate the realities of sport.

Like many others at the time, Gruneau was a radical in search of a framework. He could not accept the orthodoxies of Marxism, including the structuralist Marxism so influential at the time he wrote. But he was committed to the project of a democratic social transformation, radical transformation on the large scale. He judged the contributions of conservatives, liberals, and radicals alike by that yardstick.

The book was written at an historical moment when speaking to intellectuals seemed to matter. The text is uncompromisingly highbrow—and that made it very rare in writing about sports! Gruneau had no self-consciousness about elitism, and had no skepticism about "grand narratives." He discussed discipline in sport, but did not assume that theoretical discourse itself might have a disciplinary function. At that time Foucault was just becoming a presence in English-language cultural theory, and was far from being the dominant presence he has since become.

Nevertheless Gruneau wrote about sport against an intellectual background, indeed against a tradition which he both claimed and criticized. One of the best things in the book is his nuanced appraisal of Huizinga, and his careful appropriation of the valuable themes from the debates within which Huizinga was positioned. Gruneau transformed ideas about play and creativity into a far more sophisticated social analysis than the literature on sport had ever seen—and conversely, provided the social sciences with a language for talking about a whole field of human life they had mostly ignored.

Theory is the key to Gruneau's work, but he also had an empirical story to tell. This was about the historical development of sport in Canada. The offering in *Class, Sports, and Social Development* was undoubtedly schematic, though it was a fruitful starting point. This has been shown by the author's later work, such as the splendid social, political, and cultural analysis of the growth of ice hockey as an industry in the jointly authored (with David Whitson) book *Hockey Night in Canada*. Thinking historically about sports was the right way to go.

But what kind of history was required? In his attempt to construct an undogmatic progressive standpoint, Gruneau turned to the work of historians like Edward Thompson and Raymond Williams. British "cultural Marxism" of this kind represented an alternative to structuralism which has been rather sidelined by the growth of post-structuralism in the manner of Foucault. But it was exciting at the time and had possibilities only gradually being realized in more recent work on race and gender.

However, neither Thompson or Williams (any more than Foucault) had much to say about colonialism. The intellectuals of the 1960s and 1970s who did—such as Samir Amin or Immanuel Wallerstein—were not on Gruneau's reading list. The result was a historical study of sport that was less distinctively Canadian than it might have been. Though Gruneau talked about colonialism as an empirical fact of Canadian history, this did not register as a conceptual issue. *Class, Sports, and Social Development* has little sense of imperialism as a system, nor of sport as part of a world structure of hegemony in social relations.

Other structures that, from the perspective of the late 1990s, are underemphasized in *Class, Sports, and Social Development* are gender and race. Almost all the activities discussed in the book are in fact men's sports. In recent years this point has come into focus. There is now a lively and incisive feminist literature problematising women's position in sports culture and sports institutions, and a feminist-influenced literature analyzing the masculinity of the dominant sports and the role of sports in the social construction of western masculinities.

Similarly, issues of race and ethnicity hardly figure in the book's analysis, except that racial minorities are counted among the disadvantaged. Though Gruneau cited in passing C.L.R. James's wonderful book *Beyond a Boundary*, which evokes the race politics of international and local cricket, the study did not register the striking cultural dynamics by which disadvantaged ethnic groups become recruiting grounds for certain forms of elite sports.

Paradoxically, then, Gruneau wrote a good book about sports without saying very much at all about *bodies*. The whole framework of discussion was, in that respect, surprisingly abstract. Embodiment was, perhaps, still seen as a rather esoteric philosophical problem, or perhaps questions about bodies were avoided because they were the chosen territory of the rather stupid school of biological determinism which had christened itself "sociobiology." But the lack of attention to embodiment was a weakness in the materialist class analysis Gruneau based his work on, and a reason why that framework has largely been replaced by a style of thought emphasizing discourse, social regulation, and identity.

Yet Gruneau's approach had strengths lacking in more recent works. He had a firm understanding that the activities and experiences we call "sports" were increasingly contained within institutions, themselves embedded in large-scale social structures. It follows that we can understand the activities and experiences at a personal level only by examining the dynamics of the structures at the societal level. Gruneau had a firm understanding that the patterns of sporting activity were not fixed; they were produced in history by specific and intelligible combinations of social forces. He insisted that these processes had to be grasped historically, and that they could be changed in history.

So *Class, Sports, and Social Development* still has important lessons. Above all, its intellectual vigor and optimism are impressive. It expresses a deep conviction that we can understand even the most opaque, marginalized, or complex of issues, and that our understanding can contribute to making the human world a better place for humans to live in.

R.W. Connell
University of Sydney

foreword to the 1983 edition

Richard Gruneau is one of a small number of contributors to the growing field of "sport studies" who is also a superior sociologist. He is no narrow specialist, and in earlier publications already has established strong credentials as a student of social theory, as a young scholar whose works are enhanced by careful attention to historical context, and as a sociologist whose writings wear both the scientific and humanistic faces of his discipline. This is to say, I would suggest, that Gruneau works in the vineyard of what C. Wright Mills called the "classic tradition." These virtues are manifest in the present volume.

Class, Sports, and Social Development, in my view, is a major contribution to the sociology of sport—and a good deal more. The introductory discussion of "the break from classical theory" and sociology's "crisis" displays Gruneau's command of present-day theoretical issues and brings out clearly his own nondoctrinaire theoretical perspective: here is a prolegomenon that would serve for studies of diverse institutional and cultural complexes—popular culture, say, or the mass media, or even "higher education," as well as modern sport. The perspective derives in part from Karl Marx, Max Weber, and Thorstein Veblen, and Gruneau's contemporary mentors include T.O. Bottomore, Anthony Giddens, Stephen Lukes, John Rex, and the historian-critics E.P. Thompson and Raymond Williams. As I have noted elsewhere, "his affinity for these British notables is due in part to his Canadian nationality, but has a stronger root in his admiration of radically inclined, theoretically sophisticated, historically informed scholars who write with skill and unpretentiousness" (*Fifty Years in the Sociological Enterprise: A Lucky Journey* [Amherst, University of Massachusetts Press, 1982], p. 253). The abiding concerns of these writers are the historical emergence of modern capitalist society, its social structure and social conflicts, and especially the strategic role of class divisions in social development. These are also Gruneau's concerns.

Throughout the volume Gruneau confronts a theoretical (and indeed existential) problem that I believe to be the central issue in the analysis of social life and social change. This is what he early refers to as "the dialectical relationship between socially structured possibilities and human agency." Like Marx in the past (in some of his work) and, for example, Giddens today, Gruneau rejects a view of human action as mechanically determined by social structure: men and women are not merely reactors to the circumstances of history. But, again in the footsteps of his mentors, he focuses the study on the powerful role of class divisions and class conflict in shaping institutional and cultural arrangements. Thus, in keeping with this dialectic, in the final chapter he refers to "the basic relationships in society between sports, human freedom, and constraint" and concludes the book with the assertion that "progress in the sociology of sport depends primarily upon our capacities to make the critique of sports a part of the much broader attempt to discern the alternatives within which human reason and freedom can make history." This admonition clearly holds for the critical study of *all* social development.

In a ground-clearing exercise (remindful of Emile Durkheim's stratagem), Gruneau launches the analysis of sport by evaluating alternative theoretical interpretations. A large part of the discussion of "problems of agency and freedom in play, games, and sport" (chapter 1) is exegesis and critique of Johan Huizinga's *Homo Ludens,* Michael Novak's *The Joy of Sports,* Jean-Marie Brohm's *Sport: A Prison of Measured Time,* and Allen Guttman's *From Ritual to Record.* He dissects these diverse studies— which range from Huizinga's classic on play as the universal manifestation of human agency, to Novak's idealistic "theology" of modern sport as a "metaphorical statement about human possibilities," to Brohm's materialistic and vulgar neo-Marxist portraiture, to Guttman's anti-Marxist, allegedly Weberian, and "liberal" interpretation—with perspicacity, marked by both appreciation of the contributions of these provocative books and keen awareness of their limitations. This critical examination of an important body of literature on modern sport also reveals, in passing, Gruneau's own theoretical perspective.

Elaboration of this perspective is only one of several themes that Gruneau addresses in chapter 2. With reference to play, games, and sport (and to other spheres of human endeavor), he explicates the volume's central thesis: that "unequally distributed resources are . . . the key features of social life which link problems of human agency to problems of structural change." In the course of developing this thesis, however, Gruneau takes the reader through learned (but, for me, overly abstract) discussions of the phenomenological construction of reality as a "fundamental element of all human activity," symbolic interactionism and the study of sport, games and sport as "a part of material production by knowledgeable human agents," constitutive and regulative rules of the game, and the "transformative capacity" of players and nonplayers—these among other complex subjects. He turns to the main thesis in a long section on "sport, class inequality, and social reproduction" in which works by Giddens, Williams, and Paul Willis are ably exploited in elucidating both the hegemonic role of class and creative counter-pressures in the development of sport in capitalist societies—again, the dialectic between social structure and human agency. In a further section on "the general theory of industrial society" Gruneau extends the analysis of class and sport in the context of a strong critique of the pioneer work of Veblen as well as the works of such contemporaries as Daniel Bell and Ralf Dahrendorf. Here then is a jam-packed chapter.

Chapter 3 on class, sport, and social development in Canada is something more than an "outline," Gruneau's modest term. He makes extensive use of the research of other scholars, with special attention to the recent studies of Alan Metcalfe. But the portrayal of four "critical phases" in the history of Canadian sport, extending from the games of colonial times to the state-supervised sports of the present day, includes cogent observations on a large variety of such relevant matters as the "profane" practices of the rank-and-file in opposition to class-controlled standards, taverns and gambling, cricket versus football, amateurism versus professionalism (an especially fine analysis), commercial sport, sport and social mobility, organized labor and sport, the strong influence of the United States patterns, the mass media, and the "limits and pressures of state sport." This case history, like the book as a whole, contains many riches.

The last chapter on the "limits and possibilities of modern sport" is in part a recapitulation of the book's guiding thesis, the interactive roles of social structure and human agency in social development, and in part a summary of and brief addendum to the Canadian case. The "final note" underscores Gruneau's value orientation, which I share. For here he lauds the "profane side of play" and calls for a greater degree of autonomy in the world of sport, which is within the realm of human agency.

I suspect that Gruneau's critical evaluation of class dominance in sport and his strong support of sport's "emergent" and "oppositional" side have at least some anchorage in the fact that he writes not merely as a first-rate humanistic sociologist, but as a perceptive insider. His athletic prowess is well known in Canada and elsewhere—he has won kudos in skiing on both snow and water, swimming, football, and no doubt other ludic and agonistic pastimes. He has written a book that all serious students of sport should read. And those sociologists who do not do so will be the losers.

Charles H. Page

acknowledgments

This book owes a great deal to exchanges I have had over the last few years with colleagues and students at Queen's University. I especially want to thank Dave Neice, Hart Cantelon, Rob Beamish, Bob Hollands, and Kevin Whitaker whose critical insights have helped to refine and clarify my thinking. Thanks are also due to Alan Ingham for his frequent and stimulating long-distance phone calls, and to Charles Page, John Loy, Curt Tausky, and Bill Connolly for their supportive involvement with an earlier draft of the manuscript. I also want to express my gratitude to Lee Wetherall who shared the emotional burden of this book during its early stages, and to Don Macintosh, Terry Willett, and Bob Pike for helping to create an ideal work environment at Queen's.

Much of the final work on the book was conducted in 1980-81 while I was on leave in Vancouver, British Columbia. I want to acknowledge the support of the Canadian Social Sciences and Humanities Research Council for a fellowship that provided me with the resources necessary to finish the project. Eric Dunning and Brian Sutton-Smith read parts of an early version of the book and made suggestions that were useful in later revisions. Greg Vaz, Susan Steele, Aniko Varpalotai, and Wally Clement contributed empirical material that was later incorporated into the outline of the social development of Canadian sport presented in chapter 3. I also want to thank Alan Metcalfe for his help with historical sources, and Bob Morford for providing me with office space and other necessities while I was in British Columbia. Special thanks should also go to Bob Sparks and Cathy Guild for their hospitality and for those nights at Jerry's Cove. Thanks should go as well to Dick Martin for his enthusiastic support of the project, and to Dorothy Daley for typing the final draft of the manuscript. This typing was funded through a grant provided by the Queen's School of Graduate Studies and Research. Finally, and most important, I want to thank Shelley Bentley for her perceptive comments on stylistic matters and for generally tolerating the indulgence that this book represents.

introduction

Several years ago, during one of many coffee sessions that accompany my teaching, I was taken to task by a group of students for including Johan Huizinga's *Homo Ludens* and Thorstein Veblen's *The Theory of the Leisure Class* as required reading in their course. Why was it necessary, they asked, to read books written so long ago and with such little relevance to the present day when there exists so much more current and seemingly applicable material? I responded, a bit defensively perhaps, by suggesting that these books were "classics" in sport and leisure studies and should be read for that reason.

I had to admit, however, that this was not much of an answer, and I began to question some things I had always taken for granted. Why *did* I include writings by Huizinga and Veblen in my courses in leisure studies and the sociology of sport? Was it because the actual theories these writers developed were really so relevant or necessary to an understanding of sports and leisure in contemporary capitalist societies? Was it because I had been required to read these writers in graduate school and was unconsciously subjecting my students to the same tasks that had been set for me? Neither of these explanations struck me as very satisfactory.

More plausible answers began to reveal themselves in the midst of some research I was conducting on the socioeconomic backgrounds of executives in Canadian sports organizations. While doing background reading for this research, it occurred to me that the main reason I continued to include the works of Huizinga and Veblen in my courses was because I had always found them so useful in shaping and giving direction to my own work. Time and again I began the reading for new research projects with selections from *Homo Ludens* and *The Theory of the Leisure Class*. I did this not because of any real attraction to the actual theories developed by Huizinga and Veblen, but because their writings offered both a constant source of intellectual stimulation and a valuable point of reference for developing new ideas. What continually attracted me to Huizinga and Veblen was the kind of problems they were trying to resolve and certain features of the style of inquiry they had adopted.

Recognizing this point, however, raised a whole set of new issues. For it seemed that a good deal of my own work—and much of the work done by others on sports and leisure in capitalist societies—actually ignored these problems and had basically withdrawn from a "classical" style of inquiry. Why had this occurred? Was it because the kinds of problems raised by Huizinga and Veblen had all been resolved? Was it because their particular style of work was outdated or completely passé? I was convinced that the answer to such questions was no, and this conviction strengthened my growing sense of uneasiness about the current state of theory and research in the sociology of sport.

I soon realized that many other people interested in the sociological study of sports and leisure were struggling with similar concerns. For example, throughout the 1970s at conference sessions devoted to the sociology of sport, there was a growing cry that something was fundamentally wrong with much of the work in the field. According to some people, the field faced a crisis of relevance because it lacked any substantial body of applied research. Others took the opposite view, arguing that the sociology of sport was too applied, too focused on practical questions about sport and not sufficiently concerned with the meaning of sport in society. Still others argued that the problem was one of method and theoretical approach. The crisis in the sociology of sport was tied to the positivist tendencies and structural-functionalist premises that supposedly permeated theory and research in the area.

Among these different diagnoses and the prescriptions that accompanied them were some important insights, some unfortunate excesses, and a good deal of general thrashing about. Yet, despite it all, there did not emerge any kind of consensus about the nature of the problems affecting the field. For that reason, I was particularly interested in 1978 when three leading researchers in the sociology of sport published a monograph-length "state of the art" survey on the development of the subdiscipline.[1] Two of these researchers, John Loy and Gerald Kenyon, have been very influential in promoting the sociology of sport over the last fifteen years, and I found it especially significant that they should comment in their survey on the unevenness of the literature and suggest how "progress" in the field has not been so great as they had hoped in the late 1960s. One of the major factors that Loy, Kenyon, and their co-researcher, Barry McPherson, identified to explain this lack of progress was the inability of the field to attract a sufficiently large "critical mass" of active researchers. That is, there have simply not been enough people committed to the sociology of sport to build an adequate base of quality research.

Perhaps there is some truth to this explanation, but I was not convinced that increasing the critical mass of researchers would necessarily resolve any of the problems affecting the field. I felt very strongly that the whole question of progress in the sociology of sport went well beyond questions of numerical strength and much deeper than the kinds of criticisms that had been put forward throughout the 1970s. What the field badly needed, it seemed to me, was a much different kind of critical inquiry: a critique that aimed to get to the root of things, one that challenged dominant conceptions and provided new points of departure for debate and new directions for analysis.

My primary objective in this study is to provide such a critique and develop a set of guidelines for reorienting studies of the nature and role of sport in western capitalist societies. I also want to indicate how these guidelines might be put to use in a preliminary case study of the social development of Canadian sport. By pursuing these objectives I hope to show that adequate responses to concerns about the fruitfulness and future directions of work in the sociology of sport will not be found in parochial or intramural debate, but rather in a renewed attempt to situate the study of sport in the mainstream of the sociological enterprise and to formulate new research initiatives based on a sensitivity to the best features of sociology's classical tradition.

Framing the Problem

Any critically oriented study ought to begin with a general statement about the kinds of problems that have led one to conduct the study, and about those that need to be taken up in the analysis itself. Attention must also be paid to the fundamental assumptions that underlie the perspective one chooses. I want to go on now and outline these problems and assumptions as they relate to the analysis developed in later chapters. Given that I have already tipped my hand somewhat, it should come as no surprise that I consider one of the basic problems in the sociology of sport to be a general withdrawal from certain "classical" research questions and from the style of analysis that has most often accompanied them. Much more, however, needs to be said about this. For it is my contention that this and other problems in the sociology of sport are actually exaggerated manifestations of much broader crises in contemporary sociology—crises that, ironically enough, are reflected in the very growth and popularity of "sport sociology" as a distinct subfield within the parent discipline. To clarify this argument it is necessary to turn our attention away from the sociology of sport for the moment and consider some key issues in the development of sociological writing over the last century.

Norman Birnbaum has argued that one of the most significant qualities of early sociological writing was its synthetic character.[2] Sociology did not spring full-blown into the nineteenth century complete with its own concepts and points of orientation. Rather,

> it brought political philosophy up to date by attempting to objectify some of the moral dilemmas which preoccupied that sort of inquiry. That is, it historicized conflicts which were once depicted as immutable. From political economy, sociology drew the idea of the novelty, the magnitude of the market. History gave it a sense of movement, of sequence. Social statistics, finally, supplied the elements of a concrete description of the armature of the new society. We may yet put the matter another way. Sociology attempted a description of a new social formation *sui generis*. That description, however, was fused to analysis—which derived statements about the new social behaviour and social process. The principles, however, were often enough expressions of conceptions historically specific to the nineteenth century society. The synthesis, briefly, rested upon the delicacy and justice of the historical perceptions of the first sociologists. We should not be surprised that no sooner promulgated, the synthesis began to break down.[3]

This breakdown of the synthesis which comprised the bulk of classical social theory, Birnbaum goes on to suggest, was essentially related to the inevitable "movement of society." The particular forces that had been integral in shaping sociology's first great theoretical formulations appeared to become transformed as "new densities, new mechanisms and new institutions" emerged in the late nineteenth and early twentieth centuries. The fact that the synthesis—upon which these formulations rested—seemed tied to social conditions which were in a state of considerable upheaval, logically led to a number of reevaluations of sociology's future analytic directions.

Students of the history of social thought have generally pointed to two main concerns underlying such reevaluations. First, the institutionalization of sociology as a bona fide academic discipline in the late nineteenth century seemed to necessitate a rejection of the encyclopedianism of the discipline's "first synthesis" and a more careful delimitation of the specific frames of reference for sociological analysis. Second, the legitimacy of sociological theorizing seemed increasingly reliant upon the degree to which social theory could break from the ideologically inspired philosophy of history and romanticized social reformism that had hitherto defined so much of the sociological tradition. Using these standards, it became more broadly accepted that the progress of social thought in the modern era would lie less with the synthetic evolutionary historicism and philosophical orientation of early classical theory than with the intellectual advances occurring *within* sociology itself, by virtue of the logical and empirical analysis of the sociological method.[4]

Anthony Giddens has noted that many sociologists have tended to regard these developments as a kind of watershed in the naturation of sociological thinking.[5] It has been widely accepted that if the signpost for sociology's development in the nineteenth century pointed primarily to Comte, Marx, or Spencer, it later came to point toward the analytic convergence found in the writings of those early twentieth-century theorists whose work involved a self-conscious attempt to elaborate on methodological principles—notably, Emile Durkheim and Max Weber. Yet, Giddens goes on to argue that if the designation of Durkheim and Weber as harbingers of a "modern" sociology is essentially accurate, there is considerable danger in exaggerating the extent to which their work represents a clean break from the analytic concerns of early classical theory. Each author sought, ultimately, to come to terms with the forces that had destroyed feudal society and stimulated the growth of industrial capitalism, and each was deeply interested in reconciling the dilemmas posed by capitalist industrialism for the optimal expression of human capacities. In other words, the analyses of both authors revolved around a deep concern about concrete historical paths of social development. Giddens suggests that the tendency to underestimate this concern in assessing the theoretical significance of either Durkheim or Weber has often led to distorted interpretations of the important links that each author maintained with the analytic traditions of early classical theory.

One of the most notable of these distortions was Talcott Parsons's devaluation of the focus on historical process and development in Durkheim and Weber in favor of a search through their work for an imminent universal framework for sociological theory. Giddens claims that this emphasis in Parsons's famous book *The Structure of Social Action* was put forward with such technical sophistication that it lent credence to the view that the most modern, most "progressive," analytic elements in Weber and Durkheim were their contributions to the creation of an autonomous and "objective" social science that transcended history and philosophy.[6] The increasing popularity of this view helped clear the way for the widespread incorporation of "action theory" and for a positivist conception of the sociological method into the mainstream of social science.

It is somewhat ironic that the development of these particular emphases in sociological thinking seemed to be realized most fully in the United States—especially during the 1940s and 1950s. Morton White's work on American social thought indicates that many early American social scientists had been greatly attracted to certain features of sociology's "first synthesis" in a widespread rejection of European formalism.[7] Yet, ultimately a large part of American sociology succumbed in the post-war era to the revived formalism of Parsonian action theory and the premises involved in structural-functional analysis. Accompanying this transformation, and in keeping with the "watershed" model of sociology's development, post-war social research continued to recede from the focus on social and cultural development that had characterized the writings of the "fathers" of American social thought.[8] The evolutionary traditions of the Social Darwinists, or the developmental ideals expressed in the writings of Thorstein Veblen, for example, were largely rejected in order to accommodate a more modest "scientific" concern for status and lifestyle and the research methods best suited to addressing these topics.

Many writers have speculated that the affluence and optimism of post-war American life provided an especially favorable environment for such changes in the analytic directions of social theory and research. The old social orders of early industrial America appeared to have fallen, ideology had seemingly "ended," and the status-striving and changing lifestyles of Americans appeared badly in need of analysis. In this environment, the synthetic character of American sociology itself became fragmented with the growth of a myriad of subsociologies, each devoted to the study of isolated aspects of American life and unified only by the borrowing of general theories which could be applied in order to make situation-specific analysis appear meaningful. The "mass society" interpretation of post-war America that became so popular during the 1950s was especially notable in stimulating the growth of a number of new *cultural* subsociologies: the sociology of literature, music, the arts, and, most significant for the analysis which follows, sports.[9]

But the growth of increasingly self-contained research areas, and the parallel emphasis on general theory and statistical study that character- ized so much of post-war American sociology, did not occur without a great deal of criticism. If the neopositivists and action theorists in post- war American sociology had necessarily rejected the historicism, norma- tive underpinnings, and encyclopedic character of Marxism or Darwinism, there were many sociologists who were equally critical of the extremes to which positivism and the general theory of action had been pushed. To some writers, notably C. Wright Mills, the popularity of ahistorical grand theory, of trivialized forms of abstracted empiricism, and of the bureau- cratized parceling-up of sociological analysis, represented less an ad- vance in sociological theory and methods than an abdication of all that was significant in the discipline's rich classical tradition. In the view of others, such as Alvin Gouldner, Irving Horowitz, and a generation of more orthodox Marxist writers, the popularity of an ideologically neutered structural-functionalism had simply allowed much post-war sociology to become little more than a handmaiden of the status quo.[10]

Such criticisms of the dominant tendencies of post-war American sociology had a tremendous effect on the generation of sociology stu- dents, who began their education in the 1960s. As one of those students, I can recall being raised on a steady diet of Parsons versus Gouldner or, according to some of my more traditionally minded professors, Mills versus everybody. At least one result of all of this criticism was that large numbers of sociology teachers and their students began to reexamine some of the fundamental premises of post-war social thought. At the level of research, for example, the withering criticism of the reductionist tendencies of post-war neopositivism leveled by Mills and others seemed to reawaken a concern for the sociohistorical and comparative analysis of whole societies.[11] Similarly, at the level of theory, this concern seemed to be complemented by a clear-cut attempt to depart from the Parsonian version of action theory and the assumptions involved in structural- functional analysis.[12] Because of these developments, over the past two decades sociology has witnessed a partial renaissance of its synthetic interdisciplinary character and the growth of new directions in contem- porary theory.

Yet, despite this partial renaissance and growth of new theoretical directions, there has been an ongoing concern that the discipline remains in a state of crisis. Such views may derive a degree of substance from the numbers of sociologists who appear to have retained an intransigent commitment to the tired theoretical orthodoxies of the forties and fifties, but these people increasingly seem to be the exception rather than the rule. What is more troubling is that few of the new directions in social theory and methods that have developed over the past twenty years have proven satisfactory in enhancing our understanding of the important social and political conflicts of our age. I am persuaded by Giddens's argument, for example, that the move over the past twenty years to complement structural-functionalism with "conflict theory" has offered few insights into the dynamics of the advanced societies beyond those generated by structural functionalism or orthodox Marxism.[13] Similarly, Giddens notes how attempts to reshape certain forms of functional analysis into new technocratic and "post-industrial" theories have repeatedly been shown to be severely limited by their failure to explain the upsurge of ideological conflicts in the West and the undeniable persistence of scarcity, class inequality, and domination. An even more problematic response to the dominant perspectives of post-war social thought, Giddens continues, has been the resurgence of a "crude voluntarism" which, despite some notable exceptions, has resulted in a general "retreat" from institutional analysis in sociological writing.[14] In a widespread attempt to recast sociology only in the form of phenomenological or ethnomethodological analysis, the central problems of contemporary life have not been seen to take the form of broad "issues" or "crises" of social development; rather, these problems seem to lie simply with the mechanisms by which human beings socially construct their phenomenological expressions of everyday life.

In response to all of this one can say that a continuing state of unrest seems to be one of the only constants in the development of sociological thinking during this century. At the very least, one might argue that there is a great diversity in the explanations for this state of unrest and an equally great diversity in the solutions to it—solutions that often seem to shift and change with the times. For example, I think few people today would reduce the "crisis" in post-war sociology to the bourgeois status of the disciplines' "domain assumptions," or to the conservatism of leading theorists, as Gouldner has done. Nor would there be much support for arguing that the problem is exclusively related to such things as the inability of sociology to generate a universally accepted scientific paradigm or, alternatively, to the failure of sociology to free itself from positivistic dogma. Although the current problems with sociological analysis may stem in part from the ideological character of a good deal of sociological writing and, perhaps to a similar degree, from the dilemmas in the philosophy of science which continually dog sociological theorizing, there has been a growing movement among modern social theorists to search out causes for these problems in other areas.[15]

Lodged among the many criticisms that have come out of this movement in recent years are two tendencies that I believe are of paramount significance. Each is in some way related to the inability of sociologists in all areas of the discipline to free themselves from theories and research strategies that have allowed for the absence or misrepresentation of a focus on social development in sociological writing.

The first tendency has been alluded to already. As sociology has lost its classical synthetic character, as it has progressively mapped out its own acceptable subject matter and methods, and, more recently, as it has become fragmented into numerous professionally supported subsociologies, there has been a growing tendency to substitute narrow subdisciplinary problems of research for the broad problems of human possibility and social development that stimulated the first great contributions to sociological theory. Furthermore, these subdisciplinary problems of research have often been approached in a way that separates the necessity of conducting any kind of evaluative or interpretive analysis from the demands of empirical study.

The second problem tendency is related to the first but is more focused. That is, even when sociologists actually have returned to the study of social development, they have been hamstrung by their heavy reliance on abstract typologies whose foundations rest on a seriously limited "general theory" of industrial society.[16]

The nature of this second tendency requires clarification. The "general theory" of industrial society to which I am referring is not really a conception that can be tied to any one author; rather, it is a composite of ideas drawn from a great variety of sources. It has its origins as far back as Saint-Simon and Comte, but its contemporary (and supposedly more advanced) forms can be located in a line of continuity that runs from Durkheim and Weber, in the early years of the twentieth century, to Raymond Aron, Ralf Dahrendorf, and Daniel Bell in the fifties and sixties.[17] The industrial society, the argument runs, can be set off from "traditional" society as a qualitatively different form of social organization that emerged in response to a number of important transitional processes—such as technological developments in production, population pressures related to an expended surplus, and changes in values organized around the rise of individualist and utilitarian philosophies. Because technology and the growth of technical knowledge are axial principles in this general theory, it is usually suggested that the future of industrial society and the quality of life within it will be determined primarily by elaborations that will occur within the corpus of the basic technical structure of modern life. Inasmuch as it is assumed that past types of society have been understood and accurately classified, and that the structure and logic of "modern" society are essentially known, the study of development becomes limited to two possibilities: (1) charting the nature of the social and cultural elaborations that are occurring within the basic technical structure of advanced societies; or (2) tracing the passage of "undeveloped" societies to circumstances characterized by greater complexity.

At issue here is not the empirical content of this general theory so much as the implicit limitations it contains for any kind of renewed understanding of social development. Industrial society is depicted ideal-typically in a way that seems to foreclose the possibility of any radically new form of social organization developing out of the basic framework of industrial life (for example, socialism). Furthermore, the analytic categories that underlie the "theory" have often taken on an axiomatic, universalistic, and sometimes evolutionary character that have served to close off rather than open up empirical and theoretical inquiry.[18] Classical Weberian and Durkheimian conceptions about types of rationality or social solidarity, for example, have often become transformed into static, ahistorical conceptions in a way that neither Weber nor Durkheim ever intended. Conceived in such a way, these categories have readily contributed to a general theory which has proven to be manifestly impoverished in explaining the highly variable and persistent nature of the economic and political conflicts which continue to characterize the industrial societies. For example, little in the general theory of industrial society helps explain why France and Italy have been especially prone to recurrent revolutionary political activity when England has not, or—to use an example more relevant to the study at hand—why there are such fundamental differences in the ways "modern" sports have developed their unique forms of institutional and cultural expression in Canada, Britain, and the United States.

We can summarize the key issue here in the following way: when the study of development is limited to the analysis of movement from one (apparently) known state to another—for instance, from "traditional" to "industrial" or even from "industrial" to "post-industrial" society—then we are a considerable distance from understanding the nature of the problems that underlay sociology's "first synthesis," and that later stimulated the theoretical and empirical analyses of Durkheim, Weber, and their contemporaries. We are even further from any effective rethinking of sociological theory. Indeed, to paraphrase Giddens, this particular approach to problems of social development seems little more than the lingering ghost of "action theory" and of a renewed formalism that repeatedly passes for concrete study. The "traditional" patterns of class-based societies are continually compared to the technocratic and homogeneous character of the industrial societies, as if this comparison between ideal-types automatically and accurately describes the line of development in all industrial societies and in all institutional settings.[19]

In theory, one might expect Marxism to provide an effective counterbalance to these tendencies, for Marx always emphasized the unfolding of human potentialities through class conflicts in development and the necessary role of history in the understanding of social life. However, if this emphasis has always been implicit in Marx's writings, it has not always been evident in the writings of his "interpreters."[20] This is not to say that Marx's many interpreters have rarely done justice to his method, although this case has often been argued. Rather, the point is that Marxisms's potential as an effective counterbalance to the model of development implicit in the general theory of industrial society has been hampered by a number of important problems within Marxist scholarship itself.

The most significant of these problems can be directly linked to the domination of Marxist research by Stalinist thought from the 1930s onward. Under Stalin, the potential for a vibrant Marxist sociology became subordinated to the mechanical "economism" of the party and to the ideologically rigid form of application that the party line demanded.[21] The transcendence of Marxism by a party-backed Marxist-Leninism in the twentieth century has virtually precluded the establishment of adequate analyses of development in state-socialist societies. Indeed, these very societies appear to have become a haven for the most vulgar forms of neopositivism and minimally retreaded forms of functional analysis.

But, until very recently, even the "nonofficial" Marxism found in western societies has faced serious problems from within. For example, in their rejection of a "watershed" view of advances in sociological theory that would relegate Marxism to sociology's age of prediscovery, western Marxists have been all too quick to advance their own version of the watershed metaphor—namely, that Marx is the real pivotal figure in the development of social science, and writers like Durkheim and Weber merely represent "bourgeois rejoinders" to his great synthesis.[22] The problem with this line of reasoning is that it is has often led to an unfortunate tendency in much of western Marxism to treat Marxist theory as a set of incontrovertible statements about the nature of class relationships in capitalist societies rather than as a method for studying the changing character of class dynamics. In its simple instrumentalist forms (where the various institutions in society are automatically assumed to be instruments of class rule), this version of Marxism is problematic enough. But there has been a powerful tendency in modern

Marxist writing that views the Marxian "problematic" in a way that threatens to become more and more abstract and deterministic. As John Rex has argued, recent attempts to treat Marxism simply as an abstract science of social formations may be less an indication of theoretical growth than a subtle capitulation to formalist thinking.[23]

Developing a Response

What kinds of responses can be made to the problem tendencies just described? Some valuable insights into this question can be gained by examining the issues recently discussed both in the writings of Richard Bernstein and Anthony Giddens, and in the ongoing debate in contemporary Marxism about the relative autonomy of cultural forms and the role of human agency in social transformation.[24] In Bernstein one finds an important attempt to articulate key issues of method and analysis in a post-positivist age of social and political theory; in Giddens there is an attempt to combine such concerns with an emphasis on the emergent structures of industrial capitalism, in the fashion of classical social theory. At the same time, recent debates in Marxism represent an attempt to break out of narrowly conceived materialist formulae in order to outline new ways of understanding the changing nature of human possibilities in history.

Out of the issues raised in this body of writing, we can begin to explicate an effective strategy for dealing with the two problem tendencies described above. That strategy consists simply of recovering and articulating the classical sociologists' concerns for social development in a way that acknowledges both the essential unity of critical, interpretive, and empirical analysis, and the centrality of certain basic questions about human possibilities and the denial of these possibilities in changing social circumstances. Accompanying this is the need for acute sensitivity to the assumptions and problems raised by the uncritical use of abstract models of development for understanding and assessing how human choices and possibilities are lived out in different social and cultural settings.[25] This is the strategy I shall adopt in the discussion and critique of existing writing on sport that makes up the core of this book. In the remainder of these introductory remarks I want to clarify some key features of this strategy and relate them to the basic assumptions that have guided my analysis. As a first point let me explain what I mean when I talk about maintaining the essential unity of critical, interpretive, and empirical analysis while pursuing questions about human possibilities and their denial in studies of social development.

What I am suggesting here is that any discussion of social development should be guided by a range of issues that go beyond the empirical and the analytic. Such discussions should emphasize not only empirical and analytic questions about actual changes that have occurred in the logics and patterns of social and cultural organization in societies, but also interpretive and evaluative questions about the relationships of these changes to the differential life chances and varying forms of consciousness that characterize different individuals and groups in social life. For example, I do not believe it sufficient merely to chart out the path of social development followed by a given society—or a given institution or cultural form in society—without attempting to determine probable causes for the direction of development that has occurred and to interpret and evaluate the significance of this direction for life in society as a whole. To the degree that these concerns bring one to the edge of moral and political philosophy, they may be seen to fall outside of the scientific canons of a good deal of contemporary sociology. But I believe it can be argued credibly that the integration of philosophical, political, and sociological questions has always been compatible with the synthetic traditions of classical theory and with the classical sociologists' perceptions of the meaning of social development. Using this standard, and to paraphrase C. Wright Mills, any sociologist interested in understanding the changing nature of politics, education, sports, the arts, or any prominent feature of social existence, would be well advised to concentrate on those developmental "problems" that relate the "personal troubles" individuals have experienced in different eras to changing "public issues" of social structure—or, more optimistically perhaps, to relate these troubles to social formations that limit individual capacities to a level that falls far short of what one might expect under the social circumstances in question.[26]

One must recognize, of course, that the task of defining the character of personal troubles, public issues, and unrealized capacities always contains a measure of subjectivity, and this raises one of the most fundamental of the assumptions I have made in this study. Put most simply, I argue that any examination of the changing nature of human possibilities in social development must be drawn ineluctably to a very old sociological problem: the problem of class inequality and domination. It was this problem that defined many of the personal troubles and public issues of citizens in the earliest stages of liberal democracy, and I have become increasingly convinced that too many Northern American sociologists have exaggerated its demise. In this sense, much of the following analysis owes its point of orientation, if not directly to Marxism, at least to the long-standing European tradition of class theory in sociological writing. My analysis has also been greatly influenced by some important work coming out of Britain in the field of "cultural studies," and by the writings of a group of young Canadian social scientists whose response to cultural domination by the main themes of American social thought has been the discovery of new intellectual roots in the fields of political economy and Canadian social history.[27]

One final set of issues requires consideration. It is common in socio-logical studies of sport to emphasize the importance of one's subject matter by indicating the crucial role that sports play in the daily lives of so many people in contemporary western societies.[28] I think it extremely significant to note here that the growth and development of sociological interest in sport has approximately accompanied the significant growth and development of sport itself in the post-war era. There is now an enormous amount of capital, energy, and personal attention being de-voted to sport in contemporary life, and more and more sociologists are coming to realize that such developments require research and study.

Yet, it does seem somewhat mechanistic to assess sport's significance as an area of sociological study purely on the basis of quantitative assessments of the amount of capital, time, and energy devoted to it. As Charles Page has pointed out, what also makes sport especially interest-ing for sociology is its remarkably contradictory character as a cultural form in social life—its persisting aura of unreality in the face of an obvious relationship to social structural changes, its capacity to dramatize mytho-logically the liberating character of play while often remaining an area of constraint, and its seriousness that is often framed by the complete and utter absence of utility.[29] These factors have long been the stuff of philosophical discussion, but for the sociologist they post a special challenge: to integrate the analysis of the paradoxical features of sport into a broader understanding of human agency and cultural production and their expression in patterns of development, social reproduction, and social transformation. I believe emphatically that there is much more *theoretical substance* to the study of sport than has generally been accorded to it. The tensions between freedom and constraint in play, games, and sport, for example, and the overall relationships of these apparent dualities to conflicts over profits, or the many patterns of domination in a society, are not entirely innocent contradictions.

Thorstein Veblen seemed to understand these issues, although not quite in the way I have posed them, and he made a link between class, sports, and the problems of social development a key analytic feature of his *Theory of the Leisure Class.* Yet, with a few important exceptions, this link is grossly neglected in most North American work in the sociology of sport.[30] Despite the recent startling expansion of sociological literature devoted to the study of sports, there is little to suggest that the relationships between the institutional development of modern sports and the broader problems that have characterized the social development of western capitalist societies have been explored at all satisfactorily. To some extent, this failure may be related to the degree to which the special problems of physical educators have intruded upon and shaped the subdisciplinary thrust of "sport sociology." But where they have done research on sport, card-carrying sociologists have proven no less immune to limited approaches.

Here is the real source, I believe, of the lack of progress in the sociology of sport that Loy, Kenyon, and others have noted. Disengaged from a focus on the relationships of sport to the emergent structures of industrial capitalism, hidebound by caricatured forms of typological thinking, and blinkered by its own special problems of research, far too much sociological writing on sport has degenerated into the banal application of set sociological typologies, a nit-picking concern over problems of definition, pointless collections of "social facts," or crude decontextualized discussions of the "meaning" of the sporting experience.

None of these tendencies offers the rich insight or theoretical substance one finds in a Veblen or a Johan Huizinga. Nor do these tendencies appear to be guided by a concern for the kinds of questions that initiated the first important analyses of sport and social development. Although *Homo Ludens* and *The Theory of the Leisure Class* sought to explain something about the social significance of play, games, and sports as forms of cultural expression, the ultimate purpose of these works was to relate these forms of cultural expression to a number of broader sociological problems—indeed, to those key sociological problems about social action, social structure, and social development that were central to sociology's first synthesis, and were also reflected in the writings of Durkheim, Weber, and other scholars of their generation. It is a central part of my argument in this book that the return to such problems, and to the style of critical, interpretive, and empirical analysis that these problems demand, is by no means a retrogressive strategy.[31] For ultimately the ability to transcend our heavy reliance on the classical theories and concepts of Marx, Durkheim, and Weber—or, in the case of sport, of Huizinga and Veblen—will be based on our willingness to assess the significance of the problems with which they struggled and to pursue answers relevant for our own time.

1

Problems of Agency and Freedom in Play, Games, and Sport

*As so often, the two dominant tendencies of bourgeois cultural studies—
the sociology of the reduced but explicit "society" and the aesthetics of
the excluded social remade as a specialized "art"—support and ratify
each other in a significant division of labour. . . . It is this division, now
ratified by confident disciplines, which a sociology of culture has to
overcome and supercede, insisting on what is always a whole and
connected social material process.*

Raymond Williams, 1977

At the risk of considerable simplification, one can say that two related
problems seem to have defined much of the core of sociological theory.
The first might simply be called "the problem of human agency." Its
expression can be found in the attempt to reconcile the tensions between
voluntarism and determinism, freedom and constraint, and subject and
object in social life and history. Stated more simply, the problem of agency
involves an attempt to understand the degree to which human agents,
whether individual or collective, are constrained to think and act in the
ways they do.[1] The second problem might be labeled "the problem of
class inequality and structural change." The essence of this problem lies
in the attempt to identify and explain the rise and decline of specific

socioeconomic structures and the cultural formations associated with them. Guided by these concerns, writers in sociology's classical tradition sought consciously to specify those social conditions that achieved a certain balance between freedom and domination, expression and repression at different moments in history, and to analyze the individual and collective actions that created these conditions.

I believe that to adequately understand the role of sport in social development, we must view sport in the context of the problems of human agency, class inequality, and structural change. In chapters one and two, I shall outline and evaluate some of the ways in which these problems have been presented in previous writing on the nature and social dimensions of sport, and on sport's relationship to the reproduction and transformation of given social structures and related forms of cultural expression. My discussion begins here with a focus on sport's relationship to play, voluntary action, and human freedom, and then moves on to a broader analysis of sport's relationship to class inequality and macrostructural forms and processes in social development (see chap. 2).

The Paradoxes of Play, Games, and Sports

At some point play touches all of us. We play for fun, for fantasy, for excitement. In some cases our play seems spontaneous and freely innovative. In other cases it is more regulated and orderly. Yet, no matter what form it takes, there is a sense in which play often appears to transcend the practical affairs of everyday life. In play we seem to be absorbed in a reality that has its own limits of time and space, its own purposes and special emphases. Play allows us to be totally frivolous about important things in our work-centered lives or to be completely serious about things that are trivial. In either case, because we so deeply enjoy such apparent freedom, we are prone to celebrate play's expressive qualities and creative autonomy.

There is, of course, a great deal more to human play than apparent freedom of expression, peak experiences, or transcendental fantasy. While play certainly has its aura of unreality—its sense of abstract form— the nature and meaning of this form are greatly influenced by different social structural relations and cultural formations. When people organize their play in order to play with or against others, they create rules whose expressed purpose is to define standards for playing that are binding on all the players and that insulate the activity from the society-at-large. These rules are not spontaneous individual creations, rather they are cultural products that stem from the collective social experiences of the participants. Thus, while one of the purposes of rules is to separate play from reality, the very act of rule construction has the effect of embedding play deeply in the prevailing logic of social relations and thereby of diminishing its autonomy. For this reason, the study of play is haunted by a fundamental paradox. Play gives the impression of being an *independent and spontaneous* aspect of human action or agency and at the same time a *dependent and regulated* aspect of it.

The significance of this paradox becomes more evident if we consider the institutionalized character of so much of what passes for play in modern life. Games and sports, for example, by their very nature as highly structured, institutionally defined social practices, are frequently so overregulated and instrumental that they often seem only nominally related to play in its simplest expressive form. We tend to say that games and sports are "played," but the rules, customs, styles, and purposes of many of these activities seem almost completely determined by the social and cultural environments that frame them. In some cases, most notably high-level international "amateur" or commercial sports, it is often argued that little is left of play's freedom and creatively expressive character.

This relationship between the spontaneous and independent versus the regulated and dependent aspects of play, and those activities that are ostensibly "played" (e.g., games and sport), has attracted the attention of many writers and has always confused them. The confusions have been of two sorts. First, the range of human activities that can be classified as "playful" is extremely broad. Involved are activities as diverse as kicking a stray can in the street, singing in the shower, daydreaming, children's games, community recreation, and highly organized competitive sports. The definitional line between "play" and "sport" in these examples seems determined by the ways in which social structural and cultural forces have stylized play of certain types in an institutional fashion (i.e., *a* way of playing becomes *the* way of playing), but it is always difficult to know exactly where this line occurs.[2] One may find moments of play in big-time sports, but is it possible to argue that such sports in themselves are inherently playful?

The second set of confusions is even more complex. For all the generality of the themes discussed in the social analysis of play, games, or sports, many writers often appear to be writing about another subject altogether—a subject embedded in the seemingly paradoxical relationships between the autonomous and determined character of play, games, and sports, but not evident in the terms of discourse commonly used in the analysis of these activities. The real subject in question here is the relationship of play, games, and sports to the broader problems of human agency and freedom in social and individual life.

Consider, for example, some of the questions scholars have raised (not always consciously) in their assessments of the social significance of play, games, and sports. Is play an assertive, expressive act that involves an attempt to expand one's personal powers and exercise a form of creative control over an immediate environment? Or is it nothing more than simple fantasy, an escape from reality? If a free form of individual play is a dramatic culture-creating force, as so many writers seem to assert, does its organization into social or collective forms introduce such constraints that play loses its free culture-creating capacities and thereby becomes nothing more than a mirror of limiting social conditions? To what extent and under what circumstances can sport be seen as a negation of play or, conversely, as an example of play's "essential" character extended into the broader spheres of institutional life in society? Can it be said that play, games, and sports have any "essential" qualities at all? These questions are all ways of asking when and in what ways human beings exercise their powers as conscious, knowledgeable, historical actors both in and through play, games, and sports. Most of the questions also suggest concern about the nature of the social conditions under which specific actions might occur, about the kinds of limits these conditions set upon agency, and about whether these limits curtail freedom or provide the circumstances for its effective exercise.

Now on the last issue in particular, there has been a great debate among students of sport over the degree to which voluntary human actions and the free, playful expression of human powers are evident in the individual and collective experiences provided by games and sports. Much of the writing on sport dramatically proclaims that games and sports are notable forums for the voluntary expression of freedom, creative mastery, enjoyment, self-awareness, and human development. However, there are many writers who have been extremely critical of such assumptions. For example, in some theories it is suggested that sport is "determined" by social and cultural forces in a way that insures its separation from human freedom and human creative capacities. In other theories it is suggested that sport is cut off from human freedom only under certain circumstances. And, in still other theories, it is suggested that sport offers only nominal or illusory freedom at the expense of the development of people's powers to act politically in an unjust world that requires transformation.

It is not within the limits of this chapter to explore in detail these various theories or to situate them in the context of the broader intellectual traditions from which they draw their inspiration. Rather I shall focus my discussion on four writers whose works consciously stake out significant theoretical positions on the nature of play, games, and sport and the relationship of each to human agency and freedom. I submit that none of these writers has adequately met the challenge of resolving the paradoxes of play, games, and sports that were outlined at the outset of this chapter.

Johan Huizinga on Play as the Creator of Culture

One of the major features of eighteenth- and nineteenth-century political economy was the degree to which labor was emphasized in the organizational logic of social life. The starting point for any analysis of social development was usually defined with direct reference to *necessity* because, in order to survive and reproduce their species, human beings were forced into a necessary relationship with nature.[3] In such analyses, forms of consciousness and the idea of human spirit were at best usually regarded as residual considerations. At worst they were simply subsumed within the broad frameworks of utility theory and instrumental action.

There was, of course, much resistance to such analyses. Classical idealist philosophy and historiography, which asserted the primacy of mind and consciousness in human development, were one of the most notable examples of this resistance. Strong opposition also came from a vast body of theological writing which emphasized the spiritual rather than the material nature of human existence. In each case, writers sought to maintain that there existed a suprarational element in human societies that could not be explained by man's relationships to nature or by rational-purposive activity.[4]

Johan Huizinga's work clearly belongs to these broad traditions of idealist thought and theological writing. To a great extent, his work can be seen as an attempt to preserve some notion of the autonomous and creative human spirit in the face of the secular analytical and empirical procedures associated with the natural and social sciences of his day. Huizinga believed that the best way to preserve this notion was to emphasize the significant nonpurposive element in human life and in history. Nowhere, he suggested, was this nonpurposive element more evident than in play.

In *Homo Ludens* Huizinga argued that play is a primary and generative feature of social existence. Play is far more than a simple antithesis to labor, and far more than an element of life whose sole purpose is to perform certain biological and psychological functions in human growth and development. Neither of these explanations grasps the central fact that humans play for *fun* and that play is a meaningful activity. There is something "at play," Huizinga suggests, which "transcends the immediate needs of life [and] imparts meaning to the action," and this "meaningful" aspect of play implies "a non-materialistic quality in the thing itself."[5]

This nonmaterialistic quality is closely associated with play's nonpurposive character and the degree to which we consciously attempt to insulate or separate our play from "real life." The fact that humans diligently pursue the unnecessary and the nonutilitarian for the sake of the activity itself is a key feature that underlies our creative impulses, our ritualized forms of behavior and, ultimately, our humanity. According to Huizinga, the fundamental spirit which underlies the "significant form" of play and its expression in the contest can be seen to infuse all areas of cultural life including law, statecraft, and even war—so that it may be argued that culture itself moves and develops both *in* and *through* play.

However, Huizinga is not satisfied to argue simply that the spirit of playfulness provides the driving force in the advancement of western civilization. He also attempts to graft this argument onto an interpretation and evaluation of the present and future course of human development. This evaluation is made by first recognizing the fundamental difference between the unrestrained and innovative character of play's "significant form" as the *creator of culture,* and the structured more regulated character of those derivations of play that represent *creations of culture* (e.g., sports and games). By assessing the degree to which those creations of culture—nominally known as play—measure up to the standard of creativity and innovation embodied in the spirit of play in its most basic form, Huizinga generates a frame of reference for evaluating the quality of life in different historical periods. Following this logic, the body of *Homo Ludens* is devoted to a sweeping theoretical appraisal of the relationship between play, cultural innovation, ritual, and social development which opposes the secularization of the play element in modern times and its subjugation to the rational and calculating logic of industrial life. When Europe "donned the boiler suit," Huizinga concludes, the play element was weakened in all the basic forms of cultural expression, such as law or politics, and people no longer maintained any creative attachment to them. Instead they began to seek diversion in the surrogate play of modern sports and the excesses of the spectacle.

I do not intend here to provide a detailed accounting and assessment of Huizinga's theory. It should suffice simply to note some of the key issues that his analysis raises about human agency and freedom as features of play, games, and sports in social development. The first of these issues is Huizinga's understanding of the culture-creating capacities of human agents.

For Huizinga, play is first and foremost *voluntary activity.* It is also activity that is "free." Although Huizinga is not specific about defining the freedom that is characteristic of play, he seems to imply that it is evident in two related senses. First, play is free because all humans are free to engage in the nonpurposive activities that contribute so crucially to cultural creation. However, in order to be truly free to pursue activities for their own sake, these activities have to be freed from the restraints imposed upon them by necessity. This freedom requires the intentional creation of boundaries which set play apart from material "reality." These boundaries are largely temporal and spatial, and they are constituted as boundaries either by imagination or by the more formal specification of rules that define a separate "order" to which one voluntarily submits. The fact that humans create these rules and voluntarily submit to them in order to free themselves from necessity, Huizinga seems to suggest, is both a good indication of the suprarational character of human beings and a valuable evidence of the necessity of order in cultural life as a condition of freedom.

Underlying all of this is Huizinga's main assumption about human agency. He argues that humans are imbued with an essential and universal capacity for play that is generative of human cultural creations. Added to this is the notion that this generative capacity, this distinct spiritual essence, is represented and sustained in the "formal" characteristics of play as a free, separate, and creatively expressive process. The moral conclusion that Huizinga logically draws out of these assumptions is straightforward: the more we divide ourselves from material life and submit to the representational, nonpurposive orders that we create for this purpose, the closer we come to realizing our humanity. The more these orders become reconstituted toward some instrumental end, the further we are from realizing our humanity.

There is, however, an additional twist to this, for Huizinga's analysis attempts to show a definite link between the pursuit of play for its own sake and the "objective" conditions in society which manifest our need for a kind of spiritual transcendence. In particular Huizinga suggests how the personal rapture or "seizure" involved in individual play has a distinct collective and constitutive significance in its association with sacred rituals. Drawing on several anthropological studies of sacred rituals, Huizinga notes how rituals provide exaggerated interpretations of social order that help individuals make sense of that order and of their higher relationships to the sacred realm upon which all of life is sustained. Social rituals act as re-creative and aesthetic representations which help people to grasp not only what they *are* in a limited material sense, but also what they *become* in a higher spiritual and metaphysical sense. In this way, the "unreality" of play becomes the bedrock of a higher reality.

This point requires clarification. Huizinga argues that sacred rituals draw a clear line between the sacred and the profane. Implicit in his argument is the additional view that such rituals help to resolve the fundamental contradiction between individual wants and collective needs by providing (as Emile Durkheim might have put it) a basic lesson about religion and moral authority; that is, freedom and happiness can only exist in their association with, and submission to, sacred order.[6] For Huizinga, play is the genesis and the expression of our abilities to grasp and understand this order and—as he acknowledges in the introduction to *Homo Ludens*—the "simple question of what play really is, leads us deep into the problem of the origin and nature of religious concepts."[7]

I find Huizinga's analysis alternately brilliant and seriously flawed. It is brilliant in its attempt to build a theory of social development on the basis of play, in its emphasis on the meaningful and dramatic representational features of play, in its specification of the "formal" characteristics which define play in abstract terms, and in its attempts to relate the lived reality of play at the level of individual experience with the "higher" reality of religious rituals. Yet, despite—and in some cases as a result of—these positions, I think it can be argued that Huizinga's entire project is somewhat misleading.

What is most lacking in his analysis is an adequate sense of the determining character of material history and the ways in which the very practices that seek to separate play from reality are in themselves influenced by, and constitutive of, that reality. Huizinga follows the long-standing idealist tradition of projecting an actual human activity, play, into an abstract social form where a human creative capacity—self-creative but prior to and separate from material social practice—is seen to be the generative force in human civilization. Here the abstract idea of the playful individual acting in the presence of open alternatives and in the presence of enabling structures which guarantee nonpurposive action becomes the starting point for the analysis of social development.

But if play is truly a "function of the living," as Huizinga argues, and if living implies *social* activity, then this view is surely questionable. The processes of social interaction always seem to be governed by something more than pure consciousness or the "needs" of the human spirit. Indeed, I would follow Raymond Williams' well-known criticisms of idealist tendencies in cultural analysis and suggest that play, seen as activity, as a real social and cultural practice, is not in any way separate from, prior to, or generative of human experience; rather it is simply constitutive of that experience.[8] In other words, play is meaningful, not in some abstract metaphysical or theological sense, but in the active material sense of the making and remaking of human social and cultural relations and relationships. Huizinga's analysis is, of course, largely compatible with an understanding of play as constitutive activity. The difficulty arises when the constitutive is broken into temporal elements. Huizinga views play as *primary* and original, not in the acceptable sense that it is more important to the very act of human self-creation, but in the more abstract sense of play as the motor of history. Yet, I would argue that it is more precisely the sense of play as an indissoluble element of human self-creation that gives any acceptable meaning to its description as a meaningful and constitutive activity. To make it precede all other connected activities is to claim something quite different.[9]

The limitations of Huizinga's analytic separation of the ideal and distinctly humanizing features of play from material social conditions are nowhere more evident than in his criticisms of modern sports and in his somewhat romantic attachment to medieval European society. Medieval society, Huizinga argued, was "brimful of play," and in it the "higher forms" of recognized play were filled with ritual and the spirit of public festivity. By contrast, modern sports have lost their play character through the rationalization of play activities and the subordination of the contest to the "seriousness" of science and technological development. Huizinga saw this transformation as part of a movement from the sacred to the profane in western culture. Play's ritual significance and ubiquity in medieval society apparently suggests a richer, more fulfilling, and even happier age than present-day industrial society.

If we view the spirit of the medieval European festival and contest as something not blocked or repressed in any way, then it is easy to see how Huizinga arrived at this view. With its many ritual holidays and festivals, its close ties between church and state, and its comparatively ordered features of social organization, medieval Europe seems rather idyllic when contrasted to the long working hours, intolerable work conditions, and the ideological and social turmoil of early industrial capitalism. On the other hand, one has to ask if this view is not rather simplistic. For as Max Weber saw so clearly, the ascriptive order of medieval and, later, feudal life was not so much a festive system of social integration and playful creativity as it was a social system pervaded by brutally exploitative relationships that were given their symbolic expression in traditional cultural formations.[10] Indeed, arguing from this perspective, one might be tempted to conclude that some abstract ideal state of play was no more realized in the cultural formations of medieval Europe than in the formations of capitalist or socialist industrial societies. In his analysis of the ritualized game forms of European and Japanese feudalism, for example, Weber notes how the representational characteristics of games tended to support the logic of traditional domination by dramatizing nonrational and nonutilitarian forms of social action.[11] Thus, to borrow Weber's own terminology, it is problematic at best whether such so-called play forms can be regarded as any more humanizing or culture-creating in societies characterized by traditional domination than in societies characterized by rational-legal domination. What has occurred is simply that one set of social and cultural practices has replaced another, and *it is a question of evaluating what play, games, and sports are and what they represent in the context of these practices.* By committing the study of play to a perspective that begins by emphasizing the primacy of the generative and "unreal" features of playful action, Huizinga's legacy for the contemporary analysis of play, games, and sports has been an overemphasis on the expressive and formal properties of play viewed in an abstract and metaphysical fashion.

Michael Novak on Sport as a Civil Religion

Nowhere is Huizinga's influence on contemporary analyses of sports more noticeable than in Michael Novak's popular book *The Joy of Sports.* Novak goes beyond Huizinga, however, in his discussion of the abstract metaphysical properties of play, and he is more optimistic than Huizinga in suggesting the degree to which these properties are expressed (despite certain imperfections) in modern sports.

Novak begins by emphasizing what he believes are sport's deep ties to playfulness, spiritual freedom, and the pursuit of meaning in human existence. Sports are far more than simple amusements, Novak argues; and the emotion and drama that are so intimately associated with sport should not be trivialized simply as some kind of catharsis or childish escapism. What sports *do* offer us is an important *metaphorical statement about ultimate human possibilities.* Thus, Novak writes that sports are "true in a way that few things in life are true."[12] They embody a transcendent mythic form, a ritual elaboration of the music of the human spirit that is at once both dramatic and deeply religious.

Now in this era of mass sporting spectacles, it has become somewhat commonplace to say that sports have taken on the character of a modern religion. In most cases, however, such assertions are advanced cynically as a tacit condemnation of the excessive secularism of modern life. Yet such views, Novak asserts, are often little more than the residues of a

Puritan ethic that places too much value on labor, rejects play, and fails to grasp the significant interconnections between play and the sacred. Art, worship, prayer, and civilization itself, Novak tells us, find less fertile soil in the world of work than in play. And insofar as he views sports as nothing more than institutionalized derivations of play, they deserve to be included in any serious discussion of modern religion. Novak then expands upon this point in a number of lyrical and compelling ruminations on the essential characteristics of sport, its attractions for athletes and fans, and its present problems and future prospects. Included in these ruminations is a good deal of romanticized hagiography that has little relevance to my discussion here. I shall only note that, following Huizinga, Novak's work is a rich source of speculative material on the nature of play and on the relationships of play, games, and sports to ritual and religion. At the same time, however, Novak's work is also troubled by many of the same problems that limit the effectiveness of *Homo Ludens*. Indeed, in some cases these problems are even more pronounced in Novak than in Huizinga.

Again, many of the problems that limit the analysis are closely tied to an abstract frame of reference that seeks to articulate a *universal* "essence" or "form" for play. In particular I am referring to Novak's heavy reliance on the spiritual dimensions of human action. Novak asks us, as all theologians tend to do, to accept his organizing assumptions as matters of faith, and these assumptions cast the entire problem of social development as the analysis of *spiritual* rather than *social* possibilities. Given this, there is a strong sense in which *The Joy of Sports* is virtually innocent of sociology, political economy, or social history. Novak stresses the phenomenal, the subjective, and the transcendental, at the expense of an understanding of material social relationships. Yet at the same time, although Novak is unwilling to push sports too far into the "real" worlds of politics and power, the political implications that can be drawn from many of his arguments are often disturbing.

Consider Novak's discussion of how sport, seen as a type of *sacred form*, relates to human freedom. As humans "play" sports, Novak argues, they liberate themselves from the obsessive seriousness and confusions of everyday life. This spiritual freedom comes from an acceptance of "fixed limits" that give definition to transcendent moments of excellence and precision.[13] But what about freedom defined in distinctly social terms—freedom from domination or exploitation? Novak argues that there is little salvation for humans in social life. We are neither born free nor can we ever hope to transform totally the chaotic, violent, and exploitative character of social existence. Indeed, he suggests that politics and secular struggles are all opiates of western societies. Real salvation can only lie in the pursuit of form, in the transcendence of chaos through a commitment to order and bounded space. The play of our games and sports is an expression of our willingness to submit to these limits.

Once again something important is missing here. By defining in purely abstract metaphysical terms the criterion for establishing the connection between sports and human freedom, Novak greatly under-plays the extent to which sports can be understood as historically constituted features of social arrangements *whose fixed limits can very well be as repressive as they are liberating.* Novak is caught in the idealist trap of seeing the essence of social institutions as projections of abstract form—projections that may be blocked or repressed, yet projections nonetheless. Thus, although Novak concedes that much of modern sport is overly commercial, excessively instrumental, and prone to excesses on a grand scale, he sees these tendencies only as a debasement of the pure form that underlies our playful spirit. As a result, sport as an institution does not require radical reconstruction or transformation; it only requires adjustment, a realignment of form and content. A self-proclaimed follower of Edmund Burke, Novak argues in his concluding comments that whereas much of the criticism directed at modern sport often rings true, these criticisms only attack the "contents" of culture and not the "form." Sport is worth saving and reforming, and one can do this by introducing checks and balances that will reduce the corruption of sports, its secularization, and its evolution from an institution which provides "moments of sacred time" to one which increasingly offers profane spectacle.

I want to add one final comment on Novak's analysis. Suppose we grant for the moment that there is a powerful metaphoric quality to sport and that this quality is sustained by fixed limits—the structures that human agents consciously create in order to separate their actions from material reality. Suppose we also concede that certain aesthetic or ideal elements in human existence actually do have some sort of transcendental or universal promise, and that sports as *form* might somehow be attractive for us because they offer dramatic representations of these elements. Such arguments in themselves do not seem unreasonable, and they have been made repeatedly by different writers. For example, in making this point, Fred Inglis cites the hero of John Berger's novel about a radical painter whose life's work was to paint a masterpiece of the 1948 Olympic Games:[14]

> In sport . . . liberation is collective. I have seen games of football in which I have glimpsed all I believe the productive relations among men might be.[15]

Or, consider Inglis's own account:

> Tangled and inarticulate in the ritual grammar and theologi-
> cal vocabulary of modern sport is a remote vision of men
> joined in an activity at once happy and combative, strong in
> both friendship and rivalry, beautiful and strenuous. An
> activity rich in creative pointlessness. Many of these power-
> ful social needs have been attributed to art, and others to
> the non-productive sections of domestic life. But what of
> that characteristic of industrial society . . . which serves to
> mark off men from men, and to set them against one an-
> other? It is the strength of different games that they serve to
> rejoin men and to overcome such divisions. . . . The difficulty
> is then to talk about this possibility.[16]

The decisive word in this passage is "possibility," for metaphors of
perfectability—or abstract symbolic representations of it—are not necessarily lived out in real social practice. More often than not they are
either vague suggestions of possibility or promises of something better
than present conditions. Yet, it seems important to recognize that giving
oneself completely to the pursuit of these abstract promises often does
little to contribute to their effective realization in social life. Indeed, what
often seems to occur is that the promises themselves become confused
with actual states of human existence. For example, viewed as pure form,
most of our so-called play, game, and sporting activities offer the promise
of a fair and meritocratic contest or the opportunity for creative self-
expression free from restraint. Yet, these activities often deliver merely an
approximation of this promise shaped by existing social and cultural
conditions. As interpretations and dramatizations of the very conditions
which sustain them, play, games, and sports can be regarded as an active
part of the making and remaking of these conditions.[17] However, when the
abstract metaphorical representations of play, games, and sports are
viewed *outside* the context of this making and remaking they become
reified and separated from the process of active history. As this occurs,
the meanings encoded in play, games, and sports become depoliticized
and recreated in mythic forms that have powerful ideological overtones.[18]

Now the issue is to relate the constitutive meanings of play, games, and
sports to lived social experience without romanticizing or reifying sport's
form in some abstract fashion. One might ask that Michael Novak further
justify his rationale for deciding upon the nature of sport's form and for
relating it to human freedom. One cannot help but feel as things now stand

that Novak's Catholicism and personal views on modern politics have greatly influenced the way in which he has constructed his entire analysis. The view that people are free only when they submit to structure, that true freedom of choice lies in a certain form of "unfreedom," is a view with a historically specific and ideological history. Moreover, as Steven Lukes suggests, there is reason to be suspicious of the notion of the "abstract individual," detached from historical circumstances, who realizes himself through universalistic and idealist notions of perfection. For the very *idea* of the abstract individual, along with the related definitions of perfectability being used, are in themselves positions that have been historically and ideologically constituted.[19]

Jean-Marie Brohm on Sport as Constraint

I have argued that an adequate sense of the determining character of material history is lacking in the analyses of Johan Huizinga and Michael Novak. By contrast it is precisely this determining character that dominates the analysis of sports put forward by Jean-Marie Brohm in his controversial collection of essays, *Sport: A Prison of Measured Time.* Brohm would waste no time in arguing that the analyses of Huizinga and Novak are little more than conservative rhetoric and idealist wishful thinking. Even the title of Brohm's book, *Sport: A Prison of Measured Time,* is a direct contrast to Novak's frequent description of sport as an area of human endeavor marked by "moments of sacred time."

Brohm begins by arguing forcefully that sports are not in any sense timeless abstractions, and that they have very little to do with play itself or with some transhistorical notion of ultimate possibilities. In Brohm's words, "Such mystical conceptions present sport ahistorically, as a transcendent entity, over and above historical periods and modes of production."[20] Sport is a form of institutionalized social practice that simply mirrors the social conditions which surround it. Indeed, the very existence of institutionalized sports as we currently understand them is tied to the emergence of industrial capitalism as a distinct social formation. If we subject sport to materialist institutional analysis, Brohm continues, we find that the rhetoric surrounding sport is little more than bourgeois ideology disguised by metaphysics. According to Brohm, sports glorify meritocratic standards of hierarchy and success based on skill; they celebrate commercialism; they willingly embrace a technocratic frame of reference that subordinates the body to the machine; and they present a false view of social progress through the continued assault on the record books. At the same time, sports ostensibly serve a number of repressive ideological functions: they provide a false sense of escape and thereby act as compensatory mechanisms to alienated existence; they undermine the revolutionary potential for work; and they are symbolically tied to the coercive state, and aid in reproducing its legitimacy.

Using the style of Brohm's own terminology, *Sport: A Prison of Measured Time* can almost be seen as a "negation" of the idealist analyses of Huizinga and Novak. Brohm replaces their emphasis on nonpurposive agency and the transcendent spirit with an emphasis on the material world of productive forces and relations. For these reasons he argues that the type of regulation that defines our modern games and sports does not allow for freedom so much as it allows for the reproduction of the repressive constraints inherent in capitalism and Stalinism. Brohm contends that sport is both a "constraint in itself and a preparation for further constraints, since it removes all bodily freedom, all creative spontaneity, every aesthetic dimension and every playful impulse."[21] In other words, sports are actually antithetical to play and the freedom of expression that play so often represents. In modern sports the athlete becomes a prisoner of social forces which block all access to freedom and spontaneity. And, because the underlying structure and logic of sport embodies these forces, sport cannot be reformed or cured of its many ills. It has to be rejected in favor of a renewed commitment to playful spontaneity and fun in games.

Almost all of Brohm's arguments are powerful, penetrating, and greatly overstated. He writes in the polemical tradition of revolutionary neo-Marxism rather than from the stance of the careful and thorough Marxist scholar. Accordingly his prime purpose is to demystify, strip bare, and amplify for easy consumption the fundamental contradictions of modern sport. He notes early in the book that he has deliberately avoided writing dispassionate academic essays; rather his essays are "interventions" into the struggle to transform sport and society. In this way Brohm's work is something of a welcome alternative to the numerous uncritical celebrations of sport that have passed for social scientific, historical, and philosophical analyses in recent years. And he has gone some lengths toward showing how a Marxist analysis of sport might proceed and how it should be tied to actual political practice.

Nonetheless, there is a great deal that is analytically troublesome in *Sport: A Prison of Measured Time.* Brohm is generally correct, I believe, in arguing that the institutional shape of modern sports has been contoured by capitalist industrialism, and that sports play a role in the reproduction of relations of power and domination in modern life. I think he also does well to polemicize against a definitional frame of reference that views sport simply as a form of organized play or as an institutionalized derivation of the human play impulse. Yet, he pushes this line of reasoning much too far. It is one thing to say that sports are socially constituted institutions and elements of culture that are fundamentally different from play and that have the capacity to aid in legitimating existing material conditions. It is quite another thing to argue that sport is a completely determined product, a passive mirror of capitalist productive relations and forces; that sport and play are mutually exclusive; and that the meanings attached to sport can only be socially and ideologically reproductive.

One thing that such assumptions do is destroy any notion of human culture—and of the making of human cultural creations as social processes of a constitutive kind—by subjecting them to a crude instrumental rationalism. Instead of viewing cultural history as material practice, as Marx himself tried to do, this view makes cultural products abstractly dependent, secondary, superstructural: a realm of "mere" ideas, beliefs, and customs that are "determined" by material history.[22] What matters here is not only the problem of reductionism, but also that aspects of Brohm's analysis appear to be a left-wing variation of the separation of "culture" from material social life which has always been the dominant tendency in idealist cultural analysis.[23]

For these reasons Brohm's analysis cannot be seen to offer any kind of adequate materialist understanding of cultural forms. Instead we are given an analysis of cultural production built upon a mechanical view of the Marxist notion of determination, an overly abstract separation between historical "subjects" and socially-constituted "objects," and a non-dialectical understanding of cultural forms as straightforward reflections of reality rather than meaningful and constitutive interpretations of it.[24] It is, I believe, just plain silly to argue for a theory of institutional development and cultural production which relegates sport to the objectified status of a simple reflection of abstract capitalist categories. It is equally problematic to conclude that sports effectively and successfully socialize their participants with reactionary political views, or that involvement in sport *necessarily* functions to discourage the development of an oppositional class consciousness within capitalism. As Ralph Miliband notes, this latter view in particular "does not seem *a priori* reasonable and is belied by much evidence to the contrary; and to murmur 'bread and circuses' is no substitute for serious thinking on the matter."[25]

If we follow the view I have been developing throughout this chapter, it can be asserted, simply, that the kind of analysis developed by Brohm goes to the extreme in ignoring the fact that human beings are knowledgeable agents whose cultural creations are made and remade in the context of historically shifting limits and possibilities.[26] From this perspective, sports can be seen as active constitutive features of human experience that must be viewed in the context of a struggle over these limits and possibilities and over the appropriation of the rules and resources that define them. Depending upon their association with divergent material interests, the meanings of sports, like all cultural creations, have the capacity to be either reproductive or oppositional, repressive or liberating. For Brohm, capitalism has shaped sport in its own image, and anyone who believes that an interest in sport is in any way compatible with the pursuit of the class struggle is simply a falsely conscious dupe.

The unfortunate left-wing elitism in such thinking is rather unpalatable. To some extent this elitism may be related to the fact that much of Brohm's philosophy of sport is not inspired by Marxism so much as by the left-wing cultural criticism of the French student movement to which Brohm belonged in the late 1960s and early 1970s. The current problems with sport appear to lie less with the class domination inherent in capitalist *productive relations* than with the subordination of individual expressivity and spontaneity to the dehumanizing forces of instrumental reason and technocratic rationality. Brohm's solution to this takes its cues from Herbert Marcuse rather than from Marx, and is based in part on a romanticized pursuit of individual freedom expressed through spontaneous play and games.[27]

It is a somewhat ironic commentary on Brohm's eclecticism that these Marcusian overtones are accompanied by a good deal of economism and functionalist thinking. Brohm's few attempts to introduce "structuralist" concepts such as Louis Althusser's notion of "Ideological State Apparatuses" only exacerbates this problem.[28] Althusser's recognition of the apparent "relative autonomy" of cultural practice nominally appears to acknowledge the meaningful features of cultural formations for human agents. Ultimately, however, these meanings seem to be irrelevant except in their capacity to reproduce forces generated abstractly in the mode of production. Thus, the "relative autonomy" of cultural formations granted by Althusser can simply be translated into a set of assertions about functional interdependence.[29] Sport must be "relatively autonomous" in order to function properly as an area of reproduction and meet the functional "requirements" of the capitalist mode of production. The result of these and other influences in Brohm's work is a series of dramatic "interventions" that possibly point in the right direction, but that also show just how far the Marxist analysis of sport must go in order to transcend the tired slogans and pat formulae of left-idealism, functionalism, and abstract materialist determinism.

Allen Guttmann on Sport as Positive Freedom

Criticisms of so-called Marxist and neo-Marxist interpretations of sport occupy a good deal of Allen Guttmann's attention in *From Ritual to Record: The Nature of Modern Sports*. Guttmann acknowledges the existence of many of the problems raised by Marxist and neo-Marxist analyses of sports, but he is unwilling to reduce either the meaning or the significance of sports to radical psychoanalytic or economistic principles. At the same time, although Guttmann recognizes that the subordination of sporting performances to instrumental reason and technocratic rationality has placed certain limits on human expressivity and spontaneity, he emphatically argues that such limits are not always repressive.

Guttmann begins with the familiar argument that play belongs to the realm of freedom because it is nonutilitarian and pursued for its own sake. In its most spontaneous forms, play may be as close as humans ever get to pure freedom and unrestrained expressivity. Yet, much of our play is organized, and one must ask how play can remain in the realm of freedom once one submits to organization. According to Guttmann, the answer to this question is relatively straightforward. Following Huizinga, he notes how even the regulated "play" of games and sports remains outside the sphere of necessity and is always free in the sense that it is consciously insulated from real life and is pursued for its own sake. Moreover, the regulations that define the bounded limits of time, space, and behavior in games and sports are actually *necessary* in order to open up the possibility of cooperative action and the freedom "to lose oneself" in the pursuit of gratuitous difficulty. In organized play, Guttmann asserts, humans voluntarily surrender a portion of their absolute freedom in order to achieve a state of mutual gain. The limits associated with organization do not necessarily constrain; rather they may actually expand choices and possibilities. As formally organized physical contests, sports are more "precisely demarcated" and structured than simple play-forms. Yet, this degree of regulation does not necessarily imply that sports are somehow qualitatively different from play. Indeed, according to Guttmann, it is possible to define all sports in abstract universal terms as "playful physical contests."

There are, however, some qualifications to this type of abstract philosophical classification. Guttmann argues that although all sports share in a universal definition it must be recognized that the "Gestalt" of modern sports appears in "sharply delineated contrast against the background of primitive, ancient, and medieval sports."[30] Sports in earlier times were often closely tied to religious ritual and festivals; they were limited by ascriptive standards for involvement that stemmed from class and caste;

they had a low degree of formal organization and role specialization; and they were generally oriented toward qualitative assessments of the meaning of the sporting experience. By contrast, modern sports have become secular, meritocratic, highly rational, subject to bureaucratic organization, and increasingly oriented toward record-setting and quantitative assessments of the meaning of the sporting experience.

Such changes, Guttmann goes on to suggest, can be credibly viewed from Marxist and Weberian theoretical perspectives. Marxist and neo-Marxist explanations, however, prove on closer examination to be "unpersuasive" because they overly value economic determinations, and because they are supposedly guided more by "ideology" than by "careful empirical study." More "congruent with reality" in Guttmann's opinion is a Weberian perspective which emphasizes the growth of a rational scientific world view as the "basic explanatory factor" influencing the nature of modern sport.

Guided by this theoretical and sociohistorical framework, Guttmann moves on to a "series of speculations" about what is and what is not unique about American sports. These speculations are interesting, but they are not really relevant to my discussion here and I shall not digress to comment on them. Guttmann soon returns, however, to the core theoretical questions about agency and freedom that seem to underlie his analysis. He does so by focusing on the relationships that exist between preferences for individual and team sports and American values. Americans may have strong individualist traditions, Guttmann observes, but they are actually more prone than Europeans to participate in, and identify with, team sports. This preference occurs because, despite all of their emphasis on "frontierism" or "rugged individualism," Americans value cooperation and teamwork as much as—if not more than—spontaneity and unrestrained individual expressivity.

Yet, having made this point, Guttmann notes how it may actually be misleading to view as contradictions the expression of individualism and cooperation. The choice between one's involvement in individual or team sports, or even between spontaneous play and structured sport, is not a mutually exclusive choice between individuality or dull conformity, between freedom of expression or oppressive constraint. Rather, the choice is between differing conceptions of individualism and freedom.

One version of freedom, Guttmann reminds us, is based on the ideal of escaping from the restraints of institutional order. This view of "negative freedom" is symbolized in American thinking by the kind of pastoral utopian vision inspired by Thoreau. In a slightly different form, this negative freedom tends to underlie the praxis of the romantic neo-Marxism of

Jean-Marie Brohm and his new-left compatriots. The other version of freedom is based on the "positive" idea that submission to social order increases our opportunities to act out individual choices. The rules of social organization allow for men and women to be something more in society than they are alone. Guttmann argues that both of these concep- tions define important parts of the liberal tradition in western societies, but it is this latter view in particular that has flourished under conditions of modern democracy. In liberal-democratic societies, Guttmann states, there are certainly many troublesome situations in which the loss of personal freedom from restraint is greater than the gains of freedom of choice that stem from social organization. But on the whole, these · societies have witnessed a great gain in freedom over the last two centuries. Modern sports are the benefactors of this increase. They may be beset with "imperfections and false emphases," Guttmann concludes, but they can be seen now, more than ever, to hold forth the possibility of "relative if not absolute freedom."[31]

Guttmann's provocative book has been widely reviewed and I shall not presume to add to the substantive commentary on it except where it relates to the argument I have been developing in this chapter.[32] I will say, however, that Guttmann's book is a ground-breaking and extremely thoughtful introduction to the social development of sport and to the problem of sport's relationship to human agency and freedom. On the other hand, I think one has to recognize that the book suffers from some important limitations. For example, Susan Birrell has recently argued that Guttmann makes significant methodological mistakes in attempting to provide empirical support for his thesis that Americans prefer team to individual sports.[33] It has also been argued that Guttmann never really develops an adequate discussion of the institutionalization of sport in the West, and that he never really supplies adequate historical evidence for establishing a strong causal connection between the development of the scientific world view and the rise of modern sport. Yet, I would argue further that these criticisms only scratch the surface. For if one looks more deeply at the theoretical core of Guttmann's analysis, one can find even greater problems—problems which suggest, in my view, that *From Ritual to Record* takes us no further in resolving our confusions over the paradoxes of play, games, and sport—and related problems of agency and freedom—than either the abstract idealist analyses of Huizinga and Novak or the unsatisfactory determinism of Jean-Marie Brohm.

This last statement requires elaboration, Guttmann's work is appealing because it appears to be an effective empirically grounded response to the economism, determinism, and "ideological bias" of Marxist and neo-

Marxist criticisms of sport. Guttmann demonstrates an acute sensitivity to the active and constitutive features of play, games, and sports and, at the same time, he appears to avoid abstract metaphysics by recognizing that at different times in history, the main characteristics of games and sports are shaped by social and cultural forces and relations.

Upon closer examination, however, Guttmann's analysis is not quite as persuasive as it first seems. For one thing, his criticisms of Marxism are somewhat misleading, and his discussion of what a Weberian analysis of the social development of sport would entail is highly questionable. Moreover, whereas Guttmann's philosophical frame of reference is less extreme than Huizinga's notion of play as the creator of culture, or than Michael Novak's transcendent theology of sports, there is a sense in which Guttmann never quite escapes from idealism and metaphysics. Consider a comparison of Guttmann to Novak. Whereas Novak's metaphysics are tied to abstract conceptions of sacred form, Guttmann's are more secular, more tied to abstract conceptions of voluntary action and human will. Indeed, when reading *From Ritual to Record,* one gets the distinct impression that Guttmann has tried so desperately to avoid any sort of materialist determinism that he has erred in the opposite direction. In response to an economistic and determinist view of historical causality, he offers us vague instinct theories and an analysis of social change whose "basic explanatory factor" is tied to the development of mind—of the scientific world view. We are then asked to believe that the limits on human expression which have occasionally resulted from this scientific *Weltanschauung* are either voluntarily accepted or else are not limits at all. The limits are simply new boundaries which act to demarcate sport's separate playful order while simultaneously reflecting the increased integration of sport into a system of social organization that is more free than in the past. In other words, as a replacement for the apparent shortcomings of Marxist historical materialism, we are offered a theoretical affirmation of voluntarism and the merits of liberal democracy.

The first indication of these problems can be found in Guttmann's preliminary philosophical discussion of the nature of play, games, and sports. Here he lays the groundwork for a set of analytic tensions that runs throughout the remainder of his analysis. Briefly stated, the problem is that Guttmann wants to make abstract universal connections between play and freedom and play and sports, while at the same time allowing for the idea that the major characteristics of sports are socially conditioned. Yet, following in the tradition of Michael Novak, once Guttmann makes a universal connection between play and freedom and play and sports, he has already tipped his hand about the degree to which social forces and pressures—reflected in the organization and structure of sport—will be found to be constraining. Guttmann argues that play lies in the realm of voluntary action and freedom and, because sports are inherently playful, they also are voluntary and free. This simply disposes once again of the notion that under certain social circumstances sports might well be "unfree." Rather, it is argued *by definition* that the organization, rules, and standards for defining sport involvement have the effect of guaranteeing sport's freedom from necessity and insulating it from the constraints of the outside world.[34]

Two points are at issue here. First, as I suggested earlier, there is a fundamental difference between freedom from necessity and freedom expressed more broadly in social and political terms. The former refers to the ways in which rules allow for any given social practice to be conducted for its own sake; the latter refers to the opportunity for anyone to choose from a wide range of social practices or to create new ones. Freedom from necessity in sport is admittedly achieved by submitting to established rules and conventions, but social and political freedom may involve working against or challenging certain rules and conventions. Because Guttmann fails to differentiate between these two perceptions of freedom, his analysis tends to be extremely ambiguous. In one sense he suggests that freedom is a universal condition of sport, yet in another sense he seems to want to locate freedom outside sport, as a condition of life in society.

This raises the second point alluded to above. Even when Guttmann actually does get around to talking about freedom and sport as an aspect of social conditions, he seems to want to make this freedom in some way dependent on the more universal notion of freedom from necessity. In other words, he adopts the now-familiar stance of implying that because rules, organizations, and established traditions facilitate freedom from necessity, they also contribute to freedom in some broader sense. Yet, it is one thing to say that organizations, rules, and standards for involvement have the *capacity* to expand human choices and possibilities; it is quite another thing to imply that these social limits on spontaneous expression always do this. It seems instead to be a question of the type and quality of the limits that are created at any given point in time. If we are to understand the relationships between freedom and sport in social and political terms, then we ought to insist that sociologists and historians tell us exactly when sports actually contribute to different types of freedom and when they do not.

It is to Guttmann's credit that he tries to answer some of these questions. Moreover, even though he is philosophically predisposed to find freedom in the "play" of games and sports, he makes effective linkages between some of the major social tendencies of contemporary societies and the characteristics of modern sports. His presentation of Marxist and neo-Marxist views forces him to consider the broader social and political dimensions of sport's relationships to agency and freedom. And, although he rejects Marxism, he clearly outlines the high degree of rationalization and bureaucratization of modern sports. As noted earlier, Guttmann is drawn to this emphasis on rationalization and bureaucratization by his reading of Max Weber—perhaps the greatest theorist of modern bureaucratic organization. However, if Weber was deeply pessimistic about the penetration of instrumental reason, bureaucratic regulation, and technocratic thinking into all spheres of modern life, Guttmann is far more optimistic. There is no Weberian "iron cage" here.[35] The consequences of rationalization and bureaucratization are worrisome and frequently inconvenient, Guttmann tells us, but on the whole we have gained much more from these processes than we have lost. Rationalization and bureaucratization are part and parcel of the progress of contemporary industrial societies, and it is a bit like sour grapes to be obsessed with the problems of individual freedom from restraint when so much has been gained.

If this all sounds a lot like post-classical liberal ideology, it is because there are strong undercurrents of this type of thinking throughout Guttmann's entire analysis. The neo-Marxists are criticized for their failure to understand the "positive freedom" that stems from established rules of order and authority. And, whereas Guttmann does not go so far as Michael Novak in suggesting that blind submission to *sacred* order is our only salvation in modern life, he does suggest that submission to the *social* order of liberal democracy for the most part expands and enriches. As a result of such reasoning, Guttmann emerges from his analysis of the development of modern sport with his abstract philosophical premises intact. It is ironic, however, that in order to accomplish this, he ends up in a theoretical and ideological position that at times seems less influenced by Max Weber than by the legacy of Huizinga's conceptions of ritual and by the spirit of Emile Durkheim's famous dictum about human liberty being "the fruit of regulation."[36]

I want to be as fair as possible to Guttmann on these issues. Yet I cannot help but think that he has been somewhat unfair to analyses that have tried to show how the rules, traditions, institutional structuring, and collective representations that define modern sports are intimately associated with the class structures of western nations, the state, and with the various forms of domination often associated with them. For example, one need not be a Marxist to recognize that, for all their relative freedoms, capitalism and liberal democracy set fundamental limits on human possibilities, limits that are not always positive even when viewed in terms of already established democratic goals for social development. I suspect that Guttmann would agree with me on this. The problem lies in evaluating and deciding upon the nature of these limitations and the degree to which they facilitate freedom and forms of constraint. In making these evaluations, it is often the case that an analyst's own ideological convictions come forward.[37] I think this is what has happened in *From Ritual to Record.* Guttmann's argument that the net loss in freedom from restraint which occurs in liberal democracy is offset by net gains in social integration and the possibilities that flow from it seems every bit as ideological as the Marxist views of which he is so critical. Throughout his book Guttmann is disarmingly honest about recognizing some of the empirical and theoretical inadequacies of his analysis, yet he overlooks this latter contradiction. For this reason there is a sense in which Guttmann's book can be regarded as one more contribution to that well-populated tradition of historical and social-scientific work that equates liberalism with objectivity.

Guttmann's discussion of Marxism can also be criticized in other ways. For example, it is clear throughout his analysis that he does not have a well-developed understanding of Marxist concepts. He reduces the concept of the "mode of production" to simple productive *forces* ("industrialization" is taken to be the basic explanatory factor), and ignores the degree to which the *relations* of production figure in the productive process.[38] He also fails to recognize how the concept of alienation relates to the *totality* of social relations in a society, and not just to a given class.[39] Moreover, he reveals little sensitivity to the key Marxian notions of dialectic and contradiction, and he overstates the extent to which cultural formations must be depicted by Marxists as direct reflections of an economic base.[40]

In summary, I suggest that Guttman has given us a necessary critique of so-called Marxist and neo-Marxist views on sport that helps to sensitize us to the problems of economic reductionism, determinism, and anarchistic romanticism. The problem, however, is that he demonstrates little sensitivity to the subtleties of Marxist theory and its many variations. On the other hand, even though he is not particularly sensitive or sympathetic to Marxism, one thing Guttmann does do is try to show how economic factors and the related questions of necessity are "absolutely essential to any satisfactory interpretation of the nature of modern sport."[41] In this way, he reveals a struggle with a key feature of material history in a way that few idealist thinkers have. Accordingly, even though Guttmann seems to overstate the case for making "positive freedom" both a universal condition of sport and a specific feature of liberal democracy, his analysis is an important attempt to develop a balanced view of action and structure, freedom and constraint in the study of play, games, and sports in social development.

I want to conclude my discussion of Guttmann with just a few more remarks on Marxist and Weberian views on play, games, and sports. One major caveat should be added to any discussion of Guttmann's treatment of Marxism and neo-Marxism as frames of reference for understanding play, games, and sport in western capitalist and state-socialist societies: simply, a good number of the studies alluded to in the "sketches" Guttmann develops of Marxist and neo-Marxist analyses of sport deserve much of the criticism that they receive. For instance, many of the studies he calls "Marxist" are more properly seen as "Leninist" and "Stalinist" works. The writers of such studies often come from state socialist societies, or represent political parties in which Marxism has long been reduced to a series of catechisms and where it is subject to great pressures for theoretical orthodoxy. It is extremely misleading, however, to claim as Guttmann does that criticism of these Leninist or Stalinist analyses is an effective criticism of Marxism itself. To give just one example, the well-known Marxist historian Edward Thompson discusses community games and recreation in his *Making of the English Working Class* without falling into any of the economistic and reductionist traps that Guttmann claims are general characteristics of Marxism.

Guttmann may be on somewhat more solid ground in his criticisms of certain neo-Marxists. As noted earlier in my discussion of Jean-Marie Brohm, many of the neo-Marxists Guttmann criticizes write in a revolutionary tradition that is sometimes overly cavalier about empirical detail and factual accuracy. But such writers are not trying to impress us with their academic sophistication; rather they are trying to reveal a set of problematic "tendencies" and move us to action with voices raised in anger and disgust. Guttmann's criticisms of these voices are often accurate but seem comparatively ineffective. It is especially debatable whether he satisfactorily answers any of the neo-Marxists' criticisms about sports and sexual repression or the constraints that stem from rationalization and the penetration of technocratic rationality into sport. Indeed, although clearly at ideological odds with the neo-Marxists, Guttmann's own thesis is at times remarkably similar to their emphasis on the significance of capitalist productive forces in history and on the rationality and science that has developed in conjunction with these forces. Guttmann's position, however, is that the neo-Marxists' view of this relationship is backwards. Industrial technology and the material requirements of an industrial society did not lead to the development of rationality and science; rather, it is a case of the development of *Zweckrationalität* and a scientific world view creating the climate for industrial development.

Guttmann again claims that this view is inspired by Max Weber. By developing his analysis along these lines, he implies that Weber's work can be taken as something of a refutation of Marxism—a view Anthony Giddens has argued is extremely misleading about Weber's relationship to Marx's work.[42] The fact is that Guttmann is far less sensitive than Weber to the complex interplay between material and ideational forces in social development. For example, Guttmann's discussion of the relationship of sports to Protestantism is weakened by its inability to situate the Reformation in the broader context of class relations and status-group formation. Instead Guttmann drifts into the tenuous argument that Protestant religions were simply among the first groups to develop a strong cultural attachment to the scientific world view. His supporting examples—which depict low levels of sport involvement on the part of French-Canadian Catholics and Swiss theology majors—are neither adequate nor convincing.[43]

Conclusion: Play, Games, and Sports as Structure and Agency

In this chapter I have attempted to identify a series of fundamental paradoxes about the seemingly autonomous and independent character of play, games, and sports and their dependent and regulated character. Most significant among these paradoxes are the roles played by the constitutive boundaries which are created in and out of human experience for the expressed purpose of separating play, games, and sporting activities from necessity and from social reality. These boundaries—seen variously as rules, traditions, beliefs, and organizational structures—have been interpreted by some writers as necessary for the effective exercise of freedom in and through play, games, and sports, and they have been seen by others as somehow inimical to the exercise of such freedom.

The writers I have discussed have all incorporated elements of these paradoxical features of play, games, and sports into their various analytic projects. Although their perceptions often differ on substantive issues, I have argued that Huizinga, Novak, and Guttmann all lapse into forms of idealist abstraction as ways of explaining the nature and significance of sport and its role in social development. As a result, all three have tended either to ignore or underplay the significance of material history as a part of the constituting processes of the intentions of players, and of the rules, traditions, beliefs, and organizations which define play, game, and sporting activities at different historical moments. Jean-Marie Brohm, on the other hand, goes too far in reducing games and sports (as distinct from spontaneous play) to simple reflections of materialist categories. Brohm's analyses are also frequently functionalist. Thus, as in the case of all functionalist analyses—whether Marxist or Liberal—the constitutive features of cultural production as a whole social and material process are downgraded and recast in the form of a systemic teleology: games and sports become features of the abstract needs or "requirements" of a reified functioning structure.[44]

In contradistinction to these views, the position I have been attempting to sketch out emphasizes that play, games, and sports ought to be seen as constitutive social practices whose meanings, metaphoric qualities, and regulatory structures are indissolubly connected to the making and remaking of ourselves as agents (individual and collective) in society. To put the matter another way, rather than view any feature of play, games, and sports as some sort of transhistorical essence, need, or transcendent metaphysical form, or rather than see them as activities simply reducible to a "separate" material reality, I am opting for a view where play, games, and sports are all regarded as irreducibly constitutive of our social being. They are, in differing ways, all forms of *social practice*. As a result, even their "essential" or formal qualities cannot be conceived of independently of the organizing principles, expectations, conflicts, and disappointments that define lived social experience at any given historical moment.

My position on the relationship of freedom to play, games, and sports is built on the above assumption. Simply stated, I would adopt Steven Lukes's view that human agents (viewed individually or collectively) consist historically in a set of expanding and contracting abilities and are always faced with expanding and contracting opportunities.[45] Together, these expansions and contractions constitute varying forms of "structured possibilities" which specify "the powers of agents, varying between agents and over time for any given agent." Given this, I would insist that if we are to avoid the simplistic view that spontaneous play is always an expression of freedom, and that "structured" games and sports are always constraining; or, conversely, the view that *all* games and sports are simply organized expressions of play and thereby guarantee "positive freedom"; then we will have to be more sensitive to the dialectical relationships between socially structured possibilities and human agency.

In other words, we must struggle to avoid one-sided considerations of players as voluntary agents acting in the absence of constraining structures and of structures which do not allow for the creative and transformative capacities of players.

Obviously this struggle will require that we be quite specific about the nature of the limits and possibilities that can be associated with play, games, and sports as "structured" forms of human activity.[46] I think it crucial to recognize as a general principle that any given structure may have the capacity to both open up and close off different possibilities and choices. In the case of games and sports, for example, the rules, traditions, and organizations which define them may be both enabling and constraining. But how do we decide on the conditions which variously influence these options for different agents or groups of agents? The answer is a historical one, and requires that we situate our study of play, games, and sports in the context of understanding the historical struggle over the control of rules and resources in social life, and the ways in which this struggle relates to structured limits and possibilities.

2

Problems of Class Inequality and Structural Change in Play, Games, and Sport

... sport, like any other practice is an object of struggles between the fractions of the dominant class and also between social classes ... the social definition of sport *is an object of struggles ... in which what is at stake,* inter alia, *is the monopolistic capacity to impose the legitimate definition of sporting practice and the legitimate functioning of sporting activity.*

Pierre Bourdieu, 1978

Expansions and contractions, historically shifting limits and possibilities, socially structured possibilities—these are all terms used in the previous chapter to denote the relative and problematic character of the "freedom" available to different individual or collective agents both as a condition in and a consequence of play, games, and sports. In this chapter I want to elaborate on some of the ways in which human choices and possibilities expressed in and through play, games, and sports are influenced by the differential resources that people can bring to bear on their life situation as a result of class differences in social life. More specifically, I shall argue that the effects of these differential resources can be measured in the greater collective power of some agents to "structure" play, games, and sports in certain ways and to contour the range of meanings and significations associated with them.[1]

As a second emphasis in this chapter I want to examine in greater detail some of the major perspectives that sociologists have used to explain the expansion and contraction of opportunities and options associated with sport's relationship to social class over the last two centuries. In particular, I shall attempt to outline some of the fundamental weaknesses of these perspectives as analytic frames of reference, not only for an understanding of sports in themselves, but also for grasping the broader significance of sports as meaningful features of culture actively involved in the production and reproduction of society. This discussion will provide the foundation for presenting what I take to be a more acceptable set of guidelines for the study of class, sports, and social development.

Practices, Structures, and Power in Play, Games, and Sports

In the preceding chapter I argued that play forms, games, and sports can best be understood as real social practices rather than as abstractions, idealized forms of theological or aesthetic sensibility, or purely voluntaristic expressivity. I also suggested that, as real social practices, play forms, games, and sports ought not to be perceived as the actions of agents who are simply objective "supports" or "bearers" of "objective determinations" in history, or of abstract "system needs" of "functional imperatives." Rather, borrowing from Raymond Williams, I concluded that play, games, and sports were *constitutive* practices set in a whole social process in which humans interact with one another and generally try to make sense of themselves as agents in their association with other agents. Although the meanings, metaphoric qualities, and symbolic representations associated with the practice of play, games, and sports vary, are openly textured, and imperfectly shared, they are nonetheless connected in an indissoluble, constitutive way to the raw experiences of material history. Because these arguments were developed only indirectly in chapter one, I want to take some time now to state certain features of the arguments in more detail.

Let me begin this discussion by acknowledging the phenomenologists' claim that the interpretation and ordering of the world in a meaningful way is a fundamental element of all human activity, whether this activity is directly tied to necessity or to intentional actions motivated by a desire to separate activity from necessity. Interpretation and meaning are threaded through all of the means whereby humans "make themselves" by producing and reproducing their own means of life. This production and reproduction of our means of life and the making and the remaking of our social being goes far beyond any narrow sense of production in a purely economic sense and includes all those forms of activity whereby humans interact with one another and with nature. It is in this sense, as forms of cultural production, that we can regard play, games, and sports *in themselves* to be concrete, material social practices that are creations of human agency. In other words, play, games, and sports do not emerge "naturally" in social interaction, nor are they the manifestations of "received" states of consciousness, universal aesthetics, or the human spirit; rather they are activities people "produce" in different forms and in different ways out of the stuff of everyday experience. In this way play, games, and sports can be understood as the skilled accomplishments of players and organizers—accomplishments that involve constitutive elements of practical consciousness as human agents produce, reproduce, and produce anew the conditions of their own existence.[2]

Yet, as I suggested in the previous chapter, it is important to recognize the degree to which these constitutive forms of practical consciousness and the broader production and reproduction of the conditions of human existence derive their substance from—and are simultaneously bounded by—historically indentifiable structures through which, and sometimes against which, agents act. To adopt a well-known Marxist aphorism in a slightly modified form, while human agents certainly make their own history, they do not make it completely under conditions of their choosing.[3] Rather, people make history in the face of, and in conjunction with, previously established significative schemes (e.g., symbolic systems such as language) and habitualized patterns of social action. If one applies this aphorism to play, games, and sports one can say that while all of the practices that humans define as playful or sporting are made, they are not made in a way that is completely at the discretion of individual or collective agents.

For purposes of this discussion, I shall argue that there are three basic respects in which we can explicate the aphorism that while play, games, and sports are activities that are made, they are not made in a completely voluntary way: (1) in respect of the nature of the "ordered" significative schemes, such as language and gesture, through which agents act expressively in their efforts to make sense of and interpret themselves in the world; (2) in respect of habituated and institutionally established patterns of action expressed as rules, traditions, and organizations which take on a seemingly "objective" character and thereby "limit" or "order" the actions of players in various ways; and (3) in respect of the nature of the broader historically constituted social relations and allocative strategies which influence and define the distribution of material and symbolic resources in society, and the differential capacity of some people to shape the nature and meanings of the significative schemes, social patterns, relations, and rules referred to above in (1) and (2).

I shall now elaborate on some of the ways in which these schemes, social patterns, relations, and rules both enhance and limit the options available to people in—and as a result of—their participation in play, games, and sports. First, I will focus on some relationships between play and expressive, significative action. Social psychologists have often argued that play is an assertive, expressive act through which individuals attempt to exercise their personal powers in an enjoyable way. Some have gone even further to argue that play is a form of intentional action directed toward vivification and a degree of control—or practical mastery—over one's immediate environment. Ironically, such an attempt at vivification and practical mastery proceeds by virtue of a conscious decision to do something impractical or unnecessary. Nonetheless, the conscious decision to act against the dictates of necessity, and the unintended consequences of such decisions, are in themselves assertive and expressive; that is, they are features of actions willfully undertaken in order to lead to some kind of gratification. We say that such actions are voluntarily undertaken when it can be argued that in the situation in question the human agent *could have acted differently* and, in some cases, when it appears that control over the particular practices undertaken *in play* or *as play* remains within the powers of the individual player or of a specific group of players.

On the other hand, these "voluntary" actions are clearly not in any way separable from the wide range of constituting significative schemes which guide and shape human interaction and which can be implicated in the production and the reproduction of society. Even in the simplest forms of "unorganized" play, the fun that is consciously pursued, the practical mastery that is expressed, and the meanings that are created, are *enabled* or allowed through the use of expressive significative schemes already in place. The player voluntarily expresses himself or herself *creatively* through the repertoire of significative schemes at his or her disposal and thereby unintentionally reproduces these schemes. Put another way, each production of a new playful act is, paradoxically, the reproduced outcome of socially constituted significative schemes that have enabled the accomplishment of the act that has taken place.[4]

There are numerous arguments in sociology that appear to be generally similar to this line of reasoning. Piaget's work with children's play comes readily to mind when one focuses on the reproductive aspects of play; and George Herbert Mead's discussions of play, games, and their relationships to the constitution of the social self through symbolic interaction are brought to mind when one emphasizes the creatively constituting features of playful action. Mead, in particular, has considerably influenced how sociologists understand the role of play and games in socialization.[5] I think one can argue, however, that the symbolic interactionist tradition has not been very effective in conceiving of the symbolic connections between human interpretations and social practice as contested issues constituted in and out of a historical struggle between agents having markedly differing material interests. Moreover, as Giddens has noted, symbolic interactionism tends to focus on symbolic actions only as meaningful representations of society rather than as actual media for the exercise of practical activities; that is, as ways of "doing things."[6] Thus, one might argue that the symbolic interactionists have downplayed *the extent to which signification itself is a mode of production*—an enabling and reproducing structure of rules and resources in social life that can be understood in close association with those disciplines (e.g., history and political economy) whose primary focus is the historical struggle over "ways of doing things."[7]

It falls well outside the limits that I have set myself in this chapter to discuss in any detail either the strengths and limits of symbolic interactionism or the ways in which any given significative system (e.g., language) can be understood as practical activity. I shall only say that the very clear and constitutive relationship between signification as a medium for the accomplishment of play, and the significative nature of play itself as a practical activity in social life (e.g., as a form of discourse), suggests the degree to which even the simplest forms of play are not completely without "limits." I would add as a caveat to this, however, that in simple play the significative schemes through which play is accomplished as a meaningful practice are not yet fully incorporated characteristics *of play* as a "formal" type of social action. In this way, the simplest forms of play, seen as intentional actions, contain within them only the "limits" set by the significative schemes that have contributed to their accomplishment as social actions. Inasmuch as these schemes are somewhat open-ended and are primarily used at the discretion of the agent in *the creation* of some act of practical mastery or gratification, they are far more liberating than constraining. The unintended consequences of such playing, however, are more difficult to establish and they suggest the need to examine questions about the nature of play and what it means to play in the context of more concrete patterns of social interaction.

The patterns of social interaction to which I am referring are those patterns of social relationships that appear to take on an objectified systemic nature in social life. Let us explore the issue of the limits and possibilities expressed in and through play that becomes more formally *organized* in its association with social relationships. We can do this by focusing on the systemic and regulated character of games and sports—activities where there has been a conscious attempt to establish collectively a set of formal boundaries designed to structure play in a certain way and insure its separation from necessity. These boundaries are defined by the creation of fixed rules that are created *specific to a given game or sport* and to which the player voluntarily submits as a condition of playing. Knowledge of these rules is the first condition for partaking in different forms of games and sports. The second condition is that players at least agree to abide by the rules that they or others have made. The degree to which these rules "count" and the nature of their specific social significance depends greatly on the extent to which they become institutionalized features of social life.

Institutions in social life are generally depicted by sociologists as distinctive patterns of social interaction whose structural features represent recognized, established, and legitimated ways of pursuing some activity.[8] To speak of the institutionalization of games and sports is to note how, in a particular type of game or physical activity, a particular way of playing has become formalized and "objectified" as the direct result of the interests of certain groups that have sought its preservation. In sport, institutionalization has meant insuring that specific codified rules become widely accepted so that particularistic approaches to the activity can be incorporated into a more universalistic pattern (that is, they become subject to a *dominant* "way of playing"). In western sport this has usually meant the creation of organizational bodies whose purpose is to regulate the sport and insure its legitimation. In accordance with this process, the structuring of sport has become increasingly systematized, formalized, and removed from the direct control of individual players.[9]

I suppose one may assert that even institutionalized sports are "free" to the extent that one has the option of either playing and submitting to the rules in place, or not playing and thereby not submitting. Moreover, it seems that the creation and protection of formal boundaries specific to games and sports opens up and allows for the expression of creative agency and the production of enjoyment and meaning. In other words, we can certainly recognize, abstractly at least, the enabling capacity of even the most formal of the structures involved in the institutional structuring of playful action.[10] On the other hand, there is a sense in which the issue of the liberating potential of sport can become rather complicated. One need only think, for example, of the rather shadowy freedom expressed in or through sport in societies that place a great premium on sporting performance but where opportunities for involvement are not widely available; or where submitting to a particular set of regulations that may not be culturally palatable to certain subordinate societal subgroups is a necessary condition for involvement in socially valued sport; or where the "way of doing" sport, or what sport "says" as a form of signification, might somehow dramatize certain elements that can be implicated in the domination of particular peoples. One might go on from this and question the ways in which the very structures that enable the playing of games and sports are intimately connected to broader limits and pressures which influence the course of social development in society. The objective moment in the dialectical production of games and sports is expressed in the fact that in order for playful action to be structured in a way that creates the conditions for dramatic metaphor and agonistic expression—or even for "positive freedom" as Allen Guttmann would say—there must be very precise limits on the range of options available to players.

As noted in the last chapter, it is all too easy to romanticize what these limits allow for and thereby become caught up in intransigent defenses of their abstract *enabling capacities.* However, I want to examine some of these limits in a way that avoids the romanticized celebration of abstract form so common in idealist analyses of play, games, and sports. The main way to avoid such romanticism, I believe, is to focus on the way in which the limits which organize action within institutionalized games and sports can be related directly to broader limits in society and to certain pressures which both support and work against these limits.[11]

Let me begin with those limits most commonly perceived as occurring within institutionalized games and sports. I would argue that in most examples of western institutionalized games and sports, the formal limiting of options within the institution appears to have occurred in two related cultural senses: (1) a *technical* sense, which involves limitations on the range of practices open to any player within the rules of the game (e.g., one cannot pass the ball forward beyond the line of scrimmage in a game of Canadian or American football); and (2) a *moral* sense, wherein only certain practices are deemed acceptable as play or sport (e.g., certain restrictions on hyperaggressive practices in certain games; or regulations about the propriety of betting; or over the definition of one's status as an "amateur" or "professional").

If we follow the work of John Searle, it is tempting to distinguish among these limits two basic kinds of rules: constitutive and regulative.[12] Constitutive rules in games, Searle argues, are the stuff upon which the game is structured as a social possibility. If we suspend them or imagine a st in which they have not been introduced, the whole range of behavior that they sustain simply would not exist. In a discussion of Searle's work, Charles Taylor cites the example of chess and argues that if one were to remove the rules that allow for the accomplishment of chess, one might still push wooden pieces on a board made of squares 8 by 8, but this practice would no longer be chess.[13] Regulative rules, on the other hand, are those which do not fundamentally alter the structure of the game but guide its execution. Taylor's example of a regulative rule is that a player say "j'adoube" when he or she touches a piece without intending to play it.

Taylor goes on, correctly I believe, to argue that the nature of the constitutive elements of social life goes well beyond the use that Searle attaches to it. Rather, Taylor suggests that the meaning of "constitutive" be extended to include all of the rules that can be associated with social practices and with the production and reproduction of society.[14] Indeed it is this broad sense of the notion of constitutive practices and structures (seen as rules and resources coordinated in systems of social interaction) for which I have been arguing throughout this study. For example, I suggest that the technical and moral limits on action I have described as characteristics specific to the accomplishment of games and sports are neither "innocent" nor "neutral." Their lack of innocence and neutrality stems from the fact that they are constitutive elements involved in the structuring of the game and in the creation of dominant interpretations of it. Moreover, all of these constitutive limits are clearly connected to other sets of rules and interpretations that only exist "outside" the game in an abstract formal sense. Due to the connected nature of these different rules and interpretations, it is highly problematic to imagine that the production and reproduction of games and sports can somehow be separated from a broader understanding of the conditions influencing the production and reproduction of social life as a whole. To think in this way violates the dialectical sense of the notion of constitutive practices, ignores the fact that games and sports are in themselves a part of material production by knowledgeable human agents, and reproduces the idealist separation of games and sports from material life which I criticized in the previous chapter.

The issue at hand, however, is to evaluate the question of the limiting nature of the various constitutive structures, dominant practices, and interpretations that characterize institutionalized games and sports. Because the various structural elements of action in institutionalized games and sports are *constitutive* rather than completely *determinate*, I have used the word "limit" rather than "determine" to suggest the degree to which players (or would-be players)—even though limited by technical and moral standards—are not always completely constrained. In addition to exploring and finding new options by acting through and within such limits, players have often been prone to exert conscious and unconscious pressures against certain technical interpretations and rules and against established moral standards for play. They have, in short, frequently resisted, contested, and protested against these rules and the official interpretations of the meaning of these rules as legislated by official bodies. And, in some cases, they have adapted and modified these rules and interpretations to their own needs.

Although many of the pressures that players or nonplayers have brought to bear on rules and dominant interpretations can be understood as narrow expressions of personal interest, there is a strong sense in which such pressures have often signified much broader forms of social discontent. Yet, I would argue that whatever form these pressures take, their effectiveness, *their transformative capacity,* can be seen to be closely related to the type and range of social resources that individual or groups of players and nonplayers can bring to bear in order to restructure, reinterpret, and transform the limits in question. In other words, the *power* of players and of nonplayers to define and apply rules, to create dominant interpretations, and to defy or seek to transform such rules and interpretations, can be expressed in terms of a differential capacity to use resources of different types in order to secure outcomes.[15] The problem, of course, is that the resources individual or collective agents (e.g., a social class) can bring to bear on the production and reproduction of rules, procedures, legitimated interpretations, and even on the abilities needed to play effectively within certain structured conditions, are never distributed randomly in society. They are, rather, the negotiated products of historically specific systems of domination and divergences of interest—systems whose objectified allocative strategies and fundamental social relations give some agents a disproportionate advantage in defining and shaping the fundamental structures through which social action proceeds, and in deflecting or incorporating pressures that are exerted against these strategies and relations.

In formulating these arguments I have drawn heavily from Anthony Giddens's recent discussions of structures and power in *New Rules of Sociological Method* and *Studies in Social and Political Theory.* Giddens emphasizes that it is highly problematic to separate the idea of the structuring of social action from the notion of constitutive rules and practices set in the context of the ever-present "reflexive rationalization of action." What Giddens means by the phrase *reflexive rationalization of action* is the capability of all agents to control their activity through "a chronic awareness of its conditions and consequences thereby connecting wants to intentions."[16] The structures that agents create to order their lives (and those of others) can be understood as the specific coordination of rules and resources in given systems of interaction. Following Wittgenstein's analysis of what it means "to know a rule," Giddens goes on to argue that the creation and application of rules of all types is not only a form of meaningful practical activity, but is also an expression of power.[17] Thus he notes that,

> "what happens" in any given situation of the application of rules to generate social interaction depends on the resources that those who are party to that interaction are able to mobilize in the encounter. "What happens" here has to include not just the "outcome" of interaction, in respect of motivations that participants bring to it, but in principle may concern the very nature of that interaction itself. For if knowledge (mutual knowledge) of rules is the condition of the production of interaction, it is not in and of itself a condition of how those rules are "interpreted" or made "to count." *These latter depend upon the relative influence that those who participate in the* interaction bring to bear on its course.[18] [Emphasis added.]

The resources that agents can mobilize to make their interpretations (and the specific practices that these interpretations engender) count, Giddens continues, are socially constituted and may range from the "command of verbal skills to the application of physical violence." In this way resources can be seen as being constituted in, and as properties of, structures. Agents "possess" resources, Giddens claims, "in the parallel sense to that in which they 'know' rules."[19] For example, authority might be seen as a "structured resource" which can be potentially drawn on by some agents in a way that "influences" the conduct of others (I would use the notions of "limit" and "pressure" here). Similarly, agents might also draw on such resources as wealth, family connections, or verbal skill. Giddens notes in particular how language skills are based on a "resource knowledge" of *acceptable* language structures—structures whose acceptability has been socially constituted and coordinated with broader rules and resources—broader structures—which define economic production or the distribution of social honor. Following such notions one might suggest how different forms of involvement in games and sports may well be enhanced by a "resource knowledge" of culturally specific "ways of playing," or by the greater capacity to mobilize certain more "objective" resources such as free time, money, or access to facilities and coaching. The first type of resources involves a set of pressures and limits on *abilities*, and the second involves a set of pressures and limits on *opportunities*.[20]

One unfortunate feature of Giddens's work on structures and power is the comparative inattention given to specifying the kinds of resources that subordinate groups or social classes can bring to bear on the transformation of those structures which limit the range of abilities and opportunities readily available to them (although one can imagine that he might refer to such practices as strikes, work stoppages, etc.). At the same time, I do not think that Giddens deals in sufficient detail with the centrality of the struggle over the making of rules governing the production and reproduction of resources of different types, or how resources created under a set of legitimate "dominant" rules ought to be allocated. Yet, such caveats notwithstanding, much in Giddens's work provides a useful foundation for studies of the significance of games and sports as socially and culturally "structured" possibilities. More specifically, his work provides important theoretical support for an emphasis in the analysis of sports and social development on the changing relationships between the pressures and limits expressed in the formal structuring of sports, and those associated with the broader structuring of economic and cultural production.

Sport, Class Inequality, and Social Reproduction

Most studies of the social development of capitalist societies suggest that the major resources human agents have been able to bring to bear on their life situations have been tied to the socially constituted "rules" (including traditions and beliefs) which govern the rational organization of the labor process, the rights to property, the creation of surplus value, and the marketability of educational credentials.[21] The social classes that have emerged in capitalist societies can be defined in *relational* terms on the basis of a differential capacity to employ and define these rules for their own benefit.[22] This is not to say that the specification of these rules has been consciously undertaken with the goal of creating a class in itself (much less a class for itself), or with the idea of defending one set of class interests against another. Nor do I mean to imply that the specification of given sets of rules has developed without opposition either within classes (e.g., between status groups or class fragments) or between classes. The point is, however, that in conjunction with changing allocative rules and resources in western societies over the last few hundred years, the distinctly *quantitative* differences between individual rules and positions in the division of labor have taken on a distinctly *qualitative* character as bourgeoisie and proletariat emerged to challenge the traditional rules and resources that sustained the class systems of feudal societies.

Consider on this point, Giddens's discussion in *The Class Structure of the Advanced Societies* of the "rules" and accompanying "rights" which lie at the very core of the development of the capitalist state:

> In capitalism, authority relationships . . . (industry and state) . . . ultimately rest upon the rights inherent in the possession and deployment of capital. In neither case are these rights legitimized, as in feudal society as the natural rights of a specific minority; their legitimacy derives from newly recognized concepts of freedom and equality. In the sphere of the economy itself, freedom of contracts effectively sanctions the dominance of the owner of capital, since the wage-labourer is forced to deliver himself into the hands of the capitalist by dint of economic necessity. This position of nominal freedom and actual bondage is reinforced and stabilized by the modern state, which recognizes "political" rights of citizenship, but separates these from industry.[23]

Giddens continues by noting how Marx's analysis is flawed by its insufficient attention to the irreducible nature of the state as an autonomous social formation, and to the particular forms of domination embedded in the general demands of coordination and the control of large state operations. I do not want to engage in a discussion of this issue here; rather I think it necessary for present purposes simply to have noted some of the ways in which the fundamental social relations of capitalist liberal democracy have created conditions for the mobilization of differential resources by social classes and for the general reproduction of the class system.

This particular use of the word "reproduction" needs clarification. My use of this term does not suggest that the class systems of western capitalist societies are in any way fixed, rigid, or without internal pressures and tensions. On the contrary, ongoing processes of class formation and re-formation, shifting relations between class fragments, and notable changes in the statuses of certain occupational categories within the class system, are all important and visible features of the socioeconomic development of the western capitalist societies (more on this later). Yet, there is an undeniable sense in which the essential social relations out of which capitalism is constituted as a particular form of political economy have shown a remarkable durability. As Paul Willis notes in his subtle and perceptive study of social reproduction in Britain,

> the factories are filled on Monday morning and on every Monday morning with workers displaying the necessary apparent gradations between mental and manual capacity and corresponding attitudes necessary to maintain, within broad limits, the present structure of class and production.[24]

Willis goes on to argue that the social reproduction of capitalist social relations is not immutably set in dominant cultural forms, but is rather a fragile "contested settlement" expressed in and through a wide range of far more diverse cultural creations. These cultural creations, Willis argues, are constituted by "varieties of symbolic systems and articulations" and the bases and impetus of their production is the "informal social group" and its collective energies.[25] These energies are expressed in the direct attempt that agents make to develop meaningful accounts and representations of the world and to "experiment with possibilities for gaining some excitement and diversion" from these accounts and representations. They are also expressed in a kind of "profane revelatory probing" of the world and its fundamental organizing categories. It is these processes that work to provide the materials toward, and the immediate context of, the construction of subjectivities and the confirmation of identity.

Yet, Willis argues, while such cultural forms are autonomous productions—that is, they are not reducible to other elements of social practice, to other modes of production—their ". . . basic nature and their own full reproduction can only be understood . . . with respect to the way in which they help to produce the major relationships of the social group to itself, to other classes and to the (broader) productive process." Willis does not discuss "interpretations" of institutionalized games and sports directly as part of these cultural forms. But he does show, brilliantly I think, how profane "playing"—seen as the pursuit of informal mastery in spheres separated from necessity and as a medium for accomplishing the social identity of working-class youth—has unintended reproductive consequences. In this sense, Willis's work underlines the importance of examining not only the "objective" existence of rules and resources seen as abilities or opportunities, but also the meaningful features of these rules and resources expressed in dominant and legitimated interpretations and in oppositional interpretations. In examining the relationships between the institutional structuring of games and sports, and broader structures in social life, one has to be careful not to lose track of the nature and consequences of cultural resistance to dominant limits and pressures.

If one applies this type of reasoning to the study of games and sports in social development, then one must be sensitive to the meanings that players and spectators accord to the choices they make (e.g., to play or not to play, to watch or not to watch, how to play or to watch), or that they believe are available to them within certain limits and pressures. One must also attempt to evaluate the ways in which these choices and beliefs are incorporated into the broader reproduction of those impersonal rules, resources, and coordinating patterns of social relationships that are both the medium and the outcome of social interaction. Such a view does not necessarily commit one to the argument that games and sports are nothing more than straightforward cultural representations created in some determinate way by agents who have superior resources due to their class position. Nor does it mean that the limits associated with the structuring of sports automatically reflect or correspond to limits generated abstractly in the mode of production—limits that are internalized in some way by spectators and fans.[26] What this view does demand, however, is some attempt to specify those moments in the production and reproduction of meaning in games and sports, where the culturally specific pressures and limits embodied in the dominant representations of institutionally established sporting practices appear to penetrate so deeply into the whole substance of lived identities and relationships that they come to be widely regarded as the pressures and limits of universal experience and common sense.

It is in this way, as Raymond Williams notes, that Marxists speak of the incorporation of cultural forms into a set of "hegemonic" processes.[27] Hegemony, Williams argues, does not exist as some sort of passive process but must be continually "renewed, recreated, defended and modified." It is also continually resisted, limited, altered, and challenged by autonomous cultural processes that involve countering interpretations. It is not that one class, or one collective agent, has all the material and symbolic resources in societies. A dominant class has advantages, it has superior resources, but it cannot prevent human beings from thinking on their condition, from wanting to expand their powers, or from continually constituting their identities now in one way, now in another. What a dominant class can do is to define selectively through tradition and through institutions a sense of predisposed continuity and accepted mechanisms of incorporation. Indeed, these are a part of the resources which define its hegemony. Williams points out, for example, how any process of human socialization "includes things that all human beings have to learn," but that any culturally specific process, any dominant conception

> ties this necessary learning to a selected range of meanings, values, and practices which, in the very closeness of their associations with necessary learning, constitute the real foundations of the hegemonic. In a family children are cared for and taught to care for themselves, but within this necessary process fundamental and selective attitudes to self, to others, to a social order, and to the material world are both consciously and unconsciously taught. Education transmits necessary knowledge and skills, but always by a particular selection from the whole available range, and with intrinsic attitudes, both to learning and social relations, which are in practice virtually inextricable.[28]

Yet, the whole process is filled with unresolved conflicts, contradictions, and confusions. In conjunction with dominant definitions and practices are a wide range of idiosyncratic interpretations, emergent and historically residual definitions and practices, and a continual process of creative cultural formation which occurs both within and in opposition to the practices and definitions incorporated in the hegemonic process. Thus, Williams concludes, when studying the active role of cultural formations in the production and reproduction of the whole social material process, one must remember that

> *no mode of production and therefore no dominant social order and therefore no dominant culture ever in reality excludes or exhausts all human practice, human energy and human intention.* This is not merely a negative proposition, allowing us to account for significant things which happen outside or against the dominant mode. On the contrary it is a fact about modes of domination, that they select from and consequently exclude the full range of human practice. What they exclude may often be seen as the personal or the private, or as the natural or even the metaphysical. Indeed, it is usually in one or another of these terms that the excluded area is expressed, since what the dominant has effectively seized is indeed the ruling definition of the social.[29] [Emphasis in original.]

I want to argue that if we use Williams's general work on cultural production to provide additional background for analyzing games and sports in social development, we are led to focus on two issues: (1) the nature of dominant, residual, and emergent cultural practices and interpretations, including the limits and pressures associated with each; and (2) how all of these practices, interpretations, limits, and pressures appear to be incorporated into the hegemonic process at any given historical moment. To what extent and in what sense, we might ask, are the technical and moral limits associated with dominant institutionally supported sports of today—and the various actions and interpretations created within and against these limits—actively involved in the production and reproduction of class relations? To ask this question is to move one's understanding of the "play" of games and sports—as meaningful practices, structured in certain ways and in conjunction with unequally distributed social resources that are linked to broader rules and social relations—directly into the realms of history and political economy.

Let me offer a few final comments about sport as a meaningful and dramatic feature of social life before turning to more detailed considerations of the relationships between sport and social class as outlined in previous historical and sociological writing on social development in capitalist societies. Given the analysis I have been developing, it is easy to suggest some important parallels between my understanding of sports in cultural production and certain aspects of the work of those writers who have argued that sports may be seen as "cultural texts."[30] To say that sports are cultural texts is to suggest that they are imaginative works built out of social materials and which offer metasocial commentaries on social conditions and human emotions. As cultural texts, Clifford Geertz suggests that sports involve the conscious "use of emotion for cognitive ends."[31] They cannot be reduced to functional necessities, or to forums for the display and learning of dominant values as functionalist analyses would suggest.[32] Rather they offer "interpretations," particular "readings" of human experience.

Geertz's penetrating and masterful "reading" of the Balinese cockfight is the starting point for most writings which have gone on to develop the "sport-as-cultural-text" thesis. In analyzing the cockfight as a commentary on Balinese experience, Geertz emphasizes the degree to which the cockfight symbolically combines deep elements of masculinity and profane animality with a telling dramatization of Balinese status concerns. In this sense the cockfight is a story that the Balinese tell themselves about each other and about what it means to be Balinese.

Because the cockfight is a story, a representation, Geertz continues, it tends only to function in an interpretive rather than instrumental way. In this sense the cockfight is like an art form, and as with any art form, what the cockfight does is "render ordinary experience comprehensible by presenting it in terms of acts and objects which have had their practical consequences removed and been reduced . . . to the level of sheer appearances."[33] In a practical sense, the cockfight is only "real" to the cocks. As a mode of cultural expression for the Balinese, its purpose is neither "to assuage social passions nor to heighten them . . . but to display them." Thus, Geertz argues that

> the slaughter in the cock ring is not a depiction of how things really are among men, but, what is almost worse, of how, from a particular angle, they imagine they are. The angle, of course, is stratificatory. What . . . the cockfight talks most forcibly about is status relationships, and what it says about them is that they are matters of life and death. . . . A particular fusion of Polynesian title ranks and Hindu castes, the hierarchy of pride is the moral backbone of the society. But only in the cockfight are the sentiments upon which that hierarchy rests revealed in their natural colours.[34]

Geertz goes on to say that Balinese life expresses itself much differently elsewhere and that the cockfight is only one of an ensemble of texts that both constitute Balinese culture and are models of Balinese culture.

I think one can learn a great deal from Geertz's "reading" of the Balinese cockfight, but one must be wary in "reading" Geertz not to draw the conclusion that cultural texts should be considered only as metasocial forms of specialized art. To argue that cultural texts are simple models of experience, raised "above" practical reality through form and presenting this reality in terms of sheer experience, brings one dangerously close to a problematic philosophical position which views cultural models abstractly as transcendent forms that allow for the metaphorical resolution of social conflicts in a supposedly neutral manner.[35]

For the most part Geertz's own work avoids such a position, but he is somewhat ambiguous about the precise nature of the cockfight's relationships to the *social*. For example, on the one hand Geertz cites Auden's argument that "poetry makes nothing happen," and he suggests that the cockfight also "makes nothing happen": "Men go on allegorically humiliating one another . . . But no one's status really changes." Moreover, Geertz tells us, "almost every Balinese I have ever discussed the subject with has said" the cockfight is very much like "playing with fire and not getting burned":

> You activate village and kin group rivalries and hostilities, but in "play" form coming dangerously and enticingly close to the expression of open and direct interpersonal and intergroup aggression . . . but not quite because after all, it is "only a cockfight."[36]

On the other hand, Geertz seems rather leery about pushing too far the idea that the cockfight "makes nothing happen." For after having told us about the allegorical character of the cockfight, and that this allegory is separated from "practical" consequences, he goes on to emphasize that all

> art forms generate and regenerate the very subjectivity they pretend only to display. Quartets, still lifes, and cock-fights are not merely reflections of a pre-existing sensibility analogically represented; they are positive agents in the creation and maintenance of such a sensibility.[37]

So it seems that the cockfight really makes something happen after all. It is practically real for the cocks in the sense that they actually fight and die; it is practically real for the Balinese as a constitutive cultural form—not "above" reality in any way, even as a form of metaphor, but as a part of the making and remaking of reality. To separate "sensibility," "subjectivity," or "sentiment" from the production and reproduction of material life and forms of practical consciousness is to commit a crucial error in the analysis of cultural forms.

Can we say that cultural texts which dramatize hierarchy, forms of domination, or basic axes of social conflict in societies are completely devoid of practical consequences? The Balinese may "play with fire and not get burned" when passions are inflamed in the cockfight, but this says more about social stability in Balinese society than it says about sport itself. Indeed, there are numerous examples in other cultures where sporting contests have been real forums for class hostility or racial tension and where the formal limits of the game have actually provided important and symbolically powerful opportunities for overt conflict.[38]

Let us look at the matter in a slightly different way and examine the often utopian promises expressed in sport which I discussed in the last chapter. It is often argued in "cultural text" theories of modern sports in the West that sports represent metaphoric resolutions of conflicts over inequality by appealing to principles of order and meritocratic reasoning which transcend the principles upon which people are differentiated into ranks. It is along these lines, for example, that Fred Inglis has argued that sport

> bodies forth some of the main meanings available to us, and at a time of deep moral confusion, it may at its best, permit the clash of moralities, the contradiction of moral imperatives, to be known and understood and balanced. The old bitter opposition—between democracy and excellence, between the individual and the group, between heart and mind, between aristocrat and worker—these irreconcilables, rather than being at each other's throats can live in the spontaneous ebb and flow, the high tension of creative play. When this happens—and it can only happen for a moment —then a man becomes whole, to himself and to his times. He rediscovers purity.[39]

These are utopian promises to be sure. Can we say in a hierarchical and class-divided society that there are no practical consequences involved with such significations? I think not. Indeed, I think we even need to go further and ask how universal the interpretation of such meanings really is. On what basis may it be said, for example, that *all* people in society draw such meanings from sporting contests? On what basis can it be asserted that such meanings are "the main meanings available to us" at this stage in social development?

Questions about the practical and distinctly social nature of such significations are complicated, of course, by the fact that modern sports mix their messages with other realities of lived experience in complex and often contradictory ways. In one sense sports appear to go beyond representation to actually embody a set of "fulfilled" promises in social life—for example, a fair contest between equals, freely entered into and decided on the basis of merit.[40] Yet, sports do not expose the underlying terms of reference upon which definitions of fairness, equality, freedom, and merit have been constituted in the broader society. And, when one examines these terms of reference sociologically, one tends immediately to want to qualify *how* fair, *how* equal, *how* free, and *how* meritocratic things really are.

On the other hand there can be no denying that in some areas of life sports often are, in very practical terms, much more than mere appearances.[41] Canadians really do struggle against Russians in hockey; it often is black versus white in the boxing ring; and, if we take the case of the cockfight, it actually is high status people with the most "honor" to be gained or lost who "make" the matches, imprint them with their own meanings and aspirations, and mobilize them as a particular form of bias. As Geertz argues

> the really substantial members of the community, the solid citizenry around whom local life revolves . . . fight in the larger fights and bet on them around the side. The focusing element in these focused gatherings, these men generally dominate and define the sport as they dominate and define the society.[42]

What I want to emphasize here is the danger of separating the sociomoral dimensions of sports, as cultural texts, from the broader production and reproduction of the sociomoral limits of a society. This danger is very real and may cause us to ignore the extent to which some people have the capacity to transform a culturally specific set of meanings into metaphors of universal experience and common sense. The biggest danger of cultural text theories, as in all hermeneutical understandings of reality, is to overlook *why* it is that some people's "accounts" *count.*[43] To put the matter another way, one must always be careful that when attempting to understand what a cultural text *means* one does not lose sight of how it has been *made,* of who has made it, and of how the limits and pressures contained within it about how reality is or ought to be, are constitutively connected to the struggle, the forms of compliance, and the forms of resistance associated with changing patterns of inequality, domination, and subordination in the social development of any society.

Sports and the General Theory of Industrial Society

When sociologists and political theorists have sought to examine patterns of inequality, domination, and subordination in capitalist societies, and to understand the various pressures and limits involved in their reproduction and transformation, they have directed much of their attention toward the analysis of social class and to the particular organization of rules and resources that defines given class systems. In this section of the discussion I want to examine some of the major perspectives employed in analyzing the changing relationships between sports and social class in the social development of western capitalist societies. Most of these perspectives, I believe, have been severely limited by their heavy reliance on abstract typologies and the organizing assumptions of what was described earlier as the "general theory" of industrial society.

One of the earliest and best-known studies involving a focus on sports, social class, and social development is, of course, Thorstein Veblen's *Theory of the Leisure Class.* Veblen begins his analysis with the argument that "man is an agent . . . a center of unfolding impulsive activity" who seeks "the accomplishment of some objective end" in every act. In contradistinction to the view later developed by Huizinga—which saw the foundation for human agency as something expressed through play— Veblen argued that our sense of human purpose was manifested in a taste for effective work and a distaste for futile effort. As a result of this sense of purpose, Veblen argued, western "industrial" societies were embarked on an evolutionary drive for economic efficiency manifested in changes in the price system and in the increasingly important role played by engineers as the leaders of productive work.[44]

Yet, Veblen was deeply concerned that social groups existed whose temperaments and atavistic mentalities were barriers to this evolutionary development. Observing the social systems and structures which enabled the creation of vastly unequal resources in the United States of the 1890s, Veblen saw waste and acquisitiveness instead of productivity, and a lingering "barbarian" predatory temperament expressed on the part of those groups located at "the upper-end of the pecuniary scale." These "pecuniary" but "nonproductive" elements in American society he referred to as the "leisure class."

Veblen's theory of the leisure class is relatively straightforward.[45] Throughout history, predatory warlords have struggled for and seized the property of their enemies on the basis of their martial prowess and superior strength. Because ownership of property was seen to be a consequence of prowess and strength, it became synonymous with social honor. In the ensuing struggle for honor the coercive and bellicose nature of the primal "predatory" state in human culture never really died out. Indeed, it was often supported by an ongoing "pecuniary emulation"; to own property was to possess social honor. In this way property ownership set up invidious distinctions between individuals and groups. Set against this background (and contributing to it), manual labor ("productive" work in Veblen's view) became associated with weakness and inferiority. In short, it came to be understood, Veblen suggested, as "unworthy of man in his best estate." The so-called dignified individual abstained from work and became involved in the conspicuous *display* of leisure pastimes. Because sports and conspicuous leisure were excellent ways of "wasting" time and money, they put one's wealth on display. This display of status became the essential value of sports and leisure—so much so that the desire to impress observers with wasteful "survivals of prowess" became elevated to a social need. As Mills notes in his "Introduction" to *The Theory of the Leisure Class,* mere idleness on the part of the leisure class was not enough to generate status: "It had to be the idleness of expensive discomfort, of noble vice, and costly entertainment. It had, in short, to be conspicuous consumption: the obvious waste of valuable goods as a means of gaining respectability."[46]

It can be argued that many of Veblen's observations on the leisure class are extremely penetrating even though one might dispute the actual theory supporting them. There is, certainly, a rather obvious sense in which Veblen's observations seem dated and somewhat inappropriate in modern capitalist societies. Certainly, modern sport has become vastly different from the upper-class pastimes and athletic activities that Veblen attacked with his characteristic irony and satiric brilliance. Similarly, the class structures of western capitalist societies themselves have also undergone notable changes since the turn of the twentieth century.

Given these considerations, it is important that Veblen be assessed in the context of his time, especially insofar as he often seems caught up in a typically nineteenth-century enthusiasm for the potential fruits of industrial development.[47] In this regard, one might say that if Johan Huizinga's analysis of play was influenced by the degree to which his Catholic sensibilities were offended by the instrumentalities of industrialism and the reduction of all areas of experience to "necessity," Veblen was dismayed at what he saw as residual, non-instrumental leisure on the part of a parasitic class that lived off rather than in the industrial order. I suggest, however, that Veblen's view of workmanship is no more defensible than Huizinga's analysis of play, in that it attributes a *generative* status to the instinct of workmanship—which makes craftsmanship and productivity into the prime movers of the way society is seen to be (or *ought* to be) developing. This view is vastly different from saying that workmanship and craftsmanship as forms of material cultural production are important to the very act of human self-creation as constitutive social practices. Rather, what Veblen tends to do is create his own kind of problematic separation between a generative ideal in human existence and the expression of this ideal in concrete social practice.

One area where I find Veblen's work superior to Huizinga's analysis is in the degree to which the opposition of practical interests is made a central feature in the study of social development. Veblen is less oriented toward finding order in human culture than with identifying forms of conflict and suggesting how these forms can be tied to unequally distributed resources—especially those resources coordinated in and through class relations. This is not to say that Veblen's discussion is without flaws. For example, there is a strong sense in which he failed to notice the major differences between the leisure *pastimes* of the "gentrified" fractions of the American bourgeoisie and the *sports* of businessmen, professionals, and shopkeepers. Similarly, Veblen's "theory" does not account very well for the "gaming" pastimes common among the "industrious classes" (as he calls them), and for the large-scale penetration of "pecuniary emulation" into the culture of these classes. Nor would extending his analysis into the present day explain the notable incorporation of sports into the work place and their subjugation to instrumental reason and technocratic rationality. For example, what is one to make, from Veblen's perspective, of the historical development of games and sports from nonproductive leisure pastimes to highly rationalized and institutionalized social practices?

More important than any of these problems is Veblen's almost cavalier treatment of how status, expressed in and through class relationships, can be drawn upon as a social resource involved in the reproduction of the class system. As Mills notes, Veblen regarded the leisure class—with its strange combination of bourgeois and aristocratic traits—as a function-less and comic parasite, a dislocated caricature of the aristocracy of feudal Europe set in an American context.[48] Accordingly, while Veblen mocked these "kept classes," he tended to downplay their capacity to mobilize resources in the cultural realm and thereby contribute to a hegemony which supported their interests. Indeed, Mills continues, Veblen explicitly believed that the leisure class is "not in the full sense an organic part of the industrial community."[49] Given this belief, Veblen never explored fully the relationships between sports, class inequality, and political order.

Veblen's utilitarian criticisms of the leisure class, his emphasis on the importance of efficiency in industrial society, and on the role of technical innovation in history actually suggest the degree to which his work can be situated not so much in the classical tradition of class analysis as in the parallel tradition of the study of industrial development.[50] The key problem in Veblen's work on social class is not, as it was for Marxism, the transcendence of capitalism through class struggle; rather, it is to examine the movement of society to a condition where class inequalities would decompose within capitalism as skilled workmen, engineers, and technicians came to embody a matter-of-fact (and neutral) rationality in the course of their increasing leadership roles in society.

Ironically, however, as Mills points out, Veblen's faith in technology did not go far enough for him to move beyond a very simple view of scarcity, where the accumulation of material resources by the leisure class implied privation on the part of the "industrious" classes. The "moral edge of the phrase 'conspicuous consumption'" lies in the fact that Veblen felt such consumption tended to leave only a scanty "subsistence minimum."[51] For this reason Veblen tended to cast the political problems of the leisure class almost purely in distributive terms—problems that could be resolved through new allocative rules based on productivity, increased efficiency, and the elimination of "parasitic" classes.

While it would be an overstatement to suggest that Veblen's work has been the necessary starting point for all subsequent analyses of sports and social class in western capitalist societies, one can at least argue that the basic distributive themes evident in Veblen's work have been seized upon as matters of great relevance for American and Canadian sociologists interested in sport and society. For some people this emphasis has led to a narrow focus on the empirical question of the opening and closing of opportunities for participation in sports. For many others, the massive popularization and apparent democratization of sports over the last 100 years has been taken as a reliable index of the decline of class inequality and class domination as features of the social development of western capitalist societies.

Nowhere has this latter tendency been more pronounced than in the literature on sports, leisure, and social class in the United States. Consider, for example, the following observation from Gregory Stone's seminal and highly influential essay "American Sport: Play and Display": "As our organization has shifted from a system of estates, through a system of production and classes, to an arrangement of consumption and masses, play and sport have always been affected by the cleavages and processes built into such patterns."[52] Stone goes on to suggest how the "leisure class" that inspired the irony of Veblen has become a "leisure mass," and that the problems of sport as a form of leisure activity in American culture have changed accordingly.

There are, of course, many variations of such views, ranging from the extremes of Max Kaplan's observation that in "no area of American life more than its leisure activity has the outmoded concept of class become more apparent," to Harold Hodges's more cautious view that while class differences in sports and leisure activities could still be found in the 1960s, they are "diminishing in importance as we become an ever more homogeneous people." John Betts takes such views even further and suggests that the overall influence of American capitalism on sport has been "productive" and that sport's own contribution to social democracy has been "significant."[53]

Recent research on sports and social inequality in the United States demonstrates a general pattern of under-representation of people from the lowest income levels among active participants in organized sports and physical recreation. Given this research, there is reason to believe that each of the views stated above may be overly optimistic.[54] However, rather than become involved in a tiresome debate about at what point such broad *socioeconomic* differences in patterns of athletic recruitment and leisure involvement can actually be understood as *class* differences, I want to shift the focus away from distributive issues toward relational ones. This will require moving the focus of analysis away from the apparent democratization of opportunities for athletic participation in order to pose such broader questions as: *who* (i.e., which individual and collective agents) have been involved in the "structuring" of sports as sports have become institutionalized features of the western capitalist societies; and *what* has been the meaning of this structuring—and the limits and possibilities contained within it—for the production and reproduction of social relations within capitalism?

When John Betts says that the relationship of capitalism to American sport has been productive, he bases his comments solely on evidence suggesting the popularization of sport over the past 100 years and the massive expansion of opportunities for participation that has occurred with more facilities, cheaper equipment, and the apparent "erosion" of social barriers based on class, race, and ethnicity.[55] He also suggests that the meritocratic metaphoric character of sports and the real mobility opportunities existing in sport have helped contribute to this erosion.

But this is far too simple. For if we understand class as something that goes beyond distributive groupings, something based more on the social relations people enter into with one another in the production and reproduction of a whole social process; and if we understand class relations to be indissolubly connected to different practical interests, to the exercise of power, and to forms of domination; then Betts's argument is at best narrow, and at worst misleading.

Let me clarify this point. Surely it is misleading to make general inferences about the relationship between sports and the changing nature of social class arrangements in any society by focusing simply upon the so-called democratization of athletic participation. Far more important is the differential capacity of some people to define and shape the nature of sport's institutional apparatus and to contour the nature of the "meanings" of sports as cultural productions in the struggle to define a hegemony. Indeed, what Betts's perspective tends to overlook are the broader issues of power and domination in society, and the relationship of sports— whatever the "opportunities" for participation—to the reproduction of the allocative rules and social relations which influence the continuation of specific systems of inequality. Historians and sociologists who have limited their analyses to benign questions about opportunities for involvement in sports (e.g., the so-called democratization of sports), rather than actually exploring the themes of domination and subordination that stand at the core of class analysis and the study of the dynamics of capitalist society, have been too easily led to an optimistic conclusion. Such writers are inevitably led to argue that sport both "reflects" and "dramatizes" democratizing trends which testify to the success of capitalism as a form of political-economic organization—a success defined in terms of transforming the "external inequalities" of the past (such as inherited wealth) to a system of inequality based increasingly on the "internal" differences and capacities which "naturally" differentiate human agents.[56]

I think it useful to situate such perspectives in the context of the broader intellectual currents and traditions that have characterized the development of twentieth-century American social thought. Building on my earlier observations about the theoretical and methodological tendencies common in American social science during the mid-twentieth century, we can note the emergence of two cross-cutting tendencies in most of the literature on sport and social class: (1) a withdrawal from Veblen's emphasis on social development, within which the distributive emphasis is maintained but reconstituted in the form of empirical studies of participation rates in sport and physical recreation; and (2) an almost automatic integration of voluntarist assumptions about the playful nature of sport, with a set of parallel assertions about the inherently open nature of the possibilities available to human agents in capitalist, liberal democracy.

These tendencies suggest ways in which the concentration on sport's character as a social "leveler," and the optimism of those who have seen sport as a dimension of the classlessness of American capitalism, can be tied to broader social processes which have consistently lent ideological support to liberalism and individualism in this century—processes reflected in the increased concern of mid-twentieth century American intellectuals with middle-class issues of status and status striving, or with the "values" of different classes, rather than with broad theories of class and class conflict in society. In the case of this latter tendency, Charles Page has noted how the emphasis on status and status striving in American social science is highly representative of long-standing themes in American culture: ". . . an individualism that resists structural interpretations of social patterns and arrangements and processes, a voluntarism that rejects deterministic explanations of social action, a pragmatism that suspects abstract theories."[57]

The weaving of these themes together with the powerful voluntarist and idealist emphasis in the literature in the philosophy of play, games, and sports has led to an implied theory of the relationship between sport, class, and capitalism that *takes as resolved* some of the most significant questions that need to be asked about the nature of the institutional structuring of sport in capitalist societies. This is especially true in the case of questions about sport's role in the *production and reproduction* of the material process which defines the expanding and contracting limits and possibilities that exist for human agents within capitalism.

Let us examine this theory of sport and social development in more detail. First, the theory is based on a virtually uncritical acceptance of voluntarist and liberal assumptions, both about the nature of human agency as it is "freely" expressed in play, games, and sports, and about the decline of class as a limiting condition on people's capacities to structure sport in certain ways (although this latter problem is rarely confronted), and to participate and succeed within the limits associated with these structures.[58] Second, it is tacitly suggested in the theory that most forms of organized "play" in industrial societies can be seen to be part and parcel of a general movement toward an increasingly welfare-oriented and technocratic world order. The "progress" made in the organization of games and sports (e.g., state programs, international sports contests, broader bases of institutional cooperation), and the great improvements of human performances in sports are generally seen to celebrate rather than condemn the basic social and technical structure of industrial life. The reasoning which underlies such arguments is based on the degree to which the "structured" games and sports in western industrial societies have evolved from ascriptively based "folk" and "elite" recreational activities to a democratized component of mass culture and mass entertainment. Participation in organized or semiorganized sports has become the standard by which to gauge our capacities for play and, along these lines, it is argued that participation itself has evolved from a *privilege* of class and status in the nineteenth century to a *right* of citizenship in the twentieth. Similarly, this theory harbors the implied assumption that the main structures of "modern" sports will provide the model of development for sports in "underdeveloped" societies (e.g., only "modern" sports are represented at the Olympic Games or are recognized by established world federations).[59]

Not all of these points are necessarily present in any one given analysis that appears to adopt this "theory." But taken together they provide a coherent and internally consistent alternative to classical or neo-Marxist analyses where sport is depicted as a fully incorporated feature of cultural life in capitalism reflecting bourgeois values and practices and thereby reaffirming bourgeois ideology. Allen Guttmann's *From Ritual to Record is,* I believe, the most sophisticated expression of this theory to date, but many of the assumptions supporting the theory appear throughout the literature on modern sports in the form of an underlying tacit understanding of the logic of modern industrial development.

Now I want to argue that this tacit understanding is closely associated not only with liberalism as a political philosophy, but also with the long tradition of sociological analysis that has been influenced by the general theory of industrial society. Having already outlined some of the main features of this theory, I shall simply refer here to Anthony Giddens's summary of the theory's main features:

> The theory of industrial society, first of all, involves a dichotomous typology of society in contrast to the three-fold conception with which Marxism approaches changes in the modern era (feudalism/capitalism/socialism). The movement of change in modern times is regarded as a transition from "traditional society" . . . to "industrial society." . . . In the theory of industrial society "capitalism" is not regarded as a generic type of society, as in Marx, but as an historically marginal phase in the emergence of a maturing industrial order.[60]

In its most modern forms, the general theory of industrial society tends to have two main variants, the most common of which is based on the idea that technological advancements in industry have expanded the social surplus of resources to such a degree that the antagonistic classes of feudal society have simply become transformed into nonoppositional status gradations. In this setting, class conflict either disappears as a vehicle for social transformation or becomes "normatively regulated" in a way that spells the "end of ideology." In some versions of this type of analysis it is argued that *consumption* has overtaken *production* as the key feature of social life which differentiates people in society, and that this transition to the "consumer society" has aided a process of social homogenization. Related to this, it is argued that the great expansions of public expenditure on social welfare programs and on education have further transformed the old class system.

A closely related variant of this argument goes even further by suggesting that the social classes and class conflicts characteristic of capitalism have been surpassed because capitalism itself has been surpassed. Thus, in the writings of Daniel Bell and, to some extent, Ralf Dahrendorf, class conflicts have become completely institutionalized and managed features of contemporary life. This is witnessed, for example, by the apparent decline in the size and relevance of the industrial core; in the bloating of the service sectors of the labor force; by the increasing specialization and autonomy of different institutional orders which guarantee diversification in the sources of economic and political power; and by an increasing emphasis on technical skills and educational credentials—rather than on property and capital—as sources of power and influence.[61]

Although each of these variations of the general theory of industrial society appears to grasp important trends and contains some empirical validity, the entire thesis has nonetheless been subjected to a significant degree of criticism. Most notable is Krishan Kumar's definitive critique of theories of industrial and post-industrial society in *Prophecy and Progress: The Sociology of Industrial and Post-Industrial Society.* Kumar not only offers an impressive body of evidence to counter the empirical claims about the decline in class tensions in post-industrial societies, but he also outlines the subtle ways in which these claims have been influenced by romantic conceptions of progress and by the ideology of capitalism's dominant classes. Along similar lines, Robert Heilbroner has argued how modern post-industrial theorists have vastly overstated the significance of changes in the division of labor and in the expansion of opportunities for management and control of the structures which influence the distribution of material and symbolic resources.[62] In other words, Heilbroner suggests that despite all of the changes which have characterized the industrial society, it may be too much to say that we have completely eliminated the *dramatis personae* of the classical Marxian drama. Given this, Heilbroner goes on to argue that "the organizational character of industrial capitalism with its hierarchies, bureaucracies, and above all its trend toward concentration, seems likely to continue in the post-industrial society."[63]

Giddens's *Class Structure of the Advanced Societies* echoes many of these arguments and develops them in considerable theoretical detail in a broad critique of technocratic theories of social development. Giddens also notes how, in the writings of Herbert Marcuse, Alain Touraine and, to some extent, Jürgen Habermas, technocratic theories of industrial development have taken a leftward turn. In such writings it is suggested that nineteenth-century capitalism has developed through the rationalization of all spheres of life into "one-dimensional" or totalitarian forms of post-industrial societies. Social classes have not totally disappeared in these societies but, for the most part, they have been reconstituted into new technocratic forms of domination.

I noted earlier how Jean-Marie Brohm's work is Marcusian in the sense that it focuses on the determination of sport by productive forces (largely technological), rather than on the relationships of sport to social classes and the class struggle. Thus, it can be argued that even the revolutionary neo-Marxism of Jean-Marie Brohm has been influenced by variations of technocratic thinking and by the general theory of industrial society.[64] The problem with all of these theories, however, lies primarily in their status of abstract typologies which have claimed to adequately understand the "modern." What such theories do is replace a series of historical questions to be *determined* with a set of "characteristics" that are ostensibly *known.* As I suggested at the outset of this study, this has the effect of closing off rather than opening up empirical inquiry.

In the following chapter I shall attempt to sketch out the outlines of a more historically adequate analysis of sport in social development based on the theoretical principles developed thus far. However, as additional background for this analysis I want to note just a few more problems with most general theories of industrial development.

Most of the theories of industrial development that Giddens discusses in *Class Structure of the Advanced Societies* either limit the study of development to the "internal" evolution of particular societies, or they see the "underdeveloped" societies as involved in some kind of evolutionary movement from a traditional, pre-industrial phase to a more modern industrial phase. Similarly, these theories tend to adopt what Giddens refers to as an "endogenous" or "unfolding model" of social change, in which development is understood as a progressive orderly transfer "from a rural, post-feudal order to an urban industrialized economy within the boundaries of already established nation states.[65] I think one can safely assert that these tendencies have also penetrated deeply into the frames of reference used by "sport sociologists" and "sport historians" in their analyses of the growth of western sports. Such views, however, have severe limitations. Canada, for example, has a colonial past, and its class structure and cultural formations cannot be understood without some reference to the *dependency relations* it has maintained with colonial metropoles and to its own *internal* relations of dependency and development.[66]

Giddens makes this point in general terms by emphasizing the degree to which the "internal development" of any nation-state must be situated in the context of international systems of economics, politics, and cultures. He then goes on to suggest three other considerations that are useful as points of orientation for studies of social development. These points are described as:

> ... *the uneven development* of different institutions, sectors
> or regions within societies . . . *Critical phases* of radical
> change, in which the existing alignment of major institu-
> tions in a society becomes transformed, whether or not this
> occurs through the agency of political revolution. . . . A
> "leapfrog" idea of change whereby what is "advanced" in
> one set of circumstances or period of time may later become
> a source of retardation upon further development; and vice
> versa, what is "retarded" may later become a propitious
> basis for rapid advancement.[67]

Conclusion: Class, Sports, and Social Development

In this chapter I have introduced a number of theoretical considerations
that I take to be useful in reorienting the study of sport and social
development. I began by elaborating upon the notion that play, games,
and sports were constitutive social practices involved in the production
and reproduction of a whole, social material process. I then moved on to
a discussion of how the institutional structuring of games and sports is
influenced by the different resources that agents can bring to bear on
their social life situation. Along these lines, I suggested that the broad
allocative rules and social relations which define the class systems of
capitalist societies are significant influences on these resources, and that
it is important to understand the meaning of the various limits and
pressures involved in the structuring of sport in the context of the social
reproduction of class relations. In this way I have tried to make class
relations into an axial concept linking problems of human agency to
problems of structural change and social development.

Previous Marxist studies of sport in social development have developed views somewhat similar to this, although—as noted in my earlier
critique of Jean-Marie Brohm—most of these studies have been too
abstract and deterministic to offer an adequate framework for analysis.
Similarly, because such studies have often reduced sport to the level of a
completely determined ideological product, they have lost sight of sport's
active and constitutive features, its wide range of meanings, and its
capacity to develop oppositional tendencies within a given hegemony.
Indeed, I have opted for use of the concept of hegemony in my discussion
precisely because it allows for the notion that the accomplishment of
social interaction is always contested, sometimes in very subtle, other
times in quite significant, ways. This allows one to continue to understand
cultural productions as practices that are *made and remade* as individuals

produce and reproduce the conditions of their existence in situations characterized by markedly different resources. Similarly the concept of hegemony allows for the idea of reflexive human agency in a manner not shared by functionalist models of inculcation or socialization.

This view is by no means part of the orthodox consensus when it comes to the analysis of sport and social development. Most such analyses have been guided, either consciously or unconsciously, by a general theory of industrial society whose theoretical focus and assumptions have emerged in direct contrast to Marxism and class analysis. I have explored the idea that not only is this theory frequently arguable on empirical grounds, but also that, like the crude Marxism it is designed to challenge, it has often served as an uncontested ideal-typological model. The reification of this model has stood squarely in the road of concrete historical studies which stress unequal resources, social reproduction, and struggles over social transformation in a broad system of international economic, political, and cultural connections.

3

Class, Sports, and Social Development: Outline of the Canadian Case

> . . . *individuals cannot gain mastery over their own social inter-*
> *connections before they have created them. But it is an insipid notion*
> *to conceive of this merely* objective bond *as a spontaneous, natural*
> *attribute inherent in individuals and inseparable from their nature (in*
> *antithesis to their conscious knowing and willing). This bond is their*
> *product. It is a historic product. It belongs to a specific phase of their*
> *development. The alien and independent character in which it pres-*
> *ently exists vis à vis individuals proves only that the latter are still*
> *engaged in the creation of the conditions of their social life, and that*
> *they have not yet begun, on the basis of these conditions, to live it. . . .*
> *Universally developed individuals . . . are no product of nature, but of*
> *history.*
>
> Karl Marx, Grundrisse, *1857*[1]

In a recent essay outlining some of the main features of a "Historical Sociology," Philip Abrams comments on Michael Scriven's analogy between "explanatory narrative" in history and the development of the dramatic plot of a play.[1] The basis for the analogy stems from the fact that in each case the author "adopts a rhetoric which is not that of a formal proof but rather that of plausibility in-depth." The explanation resides, Abrams continues, in "an achieved sense of dramatic inevitability, an appreciation that, however surprising particular episodes in the drama may have been as they were presented, the plot as a whole rings true as a structuring." Abrams goes on to argue, however, that "plausibility in-depth" is not enough if historians and sociologists want to concern themselves with problems of human agency and the processes whereby social action is structured and restructured in different ways in history. Explanatory narrative needs to be constantly "interrogated" by theoretical explanation, and researchers ought to come to some understanding of a specific "problematic"—a field of concepts and arguments which organize explanation by making it possible to ask some questions by suppressing others.[2]

In many respects, I have been trying to develop such a field of concepts and arguments throughout this book. In this chapter, I want to use these concepts and arguments as a guide for outlining a case study of sport in Canadian social development. My focus in this case study will be on (1) the "problematic" of the institutional structuring of games and sports in Canada, and (2) the ways in which the enabling and constraining features of sport at different stages in its development have been connected to class relations and the various processes governing their reproduction and transformation.

I think it important to emphasize that the following analysis is not meant to be a detailed social history of Canadian sport. The rhetoric I have adopted is certainly not that of a formal proof, nor even of the "plausibility in-depth" that Michael Scriven suggests is a prime feature of explanatory narrative in historical analysis. Rather, I have sought to develop plausibility through a theoretically directed form of narrative that emphasizes broad patterns and tendencies in the struggle over the structuring of sport in Canadian life—patterns and tendencies within which subsequent researchers might attempt to provide a "reading" of sport as a text and come to some understanding of the changing subjectivities involved in its development.[3]

Because my intention here is only to outline the broad contours of this case study, I have concentrated on a reorganization and reinterpretation of existing sources and reference material rather than on developing the kind of primary material necessary in a more detailed historical treatment. In some instances, however, it has been necessary to provide a certain amount of this primary material in order to lend continuity and a degree of substance to the story I want to tell.[4] The story is organized around four critical phases in the "structuring" of Canadian sport.[5] Briefly stated, these are:

1. a preliminary phase of structuring during which imported and indigenous game-contests and popular recreations became increasingly subject to the limits and pressures of restrictive municipal ordinances, the incorporation of games and physical exercise into school programs of different types, and the development of leisure-oriented voluntary associations (e.g., socially oriented sports clubs);

2. a phase of consolidation and highly visible struggle when specific aspects of bourgeois class practice became formalized in many of the technical and moral rules (e.g., the amateur code) that came to define dominant meanings in sport and the "legitimate" conduct of sporting behavior;

3. a phase during which commercial forms of game activity, long associated with popular recreation, became more formally integrated into the market place and became subject to processes of commodification and cartelization; and

4. a phase when the Canadian state, in conjunction with national and internationally established sporting associations, began to broaden its influence in sport to include national and subnational programs in recreation, physical fitness, and provincial, national, and international athletics.

The Changing Structures of Colonial Games

Any discussion of sport and social development in Canada must attempt to situate the whole notion of the "structuring" of play, games, and sports in the context of the unique pattern of Canada's colonial development. Most work in Canadian social history and political economy acknowledges that two factors are essential to an understanding of the basic character of Canada as a social formation: (1) the role of social class as a key factor in conflicts over various resources in Canadian society; and (2) the idea that class structures and patterns of social development are greatly influenced by the relations of domination and dependency that occur between a metropole (or center) and a hinterland (or periphery). The metropole has a greater capacity to define allocative rules and to appropriate certain resources, and this leads to the underdevelopment, or the uneven development, of certain features of the hinterland's social organization.

Let us apply this type of analysis to an understanding of the limits and pressures associated with early patterns of class and institutional development in Canada. It can be argued, for example, that the initial shape of

Canada's class system emerged out of the cultural traditions of French and British imperial empires and out of the colonial institutions these empires generated. Particularly dominant in Canada were the implementation of ascriptive colonial policies of land allocation and the institutionalization of a mercantile system heavily funded by foreign investment and designed to extract "staples" from the Canadian hinterland in the service of European markets.[6] The initial effects of these patterns of social, economic, and political organization in late eighteenth- and early nineteenth-century Canada can be measured primarily in three areas.

First, by gearing to the international movement of staples rather than the development of secondary processing in domestic markets (especially following the British "conquest" in the eighteenth century), the growth of Canadian industry and manufacturing was retarded while commercial institutions (e.g., banking, retail trade) became overdeveloped.[7] Second, a conscious attempt to maintain traditional European patterns of landed power, in combination with the overdevelopment of commercial institutions, allowed for the early growth of a strong merchant class in the fledgling Canadian urban areas. This merchant class eventually came to share dominance with the remains of the colonial ruling class of the Conquest era, with the Church, and with the Empire Loyalist elite.[8] Finally, under colonial rule the close connection between the merchant class and the state generally opposed in principle both the laissez-faire political-economic philosophy commonly associated with industrial capitalism, and the rational utilitarian ethics that later became the cornerstone of liberal-democratic sentiment in industrial Britain.[9]

Recognizing these broad developmental patterns is important to an understanding of the range of symbolic representations and meanings associated with early forms of games and popular recreation in Canadian society. It has been popular for Canadian "sport historians" to emphasize the close association between the nature of colonial games and sporting pastimes and the supposedly democratic "frontier spirit" of the late eighteenth and early nineteenth centuries.[10] However, I think it necessary to acknowledge the degree to which this "spirit," and the fun and spontaneity ostensibly associated with colonial games, was mediated by the effects of a conservative political economy, the rigors of frontier life, and the constraints imposed by a semifeudal class structure.[11]

Let us examine some of these effects in more detail. First, as Wise and Fisher have noted, few of the settlers on Canada's "hard frontier" had the time or the opportunity to compete in any kind of regular games or *organized* forms of physical recreation.[12] When given the opportunity, people played the games that were known to them, but these games were vastly different from the organized sports of today. The early forms of colonial games and recreation were local, unorganized, and often based on oral traditions that were either indigenous to Canada's native peoples or, more commonly, imported from France and Britain and adapted to the Canadian situation. Moreover, these games and recreational activities were invariably periodic, subject to changing locales and to the natural rhythms of the days and seasons, and were greatly influenced by the "traditional" nature of class relations. Folk games of different types, and spontaneous contests of strength, speed, or agility which made use of natural obstacles or were functionally related to some work-role (e.g., rowing), were the main forms of "popular" game-contests. A number of more traditional "sporting" activities—such as purely *recreational hunting* and horse racing—also had broad appeal. However, the people with the greatest dedication to these pastimes were those who were least constrained by the demands of frontier life: the colonial estate-holders, military officers, and merchants.[13]

Social historians have yet to examine in detail the wide range of cultural meanings embodied in the occasional games and physical recreation of the early nineteenth-century Canadian frontier. One could certainly hypothesize, however, that as constitutive features of a conservative and traditional colonial culture, games and popular recreations presumably had a representational significance that was as attached to underlying notions of social ascription and colonial tradition as it was to the less ascriptively based features of social life on the frontier. Indeed, existing accounts of the time convey the sense that the games and recreational pastimes of early nineteenth-century Canada were somewhat more than just the idle play of the colonial squire or a periodic attempt by farmers and artisans to relieve the monotony of the almost constant work of frontier life.[14] In their various "folk" and "elite" forms, these games and pastimes also appear to have been symbolic statements of differential life chances and social location. As such they can be understood as cultural components in the representation of, and forms of resistance to, a pattern of domination that, if not completely feudal, was nonetheless highly paternalistic and antidemocratic in nature.[15]

I will not attempt here to articulate the extent to which different types of games and recreational activities in early nineteenth-century Canada were either oppositional or incorporative features of the cultural life of the time. It will suffice for my purposes simply to note the existence of a class-specific involvement in different types of activities and in the meanings of these activities. Gambling, for example, seems to have been widely practiced in early Canadian society, but it was condemned by the "proper" citizens when it was perceived as a "morbid habit" or when it broke out in "a moral distemper."[16] The prevalence of heavy gambling and drinking in certain rural pastimes, or among the underclasses in the emerging Canadian towns, seems to reflect a high degree of continuity to a long history of oppositional or "profane" rituals that mocked the dominant classes and contributed to community solidarity among the underclass.[17] Balanced against these practices, however, were the whole set of day-to-day relations that maintained established traditions of class deference, and those social activities of the dominant classes which dramatized superior rank.

I am suggesting, then, that underlying the simple participation in games and sporting pastimes for fun, relaxation, or excitement during this period in Canadian social development, we might discover a number of "deeper" meanings that were indissolubly connected to imported continental traditions of ascription, folk culture, and class domination. For example, there is considerable evidence that the early colonial ruling class viewed the aristocracy and gentry of early nineteenth-century Britain as a reference group and stressed in play nonutilitarian attitudes toward consumption and toward life itself.[18] In this way play and recreational activities of certain types symbolically articulated their class position in the manner of Veblen's "leisure class," and also contributed to the cultural legitimation of notions of natural superiority by symbolically excluding all forms of utilitarian rationality. Put another way, the values of manly character and conspicuous leisure which had long characterized the ritual games and field sports of European life were constitutive of much more than the mere "spontaneous enjoyment of life"; such values also served as means of self-assertion for the dominant class, and thereby contributed to a cultural legacy which stressed the "naturalness" of hierarchy, deference, and class distance.[19]

I have suggested that this cultural legacy, however dominant, was neither monolithic nor universally accepted. In addition to the residual features of transplanted folk cultures that were potentially threatening, the cultural hegemony of the early colonial ruling class *was* complicated by the vast and comparatively agrarian nature of the colony. It was also complicated by the existence of the very clear instrumental interests of merchants involved directly in colonial extraction and profit-making.[20] Canada was a paradox in this sense, for it combined a social organization consciously designed to create a long-term British settlement—complete with the stabilizing influence of a transplanted aristocracy—with a system of political economy based on the short-term goals of colonial extraction. As Arthur Lower has pointed out, for nearly seventy-five years after the British conquest, a "squire and parson" concept of society fought it out with outright commercialism.[21] Ultimately, however, the two factions became less estranged and the mercantile system combined effectively with a highly discriminatory set of land-granting policies in a way that stimulated a loose *rapprochement* between acquisitive and self-styled aristocratic groups in the Canadian dominant class. By the end of the second decade of the nineteenth century, the land-owning elite, transplanted colonial official, and wealthy staple-extracting merchant had consolidated their collective interests in the form of a merchant-gentry ruling class of considerable power.[22]

It is difficult to establish the extent to which this *rapprochement* between aristocrats and colonial capitalists extended into the spheres of cultural production. If there were differences in interpretations of how to live, however, these seemed generally subordinate to the overarching legitimacy of the ideological foundations of oligarchical rule and the coordinated interests of merchants and aristocrats. As Marx argues in his discussion of mercantile systems in volume 3 of *Capital,* the existence of a commercial-mercantile system in a society does not necessarily suggest the existence of a social group with "progressive" bourgeois interests; rather, merchant capitalists have tended historically to be "reactionary," aligning with traditional landed interests against both the growth of industrial capital and the spread of liberal values. In the Maritimes, Upper and Lower Canada, this pattern of resistance was offered considerable support by the British colonial connection which integrated the commercial features of life with the social and political aspects through the policies of colonial administration and the special status given to a quasi-official church, the Church of England.[23]

Yet, there is a sense in which the very factors which served to facilitate the integration of the heterogeneous, Canadian ruling class of the early nineteenth-century appear to have been eventually responsible for intensifying conflict within the colony. Gary Teeple points out how the lack of an industrial base in the colony (the ruling merchant-gentry preferred to *trade* in staples rather than to *produce* manufactured goods) combined with discriminatory land practices and heavy immigration to create a growing class of property-less laborers and "would-be" farmers.[24] At the same time, the imperially oriented commercial policy of the dominant class, which prohibited the export of manufactured goods and the emigration of skilled artisans, increasingly antagonized growing petit-bourgeois interests in the colony.[25] These tensions were further aggravated by the frustrations of frontier farmers over high interest rates, the shortage of available land, and by a growing religious pluralism which resulted in criticisms of the colonial linkage between church and state.[26] Added to these tensions, as Michael Cross has pointed out, cities and towns were growing rapidly and the dominant class was increasingly forced into closer physical proximity with the "lower orders."[27]

Tensions between the dominant class and the "lower orders" became more visible in the face of this marked increase in immigration and due to the gradual "filling in" of the frontier, the strengthening of petit-bourgeois reform interests, and the growing mechanization of production and trade. Most notably, by the 1820s and 1830s the cultural productions of the subordinate classes in Canada were viewed as a growing "problem" and as a threat to established traditions and privileges. Michael Cross argues, for example, how in a vast and comparatively empty frontier, the "un-civilized" pastimes and leisure activities of the "lower orders" could be tolerated and justified as a part of the natural order of things in colonial life.[28] In this sense, members of the dominant class saw their subordinates as "curious but harmless beings," were often sympathetic to their forms of recreation, and largely sought to maintain a measure of traditional tory disinterest in their affairs. However, the growing contact with the expand-ing and increasingly less docile "lower orders" led to the advocacy and acceptance of mechanisms for controlling the potentially "unruly" fea-tures of folk culture. An apparent manifestation of these "impulses" was seen by some to lie in the steady growth of taverns in the colony and in the proliferation of gambling and other "idle" activities which might serve to encourage the continuing "degeneration" of physical activity into "amusements" and "moral levity."

Several writers have commented on the movements for moral reform which swept through the colony in the late 1820s and 1830s, and it has been common to interpret such concerns as an indication of the growing significance of middle-class Methodist religious sentiment as a social force.[29] Although this interpretation contains a good deal of truth, one must not lose sight of the fact that the erosion of tory sympathy or disinterest and the rise of Methodist moral concerns to a level of public policy was only one dimension of a growing concern in all western capitalist societies over the "problem" of the poor. Both Christopher Lasch and Peter Bailey have suggested, for example, how the attempt to police the underclasses in the early stages of capitalist development in Britain and the United States led directly to an obsession with social control, an obsession that would last well into the twentieth century. Drinking and merrymaking among an urban working class were seen to disrupt the daily routine of businessmen, disorient people from their

work, encourage extravagance and insubordination, and stimulate de-
bauchery.[30] Thus, the dominant class of the twenties and thirties began to
seek the elimination of such "playfulness" from all areas of life—especially from the work place.[31]

Of course, the implementation of such policies did not always go
unchallenged. Such overt gestures of control actually may have helped to
ignite the tensions between rulers and ruled. At the same time, the
regulatory thrust of public reform was occasionally contested by the
more aristocratic fragments of the dominant class. A faction of Canada's
self-styled aristocrats seemed to support the notion that the pastimes of
the people ought to be left unregulated, inasmuch as the spontaneous,
nonutilitarian (and sometimes violent) "culture" of these pastimes was
remotely attached to the traditional order of early colonial life—an order
to which the elite's own conspicuous participation in hunting, fishing, and
horse racing was indissolubly connected. However, such defenses of
traditional recreations in Canada's development seem less entrenched
than were similar defenses in Britain, and they quickly eroded in the face
of the moral and political threat posed by activities that seemed to be
largely out of control.[32] As the social organization of Canadian society
became less traditional and more rationalized in the pursuit of profit, as
cities grew in the face of successive waves of immigration (especially after
1814), and as production began to change in response to technological
advances and new ideas from abroad, the elements of pretense and
fantasy inherent in traditional game forms were increasingly freed from
any contribution to social solidarity that they might have had. Liberated
from imported feudal traditions, and grounded in changing social conditions, the possibilities of the formal incorporation of the culture of games
into *fundamentally oppositional* social and political movements seemed
considerably enhanced. Games of disorder and ritual inversion—which
had long maintained a central role in folk culture, for example—had the
potential to take on "dangerous" new meanings in response to changing
social and political conditions.[33]

The prospect of such changes was met with firm regulative rules
defined and enforced (with varying success) by the ruling class. The
infusion of such "middle-class" values as sobriety and piety into the
culture of the ruling merchant-gentry class of the 1820s and 1830s
demonstrates a considerable degree of intraclass tension, but is no
indication of any significant disintegration in the power of this class. In a
manner somewhat similar to what occurred in Britain, the moral reform
movements merely bonded emerging middle-class asceticism and commercial concerns onto the political fears of the powerful. Edward Thompson

has argued that church and state opposition to underclass forms of recreation in Britain simply combined the "ethos of Methodism with the unction of the establishment."[34] Moral control was not a dictum that developed solely as a theological ideal free from practical considerations, nor did it symbolize completely the end of an aristocratic era and the rise of bourgeois values. The reformist concerns merely gave legitimacy to an expedient strategy of political domination. The "grand law of subordination" laid down by Pitt's moral lieutenant, Wilberforce, was a response to the belief that "moral levity" among the underclasses (and the large gatherings often associated with popular amusements) led readily to political sedition.

Thompson suggests that in late eighteenth-century England, such policies can be interpreted as part of a broader response to the perceived threat of Jacobinism. And, as Francis Hearn has pointed out, one may make a strong case for the argument that many eighteenth-century movements for emancipation from feudal domination often took on a "festival" and "playful" character.[35] The attempt to control this potentially oppositional festival character and transform people's play from "brute riot" to "decorum" was in large measure a response to a chaotic and rapidly changing socioeconomic and political situation. Given the growing class tensions in early nineteenth-century Canada, and the constant "threat" of liberal-democratic values imported from the United States, members of the dominant class in Canada increasingly feared large underclass gatherings and the political implications of "immoral" behavior. They responded not so much with welfare as with control, and introduced regulatory statutes designed to exclude the "lower orders" from areas where they were not appreciated, and to structure their behaviors in an "appropriate" way. This led naturally to rigid rules about *where* and *when* one might play. Play in the streets was made illegal, as was play on the Sabbath, and there was increased pressure placed on the gambling activities associated with underclass recreation. To cite just one graphic example of such control, Donald Guay has shown how the early attempt to "structure" and regulate horse racing in Lower Canada in the 1830s was essentially a response to the perceived threat posed by the swelling numbers of Francophone workers at previously upper-class events.[36]

Regulation of a different sort was also occurring in the play and games practiced by members of the dominant classes. The focus for this new emphasis on regulation was the "private school," generally modeled after Britain's reformed public school system. Recently, Eric Dunning has argued that the British public school reform movement represented an important break from traditional antiutilitarian attitudes toward playful activity.[37] The emphasis on discipline, religion, and "civilized" team sports that emerged as part of Dr. Thomas Arnold's program of "muscular Christianity" at Rugby School ostensibly represented a "mid-Victorian compromise" and "mutual accommodation" between growing industrial bourgeois and declining aristocratic interests. Dunning notes how this process helped to transform chaotic play into more organized games by stimulating the development of codified rules designed to "civilize" play activities by "equalizing" the participants.

Dunning's reasoning is masterful on this issue, but his entire analysis overstates, I believe, the degree to which the "reformed" public school was a concession to middle-class criticism of the aristocratic style of life. For example, Rupert Wilkinson and Walter Arnstein have each pointed out that, rather than becoming increasingly middle class, the reformed public schools merely captured middle-class talent in the promotion of gentry-class power.[38] By educating the young of the bourgeoisie as "gentlemen," the public schools really acted as a safety valve in the class system. They helped to avert class conflict, not by instilling the values of "self-help" and the entrepreneurial ethos into the sons of aristocrats, but rather by educating the young bourgeoisie in a sense of gentlemanly propriety which would subvert their individualistic tendencies and integrate them into a broader, more organic commitment to the collectivity. Arnstein concedes that the "reformed" public schools rejected undisciplined chivalric and aristocratic attitudes. But he argues that they continued to emphasize the nonutilitarian virtues of a classical education, the values of continuity and tradition more than those of utilitarian rationalism, and the belief in hierarchy rather than social equality.[39]

These conclusions are especially applicable to an understanding of the Canadian scene in the early 1830s, where the private-school concept was imported and adapted to solidify a fragmented Canadian ruling class that could model itself after the British gentry and thereby provide leadership and stability in the "new society." In a statement steeped in the very ideology it attempts to describe, Hodgins has noted that in Upper Canada College, Sir John Colborne sought

> to foster in the new institution a love of the old manly British
> Field Sports, a love which has always been a characteristic
> of English Public School men and is, indeed to the present
> day. And so in obtaining the services of English graduates
> for the College, Sir John not only obtained men who had the
> highest educational qualifications, but also those who would

encourage and stimulate among the boys a love of healthy
and manly games, which the astute governor rightly judged
to be a powerful factor in developing among the lads a
healthy self-reliant spirit that would fit them to cope in after
years with the many arduous and difficult problems inciden-
tal to the development of a new country.[40]

This somewhat tory approach to the social functions of team sports in
the first Canadian private schools is affirmed, I suspect, by the great
attention paid to cricket instead of football. Certainly crude football
games were played in Canada at this time, but the formal organization of
football, its progression beyond oral tradition, regional variation, and its
subsequent codification of rules, lagged behind such developments in
England until well into the late nineteenth century.[41] The industrial
bourgeois "push" that Dunning argues was so significant to the "incipient
modernization" of football in England during the 1840s and 1850s may
well have been retarded by the dominance of mercantile capital and the
lack of an industrial base in the colony. By contrast, the social organization and "common" rules of cricket had arisen *within* the development of
the British aristocracy and feudal tradition rather than emerging *out of*
conflict and accommodation between industrial bourgeoisie and aristocracy. Cricket became especially palatable to Canada's colonial merchants
and aristocrats because it combined an excellent and enjoyable forum for
learning discipline, civility, and the principles of fair play with a body of
traditions and rules offering a ritual dramatization of the traditional
power of the colonial metropolis and the class interests associated with
it.[42] As the Toronto *Patriot* editorialized on July 13, 1836:

British feelings cannot flow into the breasts of our Canadian
boys through a more delightful or untainted channel than
that of British sports. A cricketer, as a matter of course,
detests democracy and is staunch in his allegiance to his
King.

It seems unlikely that *all* cricketers would necessarily share these
sentiments, especially those in some of the growing numbers of teams in
smaller communities. Nonetheless, the limits and pressures expressed in
and through the predominance of the game as a form of established
"sport" were clearly influenced by *dominant* British cultural traditions.
Indeed, the game's heyday in Canada was generally limited to the mid-
nineteenth century, especially the 1860s when more British troops were
brought to Canada in order to protect the colony from the "threat"

imposed by the American Civil War. Later in the century, as the actual numbers of British-born Canadians relative to the total population declined, as the colonial class structure eroded, and as more Canadians became influenced by cultural ties to the United States, the game diminished both in popularity and importance.[43]

If cricket symbolized the power of the colonial metropole in Canada, its popularity among the dominant class during the twenties and thirties belied the significant class tensions that had been building during this period. These tensions erupted into open class conflict in the rebellions of 1837-38, but the rebels were easily controlled. Nonetheless, although politically unsuccessful, the rebellions revealed growing liberal and reformist strength in the colony, and the power of laborers and independent commodity producers as a new social force.[44] Within the confines of the political-economic system imposed by the "victorious" colonial-mercantile ruling class, the reformers achieved a measure of organizational legitimacy, and would eventually form governments.[45] Moreover, repeal of the British Corn Laws in 1846 provided a set of conditions which allowed for the ascendancy of a "liberal-tory" component to the upper class by effectively ending the colonial-mercantile domination of the "first commercial empire of the St. Lawrence."[46]

To suggest, however, that the decline of the dominant colonial-mercantile class of the 1820s and 1830s led to the full-scale infusion of utilitarian ethics and liberal-democratic political principles into the colony would be as misleading as to assume that the power of the large Canadian merchants was completely destroyed. While the "first" commercial empire of the St. Lawrence was crippled by the loss of imperial preference, a "second empire" began to develop quickly. Conditions became more favorable for Canada's petit bourgeoisie to develop as an indigenous capitalist class, and "responsible government" free from direct British control was achieved. But the colony remained a conservative staple-producing economy where dominant commercial interests, usually funded by British capital, maintained a firm hold on the state.[47]

Again, changes in Canadian sociopolitical relationships were incorporated into the progressive formalization and regulation of play. The regulative tendencies begun in earlier decades continued to intensify, rather than "easing" with the gradual infusion of middle-class ethics into social and political life. The rebellions themselves had reinforced the fear of a population with "time on its hands," and as the frontier began to "fill in" even more as a result of massive immigration during the 1840s and 1850s, the view of the "lower orders" hardened accordingly.[48] Concerned about the possible spread of disease from a growing and impoverished urban lower class, more thoroughly committed to reformist ideals which sought to replace traditional class obligations with state policies of control, and not quite so secure in their sociopolitical dominance, members of Canada's commercial-political ruling class of the preconfederation era continued to design regulations which would maintain order, discipline, and health among the working population and promote the interests of liberal civility.

One area where such programs were established after lengthy controversy between reformists and traditionalists was the tax-supported free school system.[49] Susan Houston has noted that in Ontario, Egerton Ryerson and his followers deeply feared the unfettered forces of urbanism and industrialization, and saw the "spirit" of underclass "insubordination" abroad threatening the "honest independence of the working and laboring classes, particularly servants."[50] Based on such attitudes, and on a concern for the necessity for a "fit" population for industrial production and military service, "play activities" in the school emphasized discipline and regimentation through military drills and gymnastic exercise.[51] By contrast, private schools continued to emphasize the values of leadership, fair play, and the disciplined but spontaneous enjoyment of games. In the former case, the possibilities derived from the structuring of playful exercise were indissolubly connected to limits defined by an emphasis on control and coercion. In the latter case, the possibilities derived from the structuring of games were connected to the broader resources that were a part of class privilege.

A more significant dimension of major changes in the social development of play, games, and sports during the 1840s and 1850s was the growth of the urban sports club.[52] Field sports flourished among a landed and agrarian upper class, but they were less suited to the recreational aspirations of a bourgeois class that had to locate close to urban markets and transportation centers. In conjunction with "incipient industrialization" in Canada, and the growth of new indigenous commercial (primarily banking and retailing) activities, the recreational sports club developed as a new structure for the social expression of play and games. At first— as Alan Metcalfe has pointed out in his ground-breaking study of sport and social stratification in nineteenth-century Montreal—the leadership of these clubs was limited to the professional, commercial, and military elite in the urban community (e.g., Montreal, Toronto, Halifax, Quebec, and St. John), and *their focus was social rather than competitive.*[53] Although the club leaders were representatives of the Canadian bourgeoisie, their approach to games and recreation was nonetheless tempered by strong gentry-class biases—a belief in the spirit of sociability in fair play, and the legacy of antiutilitarian sentiments about the role of games in life.[54]

Metcalfe has emphasized how even though actual membership in the elite clubs of the 1840s and 1850s was limited by ascriptive criteria, a few clubs did sponsor open competitions. Open competitions featured contact between social classes in athletic contests and demanded the formulation of universalistic rules that "equalized" all participants. However, even in such open competitions—where lawyers competed against Indians and workingmen—class distinctions were implicitly recognized by the provision of trophies for "gentlemen" and cash prizes for others.[55] A measure of commercialism invested in the contest was tolerated, but only within the context of limits defined by the dominant class.

Still, by the late 1860s the incipient industrialization of Canadian production had exerted pressures on culture and class to the extent that the entire structuring of play, game, and sporting activities was affected. In a social structural sense, this industrialization allowed for an expansion of the middle class; it allowed for the development of a changed, more rationalized conception of time that put new temporal limits on play;[56] and it allowed for the technological developments in transportation and communications which were necessary for games to grow beyond their localized character.[57] In a related *cultural* sense, the expansion of industry accompanied the growth of a more "pure" type of bourgeois values in the Canadian business community: *rational utilitarian* and, frequently, Darwinist values that were generally "unsullied" by the direct contact with ascriptive gentry class attitudes or the "gentlemanly" ethos of professionals and administrators.[58] These new conceptions differed from the "liberal-toryism"[59] that had evolved into the dominant ideology in Canada by the 1860s, and they created the moral environment for the development of more formally organized, achievement-based *competitive sports* as an addition to the loosely structured social and recreational activities that had hitherto served as the prime outlet for people's desires for physical play. This new emphasis in play and game activities occurred primarily in the expanding urban sports clubs.

Class Limits, Status Pressures, and the Amateur Code

By the mid-1860s, the urban club movement had begun to democratize, not on the basis of eliminating discriminatory patterns of membership selection and recruitment, but rather through the proliferation of the clubs themselves. Yet, such "democratization" merely reinforced existing class distinctions and shaped them into new organizational forms. These forms tended to dramatize the hierarchical arrangement of social groups and the solidification of new forms of domination that were based on equating personal worth with position in the marketplace. An example of the conflicts which developed along these lines can be found in the debate over "amateurism" and "professionalism."

During the 1840s and 1850s, as noted previously, elite sporting clubs occasionally sponsored open competitions where individuals from the upper class would compete against working men. Upperclass "trend setters," as Dunning and Sheard have called similar groups in England, were relatively secure in their positions, and competed in sport for fun.[60] Their identities and status were not at stake in any type of athletic contest, and it is unlikely that they would have been very concerned about the symbolic consequences of losing to "inferiors." Losing was nonproblematic, insofar as it did not affect the established ascriptive order in any way. Moreover, professionalism was not seen as a problem because it was assumed that it could always be controlled. Metcalfe reminds us that such occasional cross-class athletic contact should not be interpreted as a "utopian" view of friendly competition; competitions were not that frequent and class distinctions were still evident.[61] But the point is that open competitions sponsored by elite clubs did exist on occasion and facilitated contact between classes in the pursuit of games and sport.

However, there is some evidence that from the fifties and sixties on, fewer of these *elite-sponsored* open competitions were held.[62] Open competitions, often associated with church or company annual picnics, did become popular after the 1860s, but these events were not usually sponsored by members of Canada's dominant class.[63] We may theorize, perhaps, that as the Canadian class structure began to elaborate, and as meritocratic liberal values began to develop widespread support, members of the dominant class apparently became unable to tolerate the possibility of defeat at the hands of those they considered to be their social inferiors. They also may have become progressively more alarmed at the prospect that commercialism in sport could very easily get out of hand under such conditions and vulgarize traditional upper-class views of "the nobility of play." There were two possible responses to such developments: (1) withdraw completely from the world of competitive sports and establish social clubs which could be easily defended against the forces of democratization; or (2) set up formal organizations designed to structure play in a way which ensured that the "nobility of play" would remain uncontaminated by either "crass commercialism" or unrestricted meritocratic principle.[64] Members of different groups within the dominant class tended to pursue one or the other of these strategies: many of the traditional tory establishment withdrew to the socially oriented hunt and tandem clubs and vigorously defended these clubs against "lower status" bourgeois accessibility (for example, entry by the smaller indigenous industrial fragment of the bourgeoisie). The other component of the upper class consolidated a kind of "Victorian legacy" through the cult of the "amateur."[65] Thus, as Dunning and Sheard have pointed out in the case of the English Rugby football, the concept of amateurism seems to have evolved in a dialectical fashion as a conscious strategy of exclusion in class relations.[66] In this form, it became a major policy feature of the early "national" sports governing bodies which developed during the 1870s and 1880s in an effort to consolidate rules and regulate the play of different sports.[67]

By the mid-1880s, the key organizational structures in the world of games and sports were dominated by amateur agencies. Central among these were the early national sporting associations (e.g., the National Amateur Lacrosse Association), the newly formed Amateur Athletic Union of Canada, and the powerful Montreal Amateur Athletic Association. The executives of these agencies were not exclusively recruited from the top stratum of Canada's dominant class; rather the major amateur agencies were governed by a loose coalition of younger and less established members of this class whose origins lay in the business, professional, and military communities of the major urban centers. Of these three communities, the business community dominated the executive positions of amateur agencies. As Syd Wise has emphasized, the club movement and the standards of amateurism it embraced were intimately connected to the concerns for order and sobriety that were so much a part of the dominant culture of commerce of the period.[68]

It is instructive to note what parts of the Canadian urban business community many of these executives came from. Given that the 1880s represented what has been called the "halcyon" days of Canadian industrial development, one might hypothesize that many of the executives of the amateur agencies would come from the dynamic industrial sector of Canadian business.[69] But this was not the case. Individuals like W.K. McNaught—who combined his role as an executive member of the National Amateur Lacrosse Association with the presidency of the Canadian Manufacturers Association—seemed to be the exception rather than the rule. The major concentration of occupations for those business executives in amateur agencies lay primarily in the areas of finance and retail or wholesale trade.[70]

Given the broad political, economic, and cultural changes I have outlined, it should not be surprising that the industrial sector was underrepresented in the occupations of the organizers of the amateur organizations of the 1880s. I say this for two reasons. First, while the major amateur organizations did not generally recruit their leaders from the highest stratum of the Canadian upper class, the leadership was nonetheless unabashedly Victorian in focus, organization, and hierarchy.[71] The laissez-faire and rational utilitarian standards of industrial bourgeois interests were not always compatible with such traditions and views. Second—and because of the historical dominance of merchant capital in Canada—the indigenous Canadian industrial bourgeoisie had never been in a position to develop as a full-fledged component of the Canadian upper class. T.W. Acheson has noted that although few of the industrial elite in 1885 were men of humble origins, industrialists generally considered themselves to be the "proletariat" of the Canadian business community.[72] Moreover, despite the economic nationalism of the late 1870s, the American domination of Canadian industrial production—that had been stimulated by the Reciprocity Act of 1854—continued to act as a serious constraint to the development of *indigenous* and independent industrial power.[73]

But to note that the industrial development of Canada was retarded by the branch-plant character of production, and that "progressive" industrial bourgeois interests were rarely reflected among the key organizers of games and sports in Canada is not to argue that the broader limits and pressures of industrialization should be trivialized. Similarly, the fact that the small manufacturer or skilled artisan was not generally a part of the creation of an "amateur orientation" to organized games and sports should not be taken as an indication that these individuals were unimportant to the restructuring and reorientation of play in late nineteenth-century Canada. Undoubtedly, many upwardly mobile industrialists and skilled laborers utilized the dominant class as a reference group and became closely attached to the value of sobriety, fairness, and moral development in games. However, for some middle-class shopkeepers, and certainly for most laborers, the ideal of the true "gentleman-amateur" was only remotely attainable, and the pious concern with temperance and morality associated with it was not always culturally appealing.[74] An alternative arena for cultural expression was provided in the increasing development and expansion of commercial forms of games and popular recreation.

Dunning and Sheard have noted how the presence of an ascendant industrial component of the bourgeoisie in England stimulated an open, more meritocratic and commercial approach to games and sports.[75] The small-scale industrialists were often self-made men who directly oversaw the manufacturing process from a small office attached to the workshop.

Close contact with employees and a feeling of commonality in production were conducive to a low degree of status-exclusiveness and class distance. This relationship formed the foundation for "open" rugby clubs, often associated with the plant. Similar patterns can be identified in some of the Canadian sports clubs of the late 1800s. Fragmentary evidence suggests that it was frequently within these clubs that the emphasis on skill and winning began to rival the "amateur" ideal of fair play as a legitimate standard for gauging the quality of the "sporting" experience.[76]

This last point must be qualified with a caveat. Much of the economic production in Canada was based on an impersonal type of industrial organization and, given the long hours and lingering policies against Sabbath-breaking and amusements, there were few opportunities for recreation or organized sports for the industrial laborer. For example, Alan Metcalfe points out that manual laborers were almost completely absent from the club movement in Montreal until the late 1890s, and that nearly all of the recreational and sports facilities were limited to the middle-class and predominantly English-speaking wards of the city.[77] Workers' clubs that did start up (e.g., some of the Mechanics' Clubs) tended to represent labor's highest status occupations (e.g., mechanics, firemen),[78] and unless organized by white-collar workers, they rarely lasted more than a few years. There were even fewer outlets for recreation and games among factory workers and unskilled laborers. Despite all the rhetoric in some quarters about public recreation and public welfare, the main purpose of reform in Montreal appeared designed to do little more than expedite commerce and insure that middle-class morality was not offended by frequent displays of working-class impropriety.[79]

The following letter from a "factory boy" in an 1871 edition of the *Montreal Star* dramatically captures the difficulty that workers had in finding opportunities and places for organized play, games, and popular recreation:

> The charge of admittance to the floating bath is too high to permit us to make use of that establishment anywise frequently; the only other place where we are allowed to bathe—the beach beyond the Victoria bridge—is so distant as to be unavailable to the class I represent. You are aware, sir, at the same time, that if we go elsewhere than to the places named, it is at the risk of being arrested and sent to jail.[80]

This "factory boy's" troubles are clearly grounded in far broader allocative rules and social structural conditions. Most workers in the late nineteenth century worked long hours and a six-day week and were still legally prevented from becoming involved in recreational activities on Sundays. At the same time, few workers had the material resources to commute to sporting fields that were usually located in the "middle-class" districts of Canada's urban areas.[81]

Yet, many workers actively resisted attempts to regulate their cultural productions and, even in the face of limited material resources and limited free time, there was a great deal of informal involvement in canal swims, cockfights, boxing matches, and certain team games, most notably baseball.[82] Metcalfe notes, for example, that a vast "Sunday Subculture" of gaming and sporting activity existed in Montreal from the 1870s through the remainder of the century—a subculture that provided workers with momentary pleasure and excitement on their one free day a week.[83]

Workers' games and sports tended to be culturally separate from the majority of club sports practiced by the middle classes, although overlap did exist, especially among labor's highest status occupations where the middle classes were often used as a reference group. In the large urban centers during the late nineteenth century, the "proper" people in the business community controlled amateur sport, dominated city councils, and effectively ran the YMCA, high schools, and churches where sports were often played. Workers' sports, meanwhile, were often marginal, loosely organized, and commercially inclined. If organized formally, they were "structured" in conjunction with worker's associations, craft unions, factories, or businesses.

One might say that the emphasis most workers continued to place on their taverns, gaming, and sporting entertainment was undertaken as *an alternative* to struggles in broader areas of social life. However, in the period between the 1860s and early twentieth century, this argument would be simplistic. Ian Jobling argues, for example, that the issue of "limits" placed on sports participation was an important catalyst in helping to crystallize class consciousness in the struggle for the nine-hour day and the Saturday half-holiday. Similarly, Bryan Palmer has noted the great importance of sports in maintaining a sense of cohesiveness and continuity and in providing a forum for sociability among workers in Hamilton, Ontario.[84]

Commercial forms of sport, constituted in an increasingly formalized manner, were becoming ever more important to vast numbers of working-class people in Canadian society. As suggested earlier, commercialism of some type had always been an important part of traditional community games and recreation, but during the latter third of the nineteenth century, conditions were ideal for commercial sports to break out of the ideological and legal constraints surrounding them. The beginning of regular "challenge" matches stimulated the "monetization" of games, and the increasingly wide-open features of entrepreneurial activity in Canada reinforced the overriding importance of "success" in all walks of life, including the playing field. More important, the adulation and national pride associated with new "professional athletes"—like Canada's famous oarsman Ned Hanlan—helped to integrate play more formally into the market place and partially legitimate it as an area of "open" competition and entrepreneurial activity.[85] Yet, while such developments influenced spectatorship and offered limited careers in organized sport to individuals with exceptional abilities, the nineteenth century did not, in any organizational sense, represent the triumph of rational meritocratic values in the world of sports and games. Commercial sport was generally chaotic and in constant conflict with "amateurism," and as late as the early twentieth century the Victorian legacy of the "gentleman-amateur" was the axis around which the dominant standards of sport revolved.[86]

This conflict between amateur and more commercial forms of sporting activities at the turn of the twentieth century raises some interesting questions about the relationships of cultural forms to changing conditions of social organization. Although amateur and commercial approaches to sport shared certain structural similarities, they differed markedly in cultural emphasis. For example, the controllers of the major amateur agencies objected to commercialism primarily on the basis of four principles: (1) commercialism was supposed to debase play by allowing the representational character of play to take precedence over the act of playing itself; (2) commercialism was seen to emphasize instrumental "ends" more than traditional "means"; (3) commercialism was viewed as inflaming passion (often leading to violence) rather than dramatizing the values of restraint; and finally (4) commercialism was seen to be closely associated with gambling, drinking, and frivolity—all of which offended bourgeois Protestant sentiment.[87]

Yet, given the contingencies of industrial development and the continuing popularization of organized sports, many of the clubs, teams, and individual competitors who were associated with the major amateur organizations had a good deal of trouble living up to the ideals that amateurism defined.[88] As clubs proliferated, and as many became increasingly involved in intense local rivalries, there began to be a demand for even more regularized game schedules. In the face of such demands, exhibition matches and "challenge series" were increasingly replaced by more regular and rationalized formats—in effect, the beginnings of sports leagues. At the same time, the high cost of maintaining expensive athletic facilities created a situation where so-called amateur clubs often had to rent their facilities to other teams (sometimes even to "professionals") in order to cover costs. As this occurred, many of the clubs became transformed from "exclusive" to "open" and, finally, to "gate-taking" organizations in a manner similar to the British Rugby clubs studied by Dunning and Sheard.[89] Furthermore, although it was still in no way ideologically legitimate for a gentleman to want to win above all else, the idea of "scientific play" was beginning to rival "fair play" as an accepted standard for judging the sporting experience.[90]

The shift in emphasis from "fairness' to "technique" within amateurism itself seemed to make some of the distinctions between amateur and professional sporting activities less "real" and more arbitrary. The development of superior technique, whether pursued as an end in itself or as a means to an end, essentially has only one logical consequence: improved performance.

These transformations introduced a difficult and highly ambiguous situation within the definition of amateurism. For they suggested, on the one hand, that although sport, as an apparent derivation of play, was quintessentially a *democracy of ability,* on the other hand, it was a *subordinate* area of life where the development of ability could only be pursued on a casual, part-time basis. In other words, the guardians of the amateur ethos had embraced and assimilated some of the advancing sentiments of nineteenth-century utilitarianism, but only within the limits imposed by a conservative view of social organization which stressed *moral* rather than *rational* utility.[91] The *use-value of amateur sport lay in its contribution to personal growth and development, whereas the use-value of commercial sport came to be increasingly defined in economic terms.* But, as Alan Metcalfe has correctly pointed out, over the last two decades of the nineteenth century, there was increased bureaucratization in sport which facilitated differentiation between the executives in the major amateur sport organizations and the players themselves.[92] Given this development, it seems that the meritocratic side of the amateur equation was being overly credited at the level of actual play, thus introducing a situation where many clubs defined themselves nominally as "amateur" but began to converge progressively with more commercialized forms of sporting activity.

The consequences of this convergence were extremely significant. Influenced by the success of commercial sport in the United States, and finding the "elite" in the major amateur sport organizations inaccessible and unresponsive, members of many of the "open" and "gate-taking" clubs created organizational alternatives to domination by middle- and upper-class business and professional men. The organizers of the first professional leagues in baseball, lacrosse, and later, hockey, included promoters and fastbuck artists, local athletic facility owners, small manufacturers, and local businessmen.[93] In short, they were a far more broadly based group than the more established businessmen and professionals who controlled the major amateur organizations. However, the leadership in commercial sport itself *began to crystallize after the first decade of the twentieth century, as team owners and league organizers moved from an entrepreneurial to a corporate orientation.*

From Entrepreneurialism to Cartelization

The period of increasing entrepreneurial development in sport and popular recreation described above paralleled an intense period of broader entrepreneurial activity in Canadian society. Despite severe recessions in the latter third of the nineteenth century, the Canadian economy continued to expand and open up avenues of mobility within the class structure. Michael Bliss argues, for example, that most of the capitalists who dominated the Canadian upper class after the turn of the century had begun their careers as clerks and subcontractors a generation before.[94] Bliss may overstate the degree of actual mobility into the Canadian upper class during this period, and his arguments should not be taken to imply that great inequalities of condition had dissolved by the turn of the twentieth century.[95] But there can be no denying that substantial mobility did occur as Canada went through a dynamic phase of economic growth and entrepreneurial capitalism. In the sport world, many of the upwardly mobile clerks and white collar workers who identified with middle-class Victorian values saw in sport an agency which helped strengthen temperance and the business-related virtues of hard work and dedication. Such men moved into executive positions in the amateur sports organizations as they worked their way toward increased power and privilege. At the same time, as I have tried to indicate, commercial sport seemed to open up as an area of business opportunity and mobility for less privileged members of the bourgeoisie and even to considerable numbers of skilled laborers.[96]

This period of intense and "open" entrepreneurial capitalism in Canada did not last much beyond the first World War. The increased involvement of established banking interests and merchant capitalists in certain areas of the industrial sector (the area of the economy featuring the greatest degree of growth), and the accelerated rate of American direct investment in other areas of the industrial sector worked—in the form of corporate concentration—to solidify a more stable and rigid class structure. Thus Wallace Clement argues that

> during one brief period the manufacturing sector was open and immigrants with skills and some capital were able to establish themselves as a new social force, but as the ruling class moved in and consolidated these emerging firms, avenues began to close, manufacturing became concentrated and opportunities were limited.[97]

The open competitive capitalism—which is so commonly depicted as occurring during the transformation from feudal or colonial systems to industrial capitalist systems—was increasingly limited by the establishment of a highly structured, bureaucratic approach to production, an accompanying emphasis on specialization within the division of labor, and the overall shift to modern corporate organization.

It is readily apparent that the penetration of such developments into the cultural spheres of Canadian life continued to intensify throughout the late nineteenth and early twentieth century. The long-established monetary features of game-contests as spectacles (e.g., gambling and cash prizes) continued to develop a more coherent commodity form. As more workers gained better pay and reductions in work hours, they became a ready pool of consumers for a new *product* that combined drama and excitement in an atmosphere of leisure and sociability. In its earliest forms, this product took the shape of contests and matches in individual sports (e.g., rowing, boxing, and walking) that were "made" either by the contestants themselves or by local entrepreneurs. By the early twentieth century, however, the product had increasingly taken the form of regularized entertainment-oriented team games. As this occurred, commercial sport began a more formalized association with what Harry Braverman has called the "universal market" tendencies of capitalist enterprises.[98] As the buying and selling of labor power in Canada became more systematic and orderly throughout the late nineteenth and early twentieth centuries, the system of values upon which the free market in labor depended had worked to erode many of the more traditional conceptions of community and culture. In particular, time spent away from work by wage-laborers became more and more dependent upon the market place as a source of people's gratification, and this gave further impetus to the full-scale commodification of amusements and sporting spectacles. The demand for new consumer goods also tacitly reinforced a greater commitment to work effort as the vehicle for creating the necessary capital to purchase the goods in question.

I would argue that the unique pressures of the changes in capitalist enterprise in early twentieth-century Canada were manifested in the further structuring of commercial sport in two ways. First, as clubs and individuals entered into systematic market relationships with one another in sport, it became necessary to incorporate formally clubs and sport businesses. It is not surprising, for example, that the number of federal charters on record issued to sport organizations of various types rose from one to thirty in the period between 1880 and 1920.[99] Secondly, there was a growing recognition of the need to create mechanisms (economic rules) that could regulate "economic competition" between teams, and protect the developing labor and product markets in sport. In the early years of organized commercial sport in Canada (from 1870 to 1910), promoters and team owners usually acted in an individualistic entrepreneurial fashion and struggled with each other for dominance in the labor and product markets surrounding professional athletic activity. Such struggles were ultimately counterproductive, in that they made it difficult to keep leagues together for any period of time. Arguments over gate receipts, stadium and rink sizes, and franchise rights posed continuing threats to financial success in the sports business. And, while professional sport in itself was popular, individual teams developed and faded with almost predictable regularity.

The first major shift from an entrepreneurial to a corporate orientation in the Canadian sport world occurred, I believe, with the formation of the National Hockey League (N.H.L.) in 1917. Hockey had its folk origins in Canada in community pick-up games and in the occasional contests of "gentlemen" and soldiers during the long Canadian winters. However, the first *formally* structured games with codified rules occurred in the Canadian universities.[100] It was in this form, as an upper-class "college game," that hockey first began to attract attention. However, its popularization and incorporation into a commodity form for mass consumption occurred when the game was taken over by industrial entrepreneurs, was stripped of its amateur trappings, and was reconstituted as a violent spectator sport in the mining towns of Cobalt, Haileybury, Timmins, Sault Ste. Marie, and Houghton, Michigan.[101] In this form, hockey drew on a wellspring of deep-rooted cultural features in working-class life, but gave these features an expression unique to the emerging structures of Canadian capitalism.

By the 1920s, hockey, led by the N.H.L., had become Canada's major team sport, and by the 1930s, the owners of N.H.L. franchises had learned (after years of bidding wars for players) that profit maximization could only be hampered by unrestricted individual "economic" competition. As Colin Jones indicates, the owners recognized that in order to maximize individual profits they had to maximize joint profits.[102] In other words, the league had to function as a cartel, restricting business practices and ensuring that franchise owners acted like the participants in a joint venture.[103] The period following this realization has been characterized by corporate concentration and growing league control over both the product and labor markets in hockey. At the same time, as the league solidified, it consolidated massive capital gains based on the appreciation of franchise values and on windfall profits.[104] By contrast, Canadian professional football developed more within the ambiguity of amateurism that I described earlier, and was in constant contact with university sport programs that maintained an amateur orientation. Most of the "professionalizing" forces in football developed in western Canada and were stimulated by strong relations of regional hostility with the amateur-oriented East and by closer cultural ties with more professionalized football programs in the United States. As a result of these pressures, the Canadian Football League was extremely slow to develop a national and standardized set of rules. Indeed, Canadian professional football did not consolidate and undergo a partial move to joint profit maximizing behavior until after 1950.[105] The question of American pressures in the social development of Canadian sport is an important one, for it seems clear that as the British influence on sport softened, the United States soon began to imprint its own metropolitan influence on organized commercial sporting activities. Sports in the United States were often more "progressive" in their attachment to more fully developed industrial bourgeois cultural forms, and American society generally provided a favorable environment for an emphasis on more democratized and commercialized types of sporting activity.[106] The underrepresentation of petit-bourgeois and working-class interests in the control of Canadian amateur sport could be compensated for by involvement with American sports clubs in binational commercial enterprises. Attendant to this, it may be suggested that an excessively rigid amateur code did not always allow for the type of sporting involvement that captured the interest of the Canadian working-class community.[107] The rapidly developing national and semi-meritocratic emphases of binational commercial sports were especially compatible with petit-bourgeois and working-class interests, hopes, and aspirations, and dramatized their growing commercial strength.

But for the working class, the change from the binational, *player-controlled,* or *club-oriented* commercial sports that one occasionally found in the late nineteenth century to the slick American-dominated corporate sports of the present day, has been something of a cultural betrayal. As commercial sports grew in popularity and developed market relations to outside business interests, as wealthy patrons of commercial teams increased their influence, and as cartel structures were created in the sports world, relationships between commercial sports and the working class tended to become progressively contradictory. Actual working-class influences on decision making became limited as mobility into executive positions became restricted to individuals with capital; working-class athletes generally became transformed from journeyman players to contractually bound laborers; and what began as a dramatization of meritocracy and greater freedom revealed itself, paradoxically, to also be an abstract symbolization of constraining commodity relations.

For the most part, these trends continue to be obvious features of modern corporate sport, but there have been some interesting fluctuations in them. For example, modern team sports have emerged out of a period of extremely repressive work conditions in the 1940s and 1950s, to a point where athletes (or, more correctly, top athletes) are usually guaranteed high salaries and a measure of financial security through increased pensions and deferred salary payments.[108] Occupations in the sports world have also gained a good deal of respectability, and this change, complete with its connotations of executive houses in the suburbs, is indicative of a process that Charles Page has wryly referred to as the "embourgeoisement" of professional athletes.[109]

Another fluctuation has been a gradual move from the individual, family, or small corporation patterns of team ownership that existed during the 1920s and 1930s, to increased interlocking with larger corporations that often have little to do with sports. As Okner has noted, this pattern was partially stimulated in the United States by the tax advantages that a professional sports franchise might offer a large corporation (although many of these advantages have been successfully challenged in recent years).[110] But in Canada, the pattern seems more closely related to the desire of businessmen to support popular, highly visible public activities for promotional purposes.

It is impossible to overstate the role of the media in supporting and reinforcing this pattern. The media have played a central role in allowing corporate sports to develop and refine their particular commodity form, while at the same time presenting this form as the essence of "modern" sport. Television in particular has presented this form of sport as a kind of "shared cultural experience," while all the time ignoring its own role in shaping this experience into a marketable and consumable video product.[111] It is no accident, for example, that hockey was Canada's first television sport of any consequence. Not only was there a demand for hockey, but hockey was the most commodified and readily "consumable" sport of the early post-war era.

During the 1960s, Canadian sports coverage broadened considerably, partly as a result of growing competition between the Canadian Broadcasting Company and C.T.V., the new private network started in 1961, and also in response to emerging rules about Canadian content in the industry.[112] Sports became an especially handy and inexpensive method of meeting Canadian content regulations while maintaining the heavy importation of American programming in other areas. Such developments were applauded by the owners of sports franchises, for television was providing an excellent source of additional revenues without having to increase costs.[113]

All of this created almost "natural" market ties, not only between sports and the media itself, but also between sports and those groups interested in high profile television advertising—most notably, the powerful Canadian food and beverage industry. Several illustrations come readily to mind. For example, for years the Bassett family, involved in Baton Broadcasting and the Toronto Telegram newspaper, were centrally involved in Canadian sport. More recently, the Western Broadcasting group has had ties to several sports franchises in western Canada, and the Global Television network has purchased the Toronto Blizzard soccer team. In the case of the beverage industry, there has long been an extremely close relationship between beer and sports. As of this writing, Carling O'Keefe Ltd. owns both the Quebec Nordiques of the N.H.L. and the Olympic Stadium advertising rights for the Montreal Alouettes in the C.F.L. Moreover, it has similar arrangements for promotional and broadcast rights to Montreal Expos games, and recently purchased control of the Toronto Argonaut football team. Molson's of Canada, which were longtime owners of the Montreal Canadians before selling their interests to Carena-Bancorp Ltd., recently purchased the team back for approximately $20 million. John Labatt Ltd. has a large interest in the Toronto Blue Jays baseball team (another partner is the owner of the *Toronto Globe and Mail*), and both Labatts and Carlings are frequent sponsors of certain government programs and "professional" sports, most notably skiing. What makes such corporate ties even more appealing for the parties involved, is that their essentially instrumental character can be masked by suggesting that a "service" is being provided to the community.[114]

Evidence seems to suggest that modern trends in the ownership and control of professional team sports in Canada are moving away from the old style entrepreneurs that dominated the earliest professional teams. Increasingly, personalities like Harold Ballard of the Toronto Maple Leafs or the Edmonton Oilers' flamboyant owner Peter Pocklington seem the exception rather than the rule. This evidence of a broad movement of commercial sports from small-scale entrepreneurial efforts, to family-based or individually owned corporate enterprises, to involvement in the periphery of the empires of Canada's dominant corporations is some-times seen as an indication of progress. Work conditions in commercial team sports have improved, the argument runs, and the ruthless pursuit of profit has been mediated by a broader corporate social responsibility. But is this view of progress an accurate one? I think not. What has really occurred is simply that commercial sports are only now beginning to become subject to the liberal concessions of welfare capitalism. Mean-while, the lines of power and control in commercial sports are becoming even more closely tied to Canada's corporate elite and its structural alliances with American capital.[115]

We may note the following examples of such alliances. Boards of directors of most Canadian professional sports teams (except for a few teams in the Canadian Football League [C.F.L.] where control lies in the hands of business and professional interests in the local community) maintain readily identifiable ties with indigenous Canadian capital in the areas of finance, trade, the food and beverage industry, and transport and communications. But (again excepting the C.F.L.) the major leagues within which these franchises operate are controlled by American inter-ests. Modern hockey and baseball, in particular, represent a classic dramatization of the doubly exploitative nature of Canada's association with the American metropole. The accumulative interests of Canadian capital in areas where these interests have always been strong are enhanced by their association with organizations where control lies in American hands.[116] And, whereas Canadian capital is involved in a profit-able relationship that maintains patterns of dependency, the interests and forms of cultural expression of most Canadians remain largely underdeveloped. This is not to say that Canadians as a whole have *lost control* of commercial sports to the United States; rather, as Wallace Clement points out in the case of the Canadian economy, it is doubtful if any real collective control by Canadians has ever been present.[117] With few exceptions, modern commercial sports have always been owned and controlled by private interests (or at least by a committee of people, usually male, from middle- or upper-class fragments in communities) and have represented the organization of these interests in corporate entities that function in an international capitalist system.

This brings us rather directly to a consideration of the relationships between commercial sport and organized labor—in theory the traditional opponents of bourgeois dominance. In one of the few attempts to understand sporting activities in the context of labor and class conflicts, Kiviaho and Simola have noted how working-class sports clubs in late nineteenth-century Finland were given considerable support by the Finnish labor movement.[118] Opportunities for working-class sports participation were stimulated, and working-class club teams provided widespread entertainment. The necessity for these labor-oriented sports organizations arose partially in response to the exclusive and restrictive character of Olympian amateurism, but also as a natural part of an attempt to support and encourage working-class culture.[119]

There is some evidence that the potential for similar developments may have existed in Canada even though the Marxist component of the Canadian labor movement never developed to the extent that it did in many European nations. Bruce Kidd[120] recently noted, for example, how during the Depression years, the Canadian Labor Party sought to support working-class sport through the creation of a Workers' Sports Association (W.S.A.) that was to offer instruction and provide support for demonstrations and athletic exhibitions.[121] The W.S.A. also sponsored a team selected to compete in the ill-fated "People's Olympics" held in Barcelona in 1936 as a workers' alternative to the Berlin Olympics.[122]

However, the cultural focus of the Canadian Labor Party's approach to sports is not immediately clear from Kidd's preliminary study. Even though radical workers' papers like the *Daily Clarion* and *The Worker* occasionally pointed out that organized sports (especially commercial sports) were "a racket," they nonetheless gave them ample coverage in their sports pages. As one editorial noted, sports provided "the only enjoyment the masses get under the rotten conditions that exist at the present time."[123] Indeed, there is little evidence that any significant attempt to articulate a distinctly working-class approach to sports ever occurred. Kidd points out that the radical working-class press tended to limit its discussion of "alternatives" in sport to little more than wistful discussions of the opportunities for sports participation that supposedly existed in the Soviet Union.[124]

It is not completely within the limits I have set for myself in this chapter to attempt to explain the inability of Canadian labor to offer workers a cultural alternative to the dramatic appeal of commercial (and to a lesser extent) amateur sports. However, a few hypotheses might be noted. First, we must recognize the extent to which the Canadian labor movement, like the industrial sector of the economy itself, was underdeveloped during the late nineteenth and early twentieth centuries.[125] Radical independent union organizers were ruthlessly persecuted and there was strong pressure from American unions (primarily the American Federation of Labor) for Canadian labor to ally itself with the American labor movement. The strength of the American influence in the industrial sector of the Canadian economy facilitated the cooptation of Canadian workers by American industrial and trade unions and guaranteed a subordination of Canadian working-class culture to their particular ideology. As Howard and Scott have stressed, this ideology emphasized interclass collaboration and negotiation rather than the necessity for class conflict.[126] This emphasis in no way implied the complete endorsement of existing social conditions, but it did contain a tacit acceptance of the essential structure of capitalism and a notion that all workers might ultimately gain access to middle-class lifestyles. As part of the negotiations with labor under these terms, sports programs and industrial recreation increased markedly and gained considerable acceptability in the world of industry. At first, the right to participate in sports in a shortened work week was something that was won by labor. But, gradually, the responsibility for these programs was often taken over by management. Where this happened the sports themselves often became simply another form of incorporation and control. As Bob Russel, a prominent western Canadian radical labor leader in the early 1900s, notes in the case of the Canadian Pacific Railway:

> The CPR . . . adopted a paternal attitude of social clubs, recreation. They provided recreational activities, baseball teams, football teams. The Royal Alexandra Hotel was used Saturday night. They had a social club and the common staff from the jobs would go down there and dance with the foreman or the foreman's wife, you understand, and the Manager would look in. It was all paternalism you understand. Well of course, the rebels that were out from Europe, they were having none of this kind of stuff you know. This was just soothing syrup to them and they'd buck these things, but you'd always have (another group of workers) that were always willing to hob-nob with the boss you see. It was a better thing . . . little gold striping or that, and the CPR developed that kind of system. . . . Instead of giving an increase in wages, they'd paint your name on the side of the car. . . . You'll see those conductors and brakemen with their silver stripes or their gold stripes. . . . Well . . . (they) . . . think this is a great honour. With seven of those gold bars across him he thinks he's a real hero and that's the kind of stuff the CPR played on all the time and of course we'd been through

that experience in the old country, you see. First of all it
started with paternalism, and then it developed into a piece
work system, then came the necessity of organizing to
defeat those things.[127]

It is quite likely that organizing *against* something like sports programs,
which were enjoyable and sometimes incorporated into labor's demands
for a shorter work week and better living conditions, was held to be
paradoxical by many workers. In this sense, only the most radical labor
organizers appeared to recognize the significance of sports structured
and controlled by workers, as opposed to sports defined and regulated by
the dominant class and incorporated into working-class culture.

Somewhat similar conditions have continued to develop throughout
the twentieth century in the case of organized commercial sports. I think
it can be argued that the close cultural ties between working-class
recreation and commercial gaming and sporting activities were generated and solidified at a time when such activities were somewhat oppositional features within the hegemony of the late nineteenth century.
However, the full-scale incorporation of commercial sports into Canadian
capitalism has paradoxically created a situation where this long-standing
cultural attachment appears to have reproductive consequences. For
when the drama and excitement of sport is assumed to be enabled by its
ties to capital—that is, when sport itself becomes indistinguishable from
commodity relations—it is difficult to say that a strong working-class
commitment to it works against capitalism.[128]

The Limits and Pressures of State Sport

Thus far I have argued that an interest (primarily a fan interest) in various
commercial sports and in different types of industrially supported recreational activities emerged during the twentieth century as the prime
outlet for entertainment and physical recreation for members of Canada's
working class. On the other hand, voluntary, organizationally sponsored
amateur sports have tended to retain a strong association with the middle
and upper strata of Canada's dominant class. Even today, where sporting
activities appear to be substantially more democratized than earlier in
this century, a number of studies have documented a positive correlation
between active sports participation and a high socioeconomic position.[129] Of course, this pattern does not hold as closely in all pastimes—
activities with clearly pronounced, working-class cultural traditions like
boxing or weight lifting tend to maintain a connection with their past. But
as a general principle, the high-skill levels of amateur sports tend to draw

on advantaged groups in the Canadian reward structure. Where democratization has occurred, it has primarily been limited to the expansion of athletic opportunities within the various strata of Canada's dominant class—a situation I have referred to elsewhere as the "bourgeoisification" of amateur sport.[130] While all of this has occurred, working-class athletes have tended to remain underrepresented at "elite" levels, and those marginal Canadians to whom Marx would have referred as the "lumpenproletariat" are virtually nonexistent in the sports world.

But this whole issue of opportunities for *participation* is much less important than the question of opportunities for *control,* and the accompanying problems of the differential resources available to define and structure sport itself. It may be that there are now greater resources for working-class participation in the semicommercialized amateur sports of the present-day but there has definitely not been any substantial improvement in working-class control over sports and recreation policies. The growth of the Olympic movement in Canada after the 1920s, and the accompanying prestige associated with international sport has continued to guarantee a high degree of exclusivity at the executive levels of the major policy-making organizations.[131] One might expect this, of course, in such Victorian carry-overs as the Canadian Olympic Association, but even in our major voluntary sports associations, the predominance of upper- and middle-status interests within Canada's dominant class is blatant.

In a 1975 study that sampled executive members from over twenty of Canada's national sports associations, Rob Beamish found that over 50 percent of the executives had fathers who had been employed in professional, managerial, or technical occupations. Over 75 percent of the executives were themselves currently involved in similar occupations.[132] Moreover, the executives were generally located in the major urban centers—Toronto, Vancouver, Ottawa, and Montreal. Beamish points out how such patterns are influenced by the organizational logic of Canadian capitalism and the distribution of social resources in Canadian society. Most workers are locked into rigid production schedules, many must moonlight to make ends meet, and there is little time or incentive for voluntary participation. Also, as Beamish explains, there is little in their work to prepare them for such tasks:

> The lives of the majority of Canadians—an overwhelming majority—involve non-creative, and non-administrative mediation in their work place. Only a very small segment of the population has daily involvement with the skills, knowledge and powers that are required and utilized in

hierarchically controlled organizations. When one combines this idea with the fact that the Canadian state (which is composed of individuals who fall into the latter division of Canadian workers and who, collectively at least, believe in the ethos of centralized control and hierarchy) has institutionalized a formal bureaucratic structure for amateur sport in Canada then the impact of the class configurations unique to Capital become apparent.[133]

The issue of the role of the state in sports and recreation that Beamish raises is complex and cannot be discussed here in sufficient detail. It should be noted, however, that over the past twenty years, the involvement of the Canadian state in the "play" of its citizens and even in "the business of play" has increased markedly.[134] What I mean by such "involvement" is a gradual turn away from social control-oriented policies in the regulation of recreation and "gaming," and noncontrol policies in commercial sports (which have facilitated capital accumulation),[135] to more welfare-oriented programs ostensibly designed to increase the quality of life in Canada and expand people's opportunities for the pursuit of athletic excellence. The modern era in the development of state sport and recreation programs goes back to Bill C-131 in 1961, which created Canada's first formally constituted federal government department responsible for sport (the Fitness and Amateur Sport Directorate) within the Department of Health and Welfare. State involvement was furthered following a 1969 government *Task Force Report on Sport* which recommended the establishment of additional bureaucratic bodies designed to work with existing voluntary associations in the planning and administration of sport.[136] We now have what amounts to a bona fide federal Ministry of Sport and numerous provincial counterparts to it, a national lottery whose proceeds supposedly help in the "development" of Canadian sport, a *National Administrative Centre* to house the amateur associations, and the full-scale development of programs designed to "certify" coaches and athletes.[137]

In the absence of much research on sport and the state in Canada, explanations for these developments can only be speculated upon.[138] One argument might be that the state's increased involvement in recreation, fitness, and sport appears simply to be an inevitable part of the expansion of the social rights of citizenship that have been characteristic of most western liberal democracies over the last fifty years. This growth of state-supported social rights (many of which have been won by the underclasses in the face of considerable opposition) has accompanied a gradual shift in the sociopolitical emphasis of liberal democratic states—a shift from the role of direct and indirect agent for the accumulative interests of capital, to the role of legal and cultural guardian of liberal-democratic ideology and agent of liberal-democratic reform.

It must be recognized, however, that although state-sponsored recreation and sport programs have a good deal of social value for large numbers of citizens, they also have important implications for social reproduction. At minimum, by symbolically suggesting that the state acts on behalf of all citizens, these programs in no way threaten the long-term interests of Canadian capital. In this regard one might agree with Nicos Poulantzas that it is only by dramatically showing that the state does not function at the behest of capitalists that the state can effectively operate on their behalf. From this perspective, the apparent concern by modern state agencies over the democratization of sports or over the expansion of recreational opportunities for Canadians may be well intentioned or even progressively reformistic. But the unintended consequences of these reforms might well be measured in terms of their contribution to the social reproduction of the class system. It is along these lines that Louis Althusser and Nicos Poulantzas want to include sport in modern capitalist states as a part of the cultural "Ideological State Apparatus."[139]

But this is far too easy. In addition to the broader theoretical criticism that can be leveled against this view, I offer the following empirical considerations. First, if we focus on the place of sport in the struggle over defining and regulating the whole social process in Canadian life, it seems true to say that direct and indirect state action in the area of sport has usually been associated in some way with dominant class interests (e.g., rules over where and when to play, over the "conduct" of popular recreations, or rules which have protected the monopoly positions of professional team sports). There is, however, evidence suggesting that in Canada, inter- and intraclass struggles and the expression of class interests in sport (e.g., the struggle over amateurism) have been more often carried on *outside* the sphere of widespread state involvement. Even now, despite the notable "statization" of sport, the nature of state involvement is often limited to and focused on the development of some kind of liaison with traditionally established voluntary associations. In this regard, modern state policies *often do have a legitimate reformist character* in their capacity to influence and expand the goals of these associations beyond their often narrowly defined "middle-class" objectives. In somewhat more general terms Paul Willis reminds us:

> The huge growth of the state in welfare and education, for
> instance, is not necessarily in the best interests of capitalism.
> It has to some extent been forced on it by competing groups
> using their own real freedom for self-advancement as they

have seen it. Of course state agencies have been utilized and modified to help cool out, or drive out, problems which capitalism produces but cannot solve. But whilst they help to solve problems these institutions cannot wholly be absorbed back into capitalism. They maintain spaces and potential oppositions, keep alive issues, and prod nerves which capitalism would much rather were forgotten.[140]

Willis may be guilty of reifying capitalism in this passage but he points out, correctly, the complexity of the relationship of the state to the reproduction of capitalism. Too much emphasis on state sport programs as features of direct or indirect rule leaves too much out of the account. Yet, one ought not to be so afraid of drawing direct or indirect linkages between the state and the class system that one overlooks the extent to which state sport programs are most often far from oppositional. Defined in terms of the creation of "nationalist" goals—such as the production of high-level athletic performances—state sport programs often do little more than mystify the relationships between sport and class structure.

One might better situate this latter comment by noting that it is very easy to make too much of the rise of "welfare-statism" as an explanation for the expanded involvement of the Canadian state in the "structuring" of sports and physical recreation. As Leo Panitch argues, even today Canada is little more than a "middle range" spender on welfare programs. Moreover, in the case of recreation and sports, there has been much less formal attention paid at the federal level to recreation which emphasizes "fun" or individual enjoyment than to fitness, organized sports, and athletic success.[141] A physically healthy society is supposedly more productive (with lower absenteeism, higher job satisfaction, fewer strikes, etc.), and there is a case to be made that the current "fitness boom" in Canada merely represents the resurgence of long-standing regulative traditions that have always been class based.[142] in the case of state support for athletic success, we now seem caught up in an international sport system where state-supported athletes often appear to have become little more than ideological laborers—symbolic agents for "liberal democracy" who oppose the representatives of communism and the Third World in a contest to affirm who has the "healthiest" sociopolitical system.[143] The subjugation of sport to "performance quotas" of the kind announced by the federal minister for sport on the eve of the 1978 Commonwealth Games,[144] and the full-scale assault on the record that develops in conjunction with international sport, appears to have led to a rationalization of the dominant forms of sporting practice that goes well beyond Johan Huizinga's wildest fears.

Conclusion: A Summary of Basic Themes and Patterns

My purpose in this chapter has been to use the theoretical considerations developed earlier as a basis for outlining some of the main contributing features, contested issues, and alternative meanings associated with the institutional structuring of sporting practice in Canadian society. My discussion has focused primarily on the differential capacity of certain classes and class fragments to structure the playing of games and sports in certain ways, and to mobilize particular forms of bias through this structuring. In doing so, I have suggested that the dominant forms of institutional structuring were frequently contested and subject to varying interpretations. The mobilization of bias—and characteristic responses to it in the form of acceptances, partial acceptances, and outright rejections—appears to be constituted in, and constitutive of, the production and reproduction of the social processes involved in the complex and often contradictory nature of class formation, re-formation, and cultural production in Canadian life.

The basic perspective employed in my outline was to concentrate on inter- and intraclass struggles and their relationships to patterns of domination and dependency. I began by noting how in late eighteenth- and early nineteenth-century Canada, the dramatic representational value of "leisure class" games was the signification of superior rank and traditional aristocratic power. People participated in minimally structured games and sports for fun, relaxation, and sociability, but in ways culturally specific to their social location. Changes in class formation and the growing strength of bourgeois conceptions of social life soon developed to rival the power of imported aristocratic conceptions. These interests were initially accommodated within the hegemony of a ruling merchant-gentry class, but their presence gradually began to change the features of this hegemony. In the case of games and sports, the idea of the "disciplined" enjoyment of games contained a set of bourgeois cultural limits and pressures whose expression could be seen in the legislated control of underclass amusements and the expulsion of undisciplined "play" from the work place.

Further elaboration of class formation and struggle in Canada centered around the control of rules and resources in the area of industrial production and the extension of this struggle to the cultural sphere. Amateurism emerged in this period as a regulative strategy of social closure by an insecure and somewhat reactionary bourgeoisie surrounded by the expansion of democratic "rights" and entrepreneurial capitalism. By contrast, commercial sports dramatized the expansion of the rational market and the spread of entrepreneurial ethics beyond the spheres of the dominant class in a form that many members of the economic and political elite found threatening. At the same time commercialism offered the Canadian worker opportunities for excitement and entertainment in a cultural milieu far more appealing than the Victorian, temperance-minded amateur clubs and associations. The dominant form of commercial sports, however, soon became a limiting celebration of capital accumulation far removed from worker's control.

In recent years, more formally organized state programs—less directly concerned with social control than with health and welfare—have entered as new elements in the structuring of sport in Canadian society. And, in the formal sense at least, it can be argued that the technical and moral rules which now constitute sport *as an institution* are primarily constituted in and out of the transactions which occur between well-placed "volunteers" in the traditional amateur associations, owners of commercial sports ventures and related businesses, and state bureaucrats. Active resistance and pressures in the form of oppositional conceptions from Canadian Labor are almost nonexistent, as are pressures from the chronically poor and marginal members of the society.

As a result of all of these considerations one might be tempted to say that in the current institutional structuring of Canadian sport, the mobilization of "middle-class" bias is complete. The opportunities and socially constructed abilities of large numbers of Canadians are not readily compatible with active involvement and success in noncommercial sports or with formal involvement in the creation of policy and its implementation. Similarly, hierarchy, technocratic approaches to the body (a kind of athletic "piece-work" system), and rational utilitarian ethics—coordinated in a market model of competition and a linear quantitative conception of "excellence"—have become virtually synonymous with the dominant conception of the term "sport." Yet, it is important to recognize that there continue to be a number of important counterpressures to such tendencies. What are these counterpressures, and how significant are they in defining the limits and possibilities of modern sport? How do such counterpressures relate to broader problems of agency and freedom in social life? It is to a final consideration of such questions, viewed in the context of what I have tried to accomplish in this entire study, that I now want to turn.

4

The Limits and Possibilities
of Modern Sport

*The interest of the social scientist in social structure is not due to any
view that the future is structurally determined. We study the structural
limits of human decision in an attempt to find points of effective
intervention, in order to know what can and what must be structurally
changed if the role of explicit decision in history-making is to be
enlarged. Our interest in history is not owing to any view that the future
is inevitable, that the future is bounded by the past. That men have lived
in certain kinds of society in the past does not set exact or absolute
limits to the kinds of society they may create in the future. We study
history to discern the alternatives within which human reason and
human freedom can now make history. We study historical social
structures, in brief, in order to find within them the ways in which they
are and can be controlled. For only in this way can we come to know
the limits and the meaning of human freedom.*

C. Wright Mills, 1959

At the beginning of this study I claimed that "classical" works on the role
of play, games, and sports in social development assumed their importance
as analytic foundations for future research because they consistently

addressed the fundamental philosophical, theoretical, and moral problems of western social thought. Most notable among these problems were concerns over agency, freedom, and constraint seen as features of human possibility in the development of industrial capitalism. I suggested that although important on their own terms, the actual contents of the theories of classical writers are often less significant than the problems these writers tried to address, and the scope and critical approach that they took to the analysis of their subject matter. Using Johan Huizinga and Thorstein Veblen as examples, I noted how a reexamination of the fundamental issues with which they struggled is a necessary step to free us from our continuing dependence on their work as a starting point for understanding the nature and significance of sport in contemporary western societies.

I have now worked through a great variety of material, including discussions of the strengths and weaknesses of the analyses of Huizinga and Veblen and of a number of other writers who have tried to understand the social dimensions of modern sport in provocative and penetrating ways. As I have worked through this material I have tried to sort out what seems to be right and wrong in these various perspectives on sport and society and I have tried to develop a more adequate field of concepts and arguments as a guide to our understanding of sport and social development. Following this, I have attempted to use many of these concepts and arguments as the theoretical foundation for a preliminary case study of the various forms and phases of institutional structuring that have characterized the social development of Canadian sport over the last two centuries and the various struggles over the control of rules and resources that have accompanied this structuring. In this final chapter I want to review some general features of the previous discussion, and comment further on the limits and possibilities, forms of freedom and constraint, that are expressed in and through sport as we understand it in modern capitalist societies.

Toward a Critical Theory of Sport

Let me return first to the images of play, games, and sports as forums for freedom and constraint that have been held by mainstream students of sport and by many of their left-wing critics. Without wanting to reduce their analyses to a caricature, I have identified a number of problematic tendencies that frequently characterize the work of both groups.

One of the most problematic of these tendencies is the inclination to idealize and romanticize the abstract and enabling features of those structures which define play as a form of social action. The result of this tendency is often one or another (or some combination) of two types of arguments about the relationships between play and sport in society: (1) play is viewed as *formally homologous* with sport so that, certain minor problems aside, it is claimed that sport is a universal forum for positive freedom, creative expressivity, and enriching metaphor; or (2) play is seen to be *debased* in sport, in the sense that the various structures which constitute sport reflect society in ways that block and repress play's realization in social and cultural forms. In the first case, sport is seen as an extension of human agency, the voluntary construction of a universal playful essence. In the latter case, sport is an object of social determination, a model of structural constraint.

Another problematic tendency is the degree to which assumptions about sport as a form of play and expressive agency, or as a form of structural constraint, are threaded through with parallel theoretical assumptions about structures and agency in social life and social development in general. For example, the strong voluntarist emphasis in much of the writing on sport is often neatly matched with abstract voluntarist conceptions about social organization itself and the kinds of limits that social structures place on agency. Indeed, the idea of the enabling character of the structures which constitute sports as social possibilities is often given ready "empirical" support by the suggestion that the broader social conditions influencing the creation of these structures have themselves been moving toward a progressive opening-up of human possibilities. In other words, many contemporary students of sport have been willing consumers of an ideal-typical general theory of industrial society within which it is asserted that: (1) formerly constraining class limits on human agency have decomposed (primarily due to fundamental changes within the "industrial" societies or their evolution to some sort of "post-industrial" phase); and that (2) modern cultural forms have been automatically influenced by, and have participated in, this process of decomposition. Those less willing to accept this theory in its most voluntaristic form have tended to fall back on a mechanistic view which sees social life as so totally incorporated into the logic of class and technocratic oppression that people are drawn to games and sports only as a cultural means of escape. Yet, it is argued, this escape is illusory. What passes for sport today is itself nothing more than a product of the technocratic rationality of capitalist productive forces. By failing to confront capitalist domination directly, and by attempting to escape from it through sports, people tacitly accept structures which are the embodiments of bourgeois repression and thereby damn themselves to a reproduction of the society that enslaves them.

I have argued that there is considerable substance to this argument but, in most cases, the argument is made far too crudely. My position is that our understanding of sport as an element of culture will only be advanced by rejecting all of the old stereotypes, ideal-typical categories, and dualistic conceptions that have dominated past research. For instance, the mainstream conjuncture of idealist and voluntarist thinking in the study of sport has been exceedingly good at pointing to the deep, meaningful features of play, games, and sports, to the importance of play and games in self-creation, and to the richness of games and sports as rituals and metaphors. But this school of thought has never been able to theorize adequately about the ways in which the very structures which ostensibly enable the separation of such activities from "reality," are in themselves constitutive of that reality and represent the mobilization of particular forms of bias. On the other hand, although the reductionists and structural determinists have correctly shown some of the ways in which sports are far from universally (or even relatively) free, and have provocatively emphasized the role of sport in social reproduction, they have continually been unable to understand that players and fans are knowledgeable agents rather than unreflective dupes, and that as *dramatic* cultural productions, the collective meanings of sports are always differentially interpreted and potentially oppositional.

In this study I have suggested the need to go beyond such notions by offering a view of play, games, and sports as distinctly social practices existing in, and constitutive of, historically shifting limits and possibilities that specify the range of powers available to human agents at different historical moments. More specifically, I have emphasized that the meanings, metaphoric qualities, and regulatory structures which define sports as social possibilities are all indissolubly connected to the making and the remaking of particular ways of living and to historical struggles over the monopolistic capacity to define the kind of life that people ought to live in a political community. These struggles—and their impact on the enabling and constraining features of play, games, and sports as structures *through which* and, sometimes, *against which* humans act—can only be understood in the broader context of the conflicts of interest and unequally distributed social resources that exist in any form of social organization. My emphasis in this study has been on the conflicts of interest and unequal social resources that are expressed in industrial capitalism as a social formation, and I have argued that these differences and inequities are lived out most graphically in capitalistic class relations.

I believe that these arguments hold straightforward implications for the kind of research that should be done in the sociological study of sport. All of us may well seek out practical mastery, fun, excitement, or fantasy in play, and it is important to elucidate the formal properties of the practices that enable us to carry out this search in a free and creative way. Yet, we must also ask whether the structures that are supposedly created to accomplish this search do not in some way alter our goals and carry with them a number of consequences for freedom viewed in the broadest of terms. In a society of unequally shared resources and of notable conflicts of interest, is it not plausible that the opening up of options for some people through a particular type of structuring actually implies or symbolizes the limiting of options for others? Can we say, to use a more concrete example, that opportunities to create rules, to define the dominant meanings of sports, and to compete and succeed within different definitions, have been universally accessible? Can we assert that sports, structured in different ways, have never embodied or offered representations of allocative and regulative rules of societies in a way that can be implicated in the domination of certain groups in these societies or in other societies?

I think these questions need to be extensively researched and debated as sociologists work toward developing a new critical theory of modern sport. For my part, I would be inclined to answer these questions in the negative. But from the standpoint of future research, I believe that answers to such questions do not lie in static, ahistorical discussions of the meanings of play, games, and sports. Nor do such answers lie in the uncritical application of long-established typologies of social change and development to the study of sport and society. As writers move the focus of their analyses from situations where the *structures* which constitute particular forms of "play" are effectively controlled by individual agents, to a situation where control derives from social transactions between collective agents, then they must increasingly turn to concrete studies in history and political economy for answers about the nature of the freedom created by these structures, and the social significance of the "freedoms" that are found. The most obvious task of a critical theory of sport is to define the "problematic," the field of concepts and arguments one can use in directing these historical and political economic studies.

The Dominant and the Residual in Canadian Sport

Throughout this book I have tried to begin the task of developing such a problematic and to give some indication of how it might be used as a basis for conducting a preliminary case study of the changing role and nature of sport in Canadian social development. The case study I have provided is only a first step toward mapping and explaining these changes. My argument is that Canadians have always existed in a setting of expanding and contracting opportunities and choices, and that these expansions and contractions have been intimately connected to the struggles over scarce resources, forms of technical and moral control in the society, and the differential capacity of some groups to manufacture consent and define "acceptable" ways of doing things. Much of this struggle has involved attempts to define and regulate the nature of the practical mastery, self-expression, and enjoyment that people seek in play, and to structure "proper" channels for its exercise. In the context of this struggle have been resistances, reinterpretations, and a continually changing patterning of dominant, residual, and emergent interpretations of the meaning of sport and of how it is best practiced.

The dominant moment in the institutional structuring of Canadian sport seems to be characterized by a set of limits and pressures which stem primarily from a synthesis of the commodified features of commercial athletics, the rational-bureaucratic forms of organization that can be located in state programs, and in the programs of major national voluntary sports associations. Incorporated into the limits and pressures of this dominant moment are a whole set of interconnected notions about record-setting as the standard of excellence, and about the "naturalness" of a market model of competition—a model whose cultural corollary is an emphasis on skill acquisition as a condition of "fun" and personal development. Additional support for these limits and pressures is provided by a complex and growing system of sport scientists, "certified" coaches, and practitioners whose very occupational existence depends upon the depth of the dominant moment's penetration into the popular consciousness.

Now there can be no denying, I believe, that this dominant moment in the institutional structuring of Canadian sport is characteristically "modern," which means only that it is the most contemporary expression of how those who now define and control sport's institutional rules and resources feel that sport ought to be practiced and understood. Yet, it is important to understand that this particular expression of the nature and meaning of modern sport is not necessarily a universal definition, nor does it have any special moral or philosophical claim to being the right conception of what sport is or ought to be. Indeed, I think we must be particularly wary of arguments which seek to legitimate the limits and pressures contained within the dominant moment in modern sports by virtue of their appeals to metaphysics or to a model of development which suggests some kind of "evolution" of "traditional" game-contests and areas of playful self-activity into "modern" (and, supposedly, more advanced) forms of sporting practice. We should also be wary of explanations that claim to have uncovered any one "basic explanatory factor" which has stimulated this evolution.[1] This is not to say we should adopt the pluralist and empiricist view that all "facts" and "pressures" are created equal. Rather I am suggesting only that we recognize how such things as "the scientific world view" and "technical" forces of production cannot be understood outside the context of the ensemble of social relations which characterize social life in capitalist societies at different historical moments. In this study, for example, I have tried to indicate how various technical and cultural pressures on Canadian sport were indissolubly connected to the unique *social relations* of Canadian capitalism and to the cultural development of a society caught between two powerful colonial metropoles. The dominant moment in the institutional structuring of sport today has not evolved in any orderly or rational way so much as it has developed as a result of numerous and complex mediations between different classes, status groups, and class fragments in Canadian history.

Nonetheless, for all this complexity, I think it can be asserted that the dominant moment in modern Canadian sport is composed primarily of a rather *limited set of class practices and beliefs.* For example, its emphasis on technique emerged within the bourgeoisie largely in an attempt to specify "scientific" play within "amateurism" as something different from the more instrumental and often violent emphases of the sports participated in by the underclasses or by ascendant and threatening fragments of the petit bourgeoisie. However, the ascendancy of this particular moment to the status of dominance has only occurred in the context of the widespread incorporation of sport into the "universal market," its increasing subjugation to a rational model of productive efficiency, and to the growth of regular international sporting exchanges where nation-states trade in a symbolic ideological currency. In all of these cases, it appears to have been various fragments of the Canadian bourgeoisie that have either created or controlled the structuring of sport and have contoured its "official" meanings. This bias has not necessarily occurred in any conspiratorial sense; rather it simply reflects a class-specific response to the pursuit of fun, achievement, and mastery in spheres outside of work and the management of public recreation and welfare. The bias also reflects a resource capacity to transform such a class-specific response into a broader "shared cultural experience."

We need to ask, however, on what terms does this sharing occur, and how has one particular set of structures and dominant meanings managed to win credibility over other alternative constructions? I think it is important in answering these questions to emphasize the contested nature of at least some features of the dominant moment in sports as it emerged in the twentieth century. The early struggle over "loosening" the amateur code, for example, was a bitter fight that occasionally revealed class tensions in Canadian society in bold relief. Yet, there appears to be no conflict of this magnitude in sport today and far fewer alternatives to the dominant moment. One might argue, for instance, that the dominant moment appears to have effectively selected from the broad range of possible "ways of playing" in an extremely compelling fashion. It is in this way that we can appreciate its insertion into modern bourgeois hegemony. The limits and pressures of a set of culturally specific practices and beliefs, expressed in and through the dominant moment in the structuring of modern sport, are widely regarded as the pressures and limits of everyday experience and common sense. Money values, for example, are not only affirmed as legitimate and inevitable in modern Canadian sports, but are often seen to be "naturally" expressed in a commodity form. Similarly, if "versatility" and "fair play" were once perceived as an important part of what it meant to be excellent in sports, the notion of excellence is now widely understood (at least officially) as the single-minded commitment to the achievement of abstract standards "objectively" defined (e.g., records). The pursuit of these standards is administered by sporting associations and sports businesses whose membership composition, operating goals, and organizational logic have been overwhelmingly influenced by Canada's dominant class.

I would concede that these developments have opened up a great number of possibilities in sport. For example, there are far more opportunities for *organized* sports participation today than earlier in the century; the best athletes today run faster, jump higher, and are more skilled than ever before; and we now have sporting spectacles of unprecedented scale, grandeur, and public exposure. Submission to the structures which have supported these developments is certainly "enabling," in the sense that it has allowed such developments to occur. But we must also consider the limits on human agency and freedom imposed by these structures, and their consequences for social and political freedom defined in terms beyond sport. For it seems clear that if modern sports, in their dominant form, are cultural texts—stories Canadians tell themselves about what it means to be Canadian in today's world—these stories are often told in a language that excludes a broad range of possibilities and practices and surrounds this form of exclusion in mystifying conceptions of naturalness, universality, and romantic metaphor. Indeed, as Raymond Williams has argued about all forms of hegemonic cultural productions, it is precisely in such metaphysical and metaphoric terms that the excluded area is usually expressed, because what the dominant has successfully seized is the ruling definition of the *social.*[2] Thus, if it seems important to acknowledge some of the "structured possibilities" of modern sport in any discussion of agency and freedom, it seems equally important to examine the kinds of practices that have been *excluded* by these structures and the significance of these forms of exclusion.

One important exclusion from the dominant moment in the institutional structuring in Canadian sport is a broad set of residual definitions and interpretations that might have been considered the dominant moment in an earlier phase in the structuring of sport. Fair play, the spontaneous enjoyment of games, a qualitative (rather than quantitative) appreciation of the contest, and the ascriptively oriented, nonutilitarian "amateur" ethos (viewed in a monetary rather than a moral sense) continue to exist but are gradually being squeezed out of dominant conceptions of Canadian sport. The structures which have supported such interpretations have been in a continual process of transformation since the early part of the twentieth century. Much of the old amateur code has simply become *adapted* to the dominant moment of the present, *but there are important surviving pressures against the instrumental nature of modern sports that owe their current oppositional features to older class practices that are no longer seen as the predominant way of doing things.* The power of such residual ideological features in Canada's dominant class cannot be overlooked in any attempt to understand the nature of modern Canadian sport.

Also residual, I would argue, is the conception of oppositional sporting practice which, at the highest moment of its muted expression in the early twentieth century, combined the idea of sport with socialist solidarity and the possibility of playing sports in a society where the structuring of sporting activities would occur in a *rational* rather than *rationalized* manner. It is debatable whether this interpretation ever really developed a coherent form in the Canadian labor movement, and it now appears to have been almost completely undermined—as a form of shared cultural experience—by the institutionalization of commercial sports and their full-scale incorporation into the consumer patterns of modern capitalism. Sport continues to be an area of social life that provides a sense of continuity and enjoyment for many members of the Canadian working class. And, occasionally, some sporting pastimes may even provide partial demystifications or "penetrations" of the dominant structures of capitalism and of the dominant moment in "modern" sport. Such penetrations derive in part from the mixed messages offered by sport in contemporary life and by sport's capacity to dramatize utopian aspirations for human freedom, heroic actions, and equality. Yet, the price of these partial penetrations and of the enjoyment and continuity of certain sporting practices and rituals has been the failure to acknowledge and understand the discontinuous nature of an emergent dominant form whose structures are in no way controlled by the underclasses, and whose acceptance represents a paradoxical cultural insertion into the hegemony of capitalist life.

The Emergent and the Oppositional: A Final Note on Sport, Cultural Autonomy, and Reproduction

To say that the insertion of sport into the hegemony of capitalist life is paradoxical is to make a final point about the reflexive character of human agency. For having noted the ascendance of the dominant moment in Canadian sport as a cultural form that has won a degree of apparent consensus, it now seems necessary to point to the extremely fragile nature of that consensus. The fact that the dominant moment extends broadly into all spheres of lived experience does not mean that its basic form is necessarily accepted at all levels or that this form is interpreted in a way that automatically reproduces the conditions of capitalism. I think it can be argued, for example, that many underclass Canadians have a reasonably accurate grasp, not only of how capitalism works, but also of the extent to which the major decisions that give shape and substance to the dominant moment in sports are not really their own. But how does one act in the absence of coherent alternative structures outside of one's community, family, or local group? How does one express discontent in the face of dominant institutions and cultural forms which emphasize and offer the promise of *individual solutions* to what are essentially *collective problems?* Often it is simply a question of searching for alternatives in one's private life or among the family or local group. In this regard, it is certainly possible to see something as a "racket" in the way the working-class press occasionally referred to sport earlier in the century, and still derive enjoyment from it and not internalize its most obvious ideological features.

Earlier in this book I suggested that we can think of *structures* as the rules and resources coordinated in systems of interaction that set limits and exert pressures on the intentions, choices, possibilities, and abilities of human agents. In play, games, and sports, these structures can be understood as the broad range of technical and moral rules which constitute the activities as distinctive and supposedly "autonomous" fields of human practice. These technical and moral rules in play, games, and sports, are "made" by agents who exist in a setting of much broader rules and resources in social life, and whose capacities to define rules and contour the dominant meanings associated with them derive from these broader forms of structuring. Yet, the range of meanings that agents attribute to their play, games, and sports is complex and multilayered. The structures which constitute play, games, and sports as social possibilities are mediated by their reconstituted expression in diverse cultural forms. The result, as I suggested earlier with reference to some of the work of Paul Willis and Raymond Williams, is that social reproduction and hegemony work as much through contradiction and paradox as through reflection, correspondence, or similarity.

In sport, the relationships of contradiction and paradox to social reproduction depend on the capacity of the dominant moment in sport's structuring to make a claim to universality and shared cultural experience. In making this claim, the dominant moment can draw upon certain features of everyday experience and extremely deep-rooted wants and intentions in contemporary life as the foundation for its legitimacy. It can do this because many of its claims are not wholly fictitious; that is, at certain levels of lived experience and interpretation, sport actually does maintain an important *degree of autonomy* from the dominant economic and political structures which govern the world of necessity.

What are the main features of this degree of autonomy? Most important, I believe, is the degree to which sports exist in terms of what Richard Lipsky has called the "bracketed" character of social life.[3] In other words, as Michael Novak and so many other writers have suggested, there is a very real sense in which sport's form actually is "set apart" in space and time by its constituting structures. The bracketed world provided by these structures is inhabited by a wide variety of cultural forms, all of which articulate partial features of the human condition in a way that is not completely mystified. This is often done through sport's *dramatic qualities.* Sports, in many forms, act as texts which tell us stories and provide an excitement rarely found in other areas of life. All of us enjoy this type of excitement, and most of us like stories, even if we do not care for the style of discourse that is used to tell them or the moral contained within them. In any case, we are given the opportunity to use our imaginations to inflect, distort, and interpret the significations that are presented in ways accessible to and meaningful for our own social locations.

A second way in which the degrees of "autonomy" present in sports can be understood is through *a metaphoric appeal to voluntary action and agency embodied in spontaneous play.* As an expression of agency, there are two sides to play. It has its orderly or—as Johan Huizinga would say—its "sacred" side, which makes freedom from necessity a condition of *submission* to rules of authority. It also has its disorderly, or "profane," side which makes freedom a condition of *resisting* certain rules of authority. There is a great emphasis in sociological writing on the nature of the possibilities embodied in this sacred side of play. As I noted earlier, the ritualistic contributions to community and social solidarity embodied in submission to rules of authority in and through sport has often been seen as one of sport's most compelling features. But from the standpoint of defining sport's legitimacy and popularity, equal amounts of attention should be paid to the so-called profane side of play and its development as a component of legitimation in an era of emerging new conceptions of individualism, family, and community.

One point must be made here: it is play's profane side that can never be completely incorporated into modes of domination or mystified by some higher purpose other than "fun" expressed in play for its own sake. Societies need rules, of course, but profane playing, expressed as a kind of revelatory probing of the world, is often, as Paul Willis has argued, one of the few ways in which any one human agent can challenge the forces of repression. Various forms of rule-breaking in schools, in offices, or on the shop floor, are related to this profane side of play, as is the culture of numerous social subgroups whose actions often threaten the dominant culture.

It is telling, however, that on the playing field, the profane side of play is counterproductive and does not allow for the orderly accomplishment of games as collective forums for fun and sociability. But one can make the case that even when people voluntarily submit to rules that allow for playing in an orderly way, residues of the profane side of play may still be evident. For any form of play that runs counter to dominant "ways of playing" has its symbolically profane side. In this sense, there is something to be said for the fact that long-standing cultural connections between working-class culture and an appreciation of contests and gaming activities—often regarded as a form of profane playing by the dominant class—have helped to reinforce in an enduring way the centrality of modern sport in working-class culture. Beyond this is the even deeper cultural tradition which tends to equate an escape to sport's bracketed world as a form of individual resistance to the constraints of necessity.

Finally, the attraction of sports is fueled by the possibility of becoming caught up in *metaphoric statements of ultimate possibilities*, and through the partial living-out of these possibilities in sport's bracketed world. People want to believe that their games are free and fair, and they seem to derive a great deal of satisfaction from their attachments to local or national athletes and teams. And if they are not able to exert any kind of pressures on the conditions and structures of play at the highest levels, they can at least participate in some way, either on their own or in their local group or community. Not all local sports have been completely incorporated by the dominant moment; sometimes players retain control and can enjoy the freedom that comes from making their own variations in rules and cultural emphases. The focus on the character of such activities as forms of play or as game-contests, rather than more instrumentally defined sports, allows for the continued expression of possibilities that are often excluded in the dominant moment of sport's structuring. But, even in the case of watching or participating in the practices of the dominant moment, there are circumstances where one becomes involved with activities that dramatize aesthetic features of life that are not necessarily incorporative.

All of these "possibilities" might be thought of as relatively *continuous* features of human agency and cultural experience. What gives the dominant moment in the structuring of sport its ideological character is its capacity to win space for itself—and the class interests associated with its structuring—on the basis of its claims to represent these continuous features of human choice and possibility. It is ideological not because its claim is completely false, but because it is only partially true. What are ignored are its historically constituted and *discontinuous* features. The dominant moment's claim to legitimacy is ideological because it offers a partial explanation as if it were a whole and comprehensive one. It is in this way—while people pursue the continuities at the level of everyday experience—that the discontinuities gain the upper hand, all within the illusion of consensus.[4] This is the ultimate paradox of sports with respect to the problems of freedom, constraint, and social reproduction. Structural conditions which play a role in reproducing capitalist social relations and which limit human possibilities in very significant ways are—through their symbolic and "managed" attachments to continuous and autonomous features of human agency—"voluntarily" undertaken and given widespread support.

Must this be the case? Will the dominant moment in sports today, and the kind of society which sustains it, last indefinitely? The answers to such questions depend, of course, on people's capacities to more than "partially penetrate" the constraints embodied in the structures of modern capitalism. I think we need to recognize that sports seem to be implicated in social reproduction and hegemony but only in a way that constantly threatens to break apart and become transformed. The dominant moment in sport is always potentially challenged by the very conditions of agency upon which it seeks to build its legitimacy. Human desires for fun, fantasy, and excitement, or for personal mastery, drama, or creative expression, are a shaky foundation for hegemony.

Yet, reproduction of the essential structures of capitalist life *does occur,* and in recent years there has not been much evidence to suggest that oppositional and emergent "ways of playing" have had much success in fundamentally altering the basic constituting structures and "official" meanings of sport's dominant moment. The noncompetitive games movement of the early 1970s, for example, or the important challenges posed by the struggle to equalize opportunities for women or blacks, have been important interventions, but do not appear to have had much transformative consequence. I believe part of the problem for this has been the inability of these emergent and oppositional movements to offer anything more than mildly reformist strategies.

It is extremely important that these oppositional movements have led to a considerable number of social-democratic and supposedly "humanistic" reforms. But the problem is that these reforms have not led to the kinds of transformations that could free sport from its entrenchment in capitalist hegemony. The main reason for this failure is that these reforms have rarely been tied to broader visions and theories about the optimal expression of equity and freedom in the society at large. Also, these reforms have never really been incorporated into the kinds of oppositional forces (e.g., political parties, unions, etc.) necessary to coordinate various pressures against dominant conceptions of capitalist life and channel them into the construction of *alternative structures*. This type of incorporation would demand that nonclass elements consciously link various struggles—against bureaucratization, sexual and racial oppression, and the constraints imposed on social life by the hierarchical and repressive features of state power—with the broader forms of class struggle for creating a more humanely rational society.

I believe that work in the sociology of sport could contribute to such struggles by helping to clarify the basic relationships in society between sports, human freedom, and constraint. This implies, first and foremost, an attempt to historicize the central features of sports in capitalist societies and to assess the relationships between the structures which constitute sports as social possibilities and the broader structures of social life. It also implies some attempt to articulate the terms upon which different ways of playing make their claims for legitimacy, the kinds of practical interests they represent, and the ways in which the meanings embodied in them work to reproduce and transform social relationships as a whole. This is the academic's traditional form of political practice: to develop a discourse that speaks the language of human beings as producers, as makers of reality, and not to preserve that reality as an image. *Progress* in the sociology of sport depends primarily upon our capacities to make the critique of sport a part of the much broader attempt to discern the alternatives within which human reason and freedom can make history.

a postscript, 15 years later

"History is the fruit of power, but power itself is never so transparent that its analysis becomes superfluous."

Michel-Rolph Trouillot[1]

Throughout much of the 1970s, North American sociology suffered from an identity crisis. On the one hand, a significant amount of the work done in the field seemed to tacitly accept the major organizing assumptions of postwar suburban life. Many sociologists also believed that sociology should emulate the methods of the natural sciences, including hypothesis testing and the pursuit of law-like deductive theories. On the other hand, there was growing criticism of these mainstream positions. A new postwar generation of critical sociologists took their inspiration from philosophy, history, and radical social theory rather than mainstream empirical science. They linked their vision of sociology's agenda to a critique of capitalism, a rejection of militarism and colonialism, and the struggle to expand the rights of minorities and women.

During this time of disciplinary ferment, the sociology of sport was still something of an academic curiosity: a small but vibrant sub-field with a dedicated group of international practitioners, but also clearly on the margins of sociology overall. Nevertheless, the sociology of sport was going through its own crisis of identity and direction. Several early leaders in North American "sport sociology" had come from physical education and this influenced early debates in the field and the types of problems typically studied. One legacy of the physical education influence was a tendency to be more concerned with sport for its own sake rather than with broader sociological issues and problems. Sport sociologists were more likely to focus on the apparent effects of social organization *on* sport—how sport is shaped by "society"—than on the role played by sport in the ongoing production *of* society. In addition, much of the research in the sociology of sport adopted theoretical and methodological frameworks from the parent discipline that paid scant attention either to questions of power and domination or to broad issues and problems of social development.

When I began writing *Class, Sports, and Social Development* at the end of the 1970s, these issues were very much on my mind. I set myself the task of writing a book that would combine a critique of well-known arguments in the sociology of sport with an attempt to map new theoretical ground for critical analysis. One of my goals was to show how sport was relevant to some central problems in social theory. In addition, I hoped to show how a reconsideration of certain "classical" methods and problems in social theory could enrich our understanding of the changing nature and meanings of sport in social and cultural life. This project, I believed, warranted a return to the critical, broad-ranging styles of historical and institutional analysis that characterized much of the best work in the western sociological tradition.

Students sometimes ask if my more recent work is still guided by the theoretical and methodological perspectives outlined in *Class, Sports, and Social Development.* It is a difficult question because the book was written to address a set of issues and debates that were specific to the late 1970s and early 1980s. Quite different issues and debates need to be addressed in social analysis today, and these obviously require new concepts and fresh perspectives. At the same time, the book advanced several arguments that continue to shape my understanding of the objectives of critical social analysis and how best to achieve them. Most notable in this regard was the book's argument for a critical approach to the study of sport that combines social theory with history, interpretive cultural analysis, and political economy. In recent years I have played a bit with the proportional balance between these dimensions of analysis, inflecting the cultural analysis dimension, for example, more than the political economy one. But I remain committed to a broadly synthetic approach to the study of sport that keeps history and theory, interpretive cultural analysis, and political economy together. This kind of synthetic, multidimensional approach is necessarily critical of one-dimensional perspectives that reduce the analysis of sport to purely material (eg., technological, economic) or idealist (eg., cultural/linguistic) determinants. The approach is also strengthened, in my view, when it is linked to a critique of excessively voluntaristic or deterministic interpretations of sport's relationships to power, equality, freedom, sociality, and identity.

The early chapters of *Class, Sports, and Social Development* developed a rationale for the approach described above and provided a critique of voluntarism, reductionism, and dualistic thinking in the sociology of sport. This set the stage for the introduction of an alternative field of concepts and arguments—a revisionist theoretical framework—to guide the analysis of sport in society. For the most part, this theoretical framework built upon one key argument: namely, that play, games, and sporting activities can be usefully studied as distinctive fields of social practice whose defining structures are constituted within and through broader social structures that set limits and exert pressures on the range of powers available to human agents. In addition I argued that the structures which constitute play, games, and sports as social possibilities, and as distinctive fields of practice, should be seen both as a medium and an outcome of social action. These structures can also be viewed as both enabling (opening pathways for various freedoms, pleasures, forms of disciplinary mastery, social bonding, and identity) and constraining (directing practices and the meanings associated with them into social and cultural forms that sustain relations of domination).

The book's combined emphases on social practice, on the "structured" nature of human agency, and on the enabling and constraining features of social structures, reflected a diversity of influences. However, my thinking at the time was particularly indebted to Anthony Giddens's work on the "duality of structure" and the dynamics of social "structuration."[2] Giddens's theoretical discussions of power, agency, and structure—along with some parallel ideas developed by Steven Lukes[3]—were the inspiration for my decision to pose the pivotal "problem" in the book's opening chapter in the form of an apparent paradox between freedom and constraint. I was also drawn to Giddens's work because of his emphasis on the active ongoing *production* of structures, rather than on the functional and systemic *reproduction* of structures. This emphasis has the effect of making history an organic part of social theory, a virtue that Giddens's perspective shares with many of the most compelling works in sociological analysis. But even more notably, by emphasizing how history must be seen as a set of ongoing constitutive processes, we are sensitized to the fact that dominant social structures are never immutable. Dominant groups typically exercise their powers by trying to reproduce the social structures which sustain their privileges. Nevertheless, it is always an open question whether, how, or how long, they will succeed.

Still, I wasn't persuaded that Giddens's theory of structuration on its own necessarily offered a sufficient foundation for research in the sociology of sport. Giddens certainly recognized the limiting conditions of social structures, but the theory of structuration didn't provide enough detail about those moments in the constitution of society when dominant social structures actually do form and are reproduced, especially in the face of active resistance and struggle. At the same time, Giddens's work provided insufficient direction for analyzing the discursive—the "textual"—features of social practice, despite his interest in Goffman's dramaturgical sociology.[4] In an effort to address these apparent limitations, I incorporated some of Paul Willis's ideas about the reproduction of class structures, via "profane" forms of self-affirmation in "informal" groups, into the book's theoretical framework. These ideas were set in the broader theoretical context of Giddens's work, as well as Raymond Williams's discussion of culture as *both* "practice" and "hegemony."[5] I also borrowed some ideas from Clifford Geertz's pioneering work on "cultural texts," although, in the end, I concluded that Geertz's work said far too little about how textual meanings might relate to power, inequality, and social reproduction.[6] It seemed logical that these problems could be avoided by developing a theoretical framework that necessarily bracketed the insights of interpretive cultural analysis with those of social theory and political economy. As I pursued this line of thinking, the discussion of practices, structures, and power in *Class, Sports, and Social Development* moved in a Marxian direction, albeit one more influenced by Gramscian approaches to cultural studies and by 1970's Canadian political economy than by Marx himself.[7]

One unfortunate consequence of all this was that the book's theoretical framework essentially ignored the bodily dimensions of power and social reproduction in and through sport. In retrospect, the omission is particularly glaring because I was reading Pierre Bourdieu in the late 1970s, and the relationships between bodily practices and power figure prominently in his work. More notably, a number of Bourdieu's ideas about the need for a theory of practice, and about the social production and reproduction of boundaries that define distinctive "fields" of practice, were influential in developing the book's analysis.[8] But my attraction to Giddens's ideas, mixed with an implicit Gramscian concern with the formative role of ideas in political struggles, led me to focus more on conscious agency than on unconscious bodily practices in the constitution of society. This inattention to unconscious bodily practices, and, more broadly, to issues of embodiment in sport, was reinforced by my attraction to the methods of Marxian historical materialism, an intellectual tradition that has never shown much concern for the body. Reading Bourdieu and Michel Foucault in subsequent years has persuaded me that *both* conscious agency and often unconscious bodily discipline and embodiment require consideration in any adequate theory of social practice, social structure, or power.[9]

Commentators over the years have occasionally suggested that *Class, Sports, and Social Development* is a Marxist book. The claim is debatable, to say the least, because of the pervasive influence in the analysis of non-Marxist writers, such as Veblen, C. Wright Mills, and Giddens. Still, there are several respects in which the book is obviously indebted to Western Marxism: 1) in the critique of one-dimensional "idealist" and "materialist" perspectives on sport in favor of a more dialectical materialist approach that views sport as a set of *social* practices; 2) in the privileged role given to class structure in determining key allocative and expressive rules and resources in the constitution of sport in society; 3) in the emphasis on postcolonial class struggles and capitalist class domination in the institutionalization of Canadian sport; and 4) in the implicit definition of "freedom" as the opportunity for self-creation in the absence of constraints associated with capitalist class structures.

In the years since the book was originally published, Western capitalism has tightened its grip on social and cultural life around the world. Sport in particular has been swept up in a globalizing commodity logic at a pace far in excess of what I would have predicted in the early 1980s. In the book, I argued that the "dominant moment" in the institutional structuring of Canadian sport developed through a complex set of negotiations and struggles involving various class and non-class agents. But, the terrain on which these negotiations and struggles occurred was the field of capitalist core-periphery relations, postcolonial state formation, and uneven Canadian industrial development. It was too much to say that capital alone provided the rules and resources that shaped the dominant structures of the field of sporting practice, but capitalist class structures, and the relentless expansion of commodification, were immensely important. They are even more important today, and not just in western nations. That is why "specters of Marx"—to use Jacques Derrida's recent phrase—refuse to go away.[10] It is why the critical analysis of capitalist labor processes, class structures, state policies, and capitalist influences on the social organization of space and time, still matter, and why the task of developing sophisticated neo-Marxist perspectives on sport seems more urgent now than ever. That said, there are obviously other significant forms of domination beyond class, state, and the labor process that require critical attention in the sociology of sport. There have also been important shifts in the nature of contemporary capitalism that require new concepts and perspectives, especially in respect to the increased importance of communication and culture in the capitalist division of labor and the accumulation process, and the changing social organization of space and time in human life.

Shortly after completing *Class, Sports, and Social Development,* I realized that the book didn't say enough about the role of media in the making of contemporary sport. Nor did the book offer any sustained analysis of the significative and interpretive dimensions of sport, despite the attention I gave to Geertz's analysis of the textual features of Balinese cockfighting. Recognition of these limitations prompted me to undertake research on sport and communications media for much of the remainder of the 1980s.[11] During this time, the analysis of culture and communications came to play a more central role in my understanding of both the social production of sport in society and the broader dynamics of capitalist production. Along the way, I struggled to develop a more nuanced understanding of the ideological dimensions of media production and media discourse, as well as of the diversity of meanings associated with self-identification and the consumption of commodities in capitalist life. I also became more aware of the changing aspects of space and place in social life, the ways that all social and cultural relationships are spatial in form, and the time-space compression that is such an important feature of capitalist modernity.[12]

Global capitalism was undergoing a period of crisis and transition that I was only vaguely aware of while writing *Class, Sports, and Social Development.* The long postwar economic boom that had sustained the development of affluent consumer societies in North America and Europe came to a skidding halt in the global deflation of 1973-75, thereby setting the stage for the economic restructuring and neoliberal economic policies that would come to dominate western economies and governments through the 1980s and 1990s. In this restructuring, the information, media, and entertainment industries became increasingly visible and important features of life around the world. Communications satellites, digital information technologies, and deregulated markets all helped broaden the spatial reach of the growing industries of information exchange and symbolic production, both within different societies and between them. These changes in turn were an important part of an emergent global reorganization of the capitalist division of labor, featuring the consolidation of transnational "free trade" agreements in several parts of the world; the erosion of centralized manufacturing and industrial work across the northern nations; and capital's relentless push for "flexibility" and customization in production and in marketing.[13] In this context, the economic and cultural importance of sport for capital grew markedly. Increasingly integrated into global media conglomerates, transnational merchandising systems, international tourism, and urban redevelopment, the contours of sport as a field of practice were reworked and redefined. The analysis of sport's relationships to various forms of freedom and constraint, liberation and domination, in this context, needs to be sensitive to new structures, meanings and struggles that condition sporting practice.

Many of these new struggles are about questions of power, identity, and equality in realms that often seem far removed from the terrain of class and state politics. Since the 1970s there has been a widespread disaggregation of older industrial workforces in Europe and North America, accompanied by intensifying social and cultural differentiation, diversification, and heterogeneity in global networks, cultural flows, and social relations. In conjunction with this, many of the more established prewar and postwar forms of cultural "identity" (associated, for example, with class, gender, race, nation, and sexual preference) in many parts of the world, and especially in the west, have become destabilized and subjected to new forms of negotiation.[14] The contemporary industries of media and entertainment have become increasingly significant sites for these negotiations. In this context, sport has become more important than ever as a site for dramatizing diverse and often contradictory forms of social identification, not only with nations and cities, but also with race, gender, class, and a dizzying array of consumer goods and lifestyles.[15]

Class, Sports, and Social Development discussed non-class dimensions of power and struggle in respect to status distinctions, Canadian national-popular struggles, technocratic ideology, and state intervention. More notably, the book concluded with a call for coalition building between more traditional class-based forms of opposition and newer social movements associated with various non-class struggles. But the book overwhelmingly emphasized class struggles, class identities, and class differences in the "structuring" of sport in particular ways and the meanings often associated with sports. This primary emphasis on class dynamics occurred at the expense of analyzing other centrally-important structuring practices—other sets of rules and resources—pertaining, for example, to race and gender. This limitation was significant enough when the book first came out, but it is even more notable today when many of the older sites and forms of class politics and struggle seem to have dissolved in a sea of cultural and political heterogeneity.

Recognizing and analyzing this cultural and political heterogeneity is undoubtedly a matter of considerable importance in the sociology of sport. It is not surprising, then, to find a great deal of recent research devoted to an exploration of how sport intersects with multiple sources of power and difference throughout the world. One interesting line of analysis, influenced by the "figurational" sociology of Norbert Elias,[16] emphasizes the multiple and multidirectional features of power centers and power balances as factors that contour international flows of goods, representations, and identities. Joe Maguire has argued, for example, that figurational sociology directs our attention to complex long-term processes of economic, social, political, and cultural interdependence around the world that have diminished the contrasts between the types, styles, and meanings of cultural forms and practices in contemporary life. But no single causal factor, no single center of power has fully determined the course of contemporary social development. In the case of power, in particular, the development of increasingly complex inter-connections and dependencies between formerly unequal groups over the past several centuries has led to forms of social and cultural inter-action that have blurred many of the distinctions between privileged core groups and outsiders. This process has prompted the creation of new forms of distinction, but it has also equalized power ratios and has promoted new styles of conduct and new forms of identity. These processes have been played out in the case of sport, where the decreas-ing contrasts between types, styles, and meanings of sport in global terms (e.g. the formation of international organizations, globally-standardized rules, new trans-national super leagues, etc.) has been accompanied, almost paradoxically, by an increasing variety of sporting activities, styles, and meanings.[17]

This "figurational" line of analysis, like Giddens's work, is sensitive to the problems of dualistic thinking and has the virtue of emphasizing process over structure. The figurational perspective also forces you to think about what is socially and culturally distinctive about "modern" sport, and, at its best, it necessarily leads you to think about questions of power and difference in sport in multiple, trans-cultural, and, indeed, global terms. My first encounter with a figurational perspective came indirectly while reading Eric Dunning's work in the 1970s. Dunning has been a tireless promoter of figurational approaches to the sociology of sport for more than twenty-five years, and his essays and book (with Kenneth Sheard) on the social development of rugby in Britain influenced my thinking a great deal.[18] A number of these influences are evident in the historical analysis in *Class, Sports, and Social Development*. Still I never felt that Dunning's work—or Elias's either, for that matter—offered an adequate theory of power or an engaged standpoint for social criticism. Power is discussed in various ways in Elias and Dunning's work, but it is rarely connected directly to a broader theory and critique of domination in social life, especially in respect to the changing social organization of capitalism. Even today, after a decade and a half of theoretical development and refinement, more recent figurational approaches to the sociology of sport, such as Maguire's, only pay passing attention to the specific structural dynamics of global capitalism. More important for me personally, the figurational approach to the study of power has always seemed a bit too restrained, unwilling to risk transgressing an imagined stance of scholarly detachment. The result is an approach to the study of power that potentially accommodates diversity but lacks a critical edge.

A more provocative line of analysis in the study of sport, power, and difference in recent years has focused much more self-consciously on the critique of various forms of domination. Inspiration for this line of analysis has come from radical feminism, various branches of postcolonial and postmodern theory, cultural studies, and new social movements linked to struggles around sexual preference, environmental protection, and disability. This diversity of origins is reflected in the use of often highly-divergent approaches to the study of sport and power. But, at the risk of excessive simplification, I would argue that the work of Michel Foucault has provided much of the theoretical impetus, either explicitly or implicitly, for many of the most suggestive recent critical studies.[19]

Foucault argues that power is an inevitable part of the production of society: it is omnipresent, dispersed through all discourses (even critical ones), intellectual and bodily disciplines, and social relations, and is not dependant on any singular social foundation. Researchers writing from the range of critical standpoints noted above, often drawing on ideas indebted to Foucault, have forced an older generation of social critics like me to broaden our understanding of radical politics. This new line of critical analysis has also focused attention on the problematic nature of any discussion of "constraint" that gives priority to one axis of power, or one political subjectivity, over another. At the same time, taken collectively, new critical theories of power and difference call into question the possibility of achieving any kind of "universal" emancipation or freedoms in or through sport.

The newer critical approaches noted above address several issues that warrant comment in light of the analysis developed in *Class, Sports, and Social Development*. First, the Foucauldian emphasis on relations between power and discourse in contemporary critical thought has helped me to better understand the limitations of certain categories and arguments used in the book. A good example is the book's appeal to "classical" sociology as a standpoint for reinvigorating the sociology of sport. Inspired by C. Wright Mills, I wanted to use the idea of "classical" sociology in a progressive way: to promote a critical, synthetic, and multidimensional approach to historical sociology and institutional analysis and to identify key research questions associated with the changing nature of power and inequality in industrial capitalism. But this project was only partially successful because my ability to make "progressive" use of the idea of classical sociology was limited by hidden assumptions associated with the concept.

Robert Connell has argued persuasively that the idea of classical theory in sociology developed out of a highly selective "foundation story" of the discipline's development. In this story, the field of sociology is said to have emerged as a response to the "internal transformation of European society," prompting the creation of "discipline-defining texts written by a small group of brilliant authors."[20] More specifically, the story goes, the "founding fathers" of the discipline were motivated by the desire to systematically analyze the advent of modern industrial societies: the industrial revolution, class conflict, secularization, alienation, and the modern state.[21] The problem, according to Connell, is that this story is not complete. It overlooks the extent to which nineteenth- and early twentieth-century sociology was encyclopedic in scope, concerned with global issues of evolution, empire, civilization, and progress, and engaged with non-European cultures and societies. In conjunction with these issues sociologists necessarily paid a great deal of attention to questions and debates about sexuality, racial, and gender differences. Connell even goes so far as to claim that such emphases were "core" concerns in late nineteenth- and early twentieth-century sociology.

This kind of critique is reminiscent of Foucault's descriptions of medicine and economics as "discursive formations" that are connected to relations of power. In sociology's case, Connell notes how the discipline took form in the "urban and cultural centers of the major imperial powers at the high tide of modern imperialism." Late nineteenth- and early twentieth-century sociologists were confronted with the new experiences of global difference and struggle and variously worked to explain, justify, or challenge them. However, with the ascendance of the United

States as the hegemonic center of global sociology, a new definition of "core" problems in sociology began to emerge. The central problems of sociological theory and research became more narrowly understood as the study of social differentiation, social disorder, and social development *within* the modern industrial "metropole."[22] This had the desirable effect of deleting much of the open racism and sexism of nineteenth-century sociology from the discipline's theoretical core. It also had the undesirable effect of pushing discourses of global difference, empire, civilization, imperialism, race, gender, and sexuality to the margins of theoretical discussion.

I think Connell finds more consensus around this emergent tendency in twentieth-century sociology than there really was. Still, his discussion helps to explain why my appeal to "classical" sociology in *Class, Sports, and Social Development* largely precluded any discussion of global core-periphery relations beyond Europe and North America, as well as racial and gender oppression. The die was cast the moment I linked the idea of "classical" sociology as a distinctive style of analysis to a more specific set of "classical" sociological problems associated with agency, freedom, and constraint in the development of industrial capitalism, defined primarily with respect to social class. This focus on "internal" social dynamics and struggles arising in conjunction with industrial capitalism was undertaken with progressive intentions, but it nonetheless reproduced many of the Eurocentric and Androcentric assumptions implicit in the canonical foundation story of sociological history that Connell describes.

I believe that it was—and continues to be—useful to study sport as a field of constitutive social practices viewed in the context of the enabling and constraining features of social structures. But, we don't need to appeal to "classical" sociology for guidelines on how to undertake these studies. What we need instead, as Connell's work reminds us, is better history and more inclusive ways of doing theory.[23] Not surprisingly, there hasn't been much agreement among radical intellectuals in different generations and societies—often with different preferred causes—about exactly how to do this. These "differences" are no less evident in the sociology of sport than anywhere else and raise a number of provocative questions.

For example, *Class, Sports, and Social Development* was undoubtedly limited by its almost singular emphasis on the role of class structures, class struggles, and state power in the institutional development of sport. However, this problem of singularity, often viewed as an inherent problem of Marxist or socialist perspectives, has been no less evident in much of the feminist writing on women in sport over the past two decades. It has been relatively rare for feminist theorists in the sociology of sport to pay anything more than lip service to the links between gender, race, class, and the state until very recently.[24] Nor has feminist writing on sport paid much attention to broader questions of global difference. Throughout the 1970s and 1980s in particular, mainstream North American feminist writing on sport had little to say about feminist diversity, especially as articulated through voices from "Third World" or "Southern" nations.

You can make somewhat similar arguments about the one-dimensionality of much of the literature on sport and race. Prior to the early 1990s, very few writers in this area explored the intersections between race, class, and gender in any sustained way. In addition, global perspectives on race and sport have generally remained underdeveloped. There was an important internationalist slant to some of the writing on race and sport in the 1970s and 1980s in conjunction with sporting boycotts in support of the struggle against South African apartheid. More recently, research on "globalization" seems to have stimulated a renewed interest in international perspectives on sport and race.[25] In recent years, there has also been a growing interest, particularly among sport historians, in the place of sport in histories of racial nationalism and imperialism.[26] Nonetheless, the dominant themes in the critical sociological literature on race and sport continue to be disproportionately determined by issues and struggles within the "metropoles" of North American and European societies. In one of my recent classes—where more than 60 percent of the students had backgrounds that were Punjabi, Indian, Filipino, Chinese, Malaysian, and Korean—every term paper written on the topic of "race and sport" dealt with the contemporary African-American experience.[27]

It has been immensely important, of course, for activists and scholars over the past two decades to acknowledge race as a central "structuring" feature in U.S. sport. From the standpoint of theoretical inclusiveness, it has been even more important to hear growing numbers of African-American voices in this literature. On a global scale, however, far too many voices continue to be left out of the account. The absent voices of Nike's subcontracted Asian workers can add a lot to our understanding of Michael Jordan. There is a certain quasi-imperial irony in the fact that the sheer volume of critical work on race and sport undertaken in the U.S. has shaped so much of the theoretical agenda in other places.

So, in one sense, better histories and more inclusive theories in the sociology of sport require that we address the multiply-constitutive character of a diversity of axes of power, inequality, and identity on a global scale; that we acknowledge and analyze the broadest possible range of experiences of oppression and sites of opposition; and that we hear the broadest possible range of voices of marginality. But in another sense, it is obvious that the full realization of this objective in any one theoretical or historical narrative is impossible. No single narrative can address every form of oppression, identity, or political aspiration. This is more obvious than ever today, at a time when increasingly fragmented forms of social differentiation have created a seemingly endless number of self-defined political identities around the world. Consider the case of feminism. Like Marxism, one of the strengths of feminism over the years has been the presence of significant differences within the movement with an accompanying vitality of theoretical debate. Over the past two decades, however, "feminism" has transformed into an almost incalculable list of often competing "feminisms." On this point, Manuel Castells lists Black feminism, Mexican-American feminism, Black-lesbian feminism, lesbian feminism, sadomasochistic-lesbian feminism, Japanese feminism, or territorial/ethnic self-definitions such as the "Southall Black Sisters in England" as just a few of "endless possibilities of self-defined identities in which women see themselves in movement."[28] In all of these feminist instances, claiming "identity" has been an exercise in political agency, a form of empowerment.

The pursuit of such empowerment has elevated our awareness of the importance of a wide range of micropolitical struggles around gendered "otherness," including such things as sexuality, domestic work and domestic workers, medicine, health care, housing, and—most notably for sociologists of sport—popular culture. But in the widely-popular Foucauldian perspective on these things, there is no one fixed standpoint from which to evaluate any of this. In a world where there is no truth, only power, and where power is said to circulate everywhere, politics can only be understood as an ongoing localized tactical project. Any one form of domination becomes as relevant as any other, so political struggle can easily be seen as little more than an arena of choice closely associated with one's self-defined identity.

There are significant strengths to this approach in societies where institutionalized multiplicity and flexibility create the need for radical critics to be flexible too, to continue to respond to swiftly-changing alignments and centers of power, and to create new possibilities for variable alliances in different power struggles. At the same time, though, the approach suffers from some important limitations. Nancy Fraser suggests, for example, that one notable problem with this kind of broadly Foucauldian approach to social criticism lies in Foucault's "extreme reticence on normative and programmatic matters" as well as his "reluctance to consider how all these various struggles might be coordinated and what sort of change they might accomplish."[29] Without any normative standards for evaluating if and when some forms of power are more noxious or more widespread than others, or for evaluating the conditions where different political agendas come into conflict with one another, social criticism potentially loses much of its bite. Bianca Beccalli, has suggested that in this context radicalism can easily lose its anchorage in the idea of broad collective struggle, becoming reduced to "just another form of lifestyle politics."[30]

I want to argue strongly that the challenge of writing better histories and more inclusive theories will not be met simply by celebrating a diffuse radical pluralism. We certainly need a constant sensitivity to, and respect for, societal differentiation, heterogeneity, and multiplicity, as well as a self-conscious reflexivity about various forms of privilege and how they might influence theory and research. But, in the end, we also need to evaluate such things—and the politics associated with them—in the context of what Nancy Fraser calls "the big diagnostic pictures necessary to orient political practice." The task and promise of sociological theory has always been to help us draw these big diagnostic pictures. With these pictures we can try to understand how certain forms of power become sedimented in institutions. We can try to evaluate which forms of power have become "totalized" across a wide variety of institutional sectors (and which have not), and what responses this appears to have engendered in the society. We can also try to evaluate how radical interests often compete in significant ways, sometimes aligning to challenge the most entrenched forms of domination, sometimes conflicting in ways that, ironically, work to reproduce dominant social structures and practices.

In order to do this well, a certain retreat to highly-focused standpoints for critical analysis seems inevitable. If it isn't possible to reference every site of power, every form of struggle, or acknowledge every marginalized voice in social analysis, we have to choose more modest entry points. These chosen entry points typically stem from tensions, grievances, convictions, and curiosities specific to our own biographies and social and geographical locations. My point is that it may not be a big problem to write with a largely singular focus on class, gender, race, or sexual preference after all, as long as two conditions are met. First, critical social analysts should recognize and acknowledge the socially-situated nature of their work. Second, critical analysts should consider the extent to which their preferred entry point to social analysis might be significantly enhanced by a consideration of other sociologically relevant dimensions of power.

Class, Sports, and Social Development would have been a far better book if I had followed these guidelines. I have always believed that historical narratives can be held to certain tests of credibility. But I was also sensitive to the need to situate the book as a constructed account, a politically-engaged and partial "reading" of history written from a certain point of view, rather than an objective and full account of historical "facts." Nonetheless, I wrote the book with the confidence and authority of the detached expert, standing above society, and outside privilege, a discursive style that somewhat undermined my own caveats. At the same time, my discussion of class and sports actually would have been far stronger if I had explored the mutually constitutive relations between class and such things as masculinity, internal colonialism, overt and subtle racism, and racial nationalism.

Writing better history and more inclusive theory involves the pursuit of complexity rather than totality. Whatever stories we tell about the changing nature of sport in different societies or in global social relationships will always be partial, but they can always be made more complex. One way of increasing complexity is to build on a singular entry point (e.g. class, gender, or race) in order to address a broader range of silences, structuring practices, and centers of power along the lines of my previous comments. Another way to do this is to attend to the ways that history is experienced unevenly and is shot through with contradictions and the unintended consequences of human action. The issue of unevenness is especially important, in my view, because so many theorists and researchers seem rather insensitive to it. You see this a lot when terms such as postmodernism, postindustrialism, or postfordism are casually thrown around to describe sport, suggesting some completely new set of social and cultural dynamics that has emerged to structure the properties of the whole field of sporting practice.

I am not suggesting that these descriptive categories are without value. The problem lies in the reified and totalizing way they are sometimes used. In such circumstances we can lose sight of the complexity and unevenness of social development. For example, if there is such a thing as a "postmodern" social condition, let alone postmodern sport, it is surely experienced only by certain groups of people in certain contexts. Evaluating which people experience "the postmodern condition" (intellectuals figure prominently here) and in which contexts strikes me as a very relevant sociological question. In the end, the challenge is to write theoretically-informed histories that are sensitive to multiple and uneven paths of change, histories where the structuring principles of the field of sporting practice at any given time are recognized to involve complex sets of dominant, residual, and emergent tendencies.

notes

Introduction

1   See John Loy, Barry McPherson, and Gerald Kenyon, *The Sociology of Sport as an Academic Specialty: An Episodic Essay on the Development and Emergence of an Hybrid Subfield in North America;* and the Preface to *Sport, Culture and Society,* 2d ed., ed. Loy, Kenyon, and McPherson.

2   Norman Birnbaum, "An End to Sociology?" in *Crisis and Contention in Sociology,* ed. Tom Bottomore.

3   Ibid., p. 173.

4   See Tom Bottomore, *Sociology: A Guide to Problems and Literature;* Anthony Giddens, *Class Structure of the Advanced Societies,* and *Studies in Social and Political Theory.*

5   Giddens, *Capitalism and Modern Social Theory* and *Studies in Social and Political Theory.*

6   Giddens, *Class Structure,* p. 16.

7   See Morton White, *Social Thought in America: The Revolt against Formalism.* White does not define "formalism" in precise terms; rather he suggests that formalist tendencies have taken different shapes depending upon the disciplines in question. At the most general level, however, formalism can be understood as a movement that bases explanation on sets of abstractions (e.g., formal logic) which exist independent of individual experience. White notes how many prominent American theorists in the late nineteenth and early twentieth centuries were involved in a "campaign to mop up the remnants of formal logic, classical economics and jurisprudence in America, and to emphasize that the life of science, economics and law was not logic but experience" (p. 11). The creation of an abstract "action theory" that accommodated itself very well with functionalism and systemic analysis was a movement away from experience and into a renewed type of sociological formalism.

8   See Charles H. Page, *Class and American Sociology.*

9   The interpretation of the United States as a "mass society" (e.g.,
       P. Kornhauser, *The Politics of Mass Society*) became extremely popular in the
       1950s and led to a great deal of emphasis in American sociology on the so-
       called mechanisms of "homogenization" and on the cultural consequences
       of this homogenization. "Mass culture" in a variety of forms suddenly
       became extremely important. As Bernard Rosenberg wrote in 1957, "mass
       culture is not only a wilderness . . . it is largely uncharted." The subsequent
       "charting" of mass culture, typified by the selections included in Rosenberg
       and White's seminal anthology *Mass Culture: The Popular Arts of America*
       provided the groundwork for the development of a series of subsociologies,
       defined by their narrow focus on a single dimension of cultural experience.
       The growth of a "subsociological" emphasis on sport was given impetus by
       the works of several prominent sociologists writing in the mass culture
       tradition, most notably Gregory Stone and Reuel Denney; and by the
       expanding number of writers more directly concerned with physical recre-
       ation and leisure as cultural products of the mass society (see, for example,
       the selections in Larrabee and Meyersohn's anthology *Mass Leisure*). The
       formal organizational development of a "sport sociology," however, did not
       come so much from sociology as from the field of physical education. See
       Gerald Kenyon and John Loy, "Toward a Sociology of Sport," *Journal of
       Health, Physical Education and Recreation* 36 (1965); John Loy and Gerald
       Kenyon, *Sport, Culture and Society;* and Gerald Kenyon, "A Sociology of
       Sport: On Becoming a Subdiscipline," in *Sport in American Society,* 2d ed.,
       ed. George Sage.

10   See C. Wright Mills, *The Sociological Imagination;* Alvin Gouldner, *The
       Coming Crisis of Western Sociology;* and Irving Louis Horowitz, *The New
       Sociology.*

11   Cf., a similar point made in Seymour Lipset's Introduction to T.H. Marshall's
       Class, Citizenship and Social Development.

12   This point is also made in Giddens, *Class Structure of the Advanced Societies.*

13   Ibid., pp. 14-19.

14   These "exceptions" represent some of the most provocative of the work
       now coming out of the long tradition of the *Geisteswissenschaften* in Ger-
       many. See, for example, Hans Georg Gadamer, *Philosophical Hermeneutics;*
       the essays in Paul Connerton, *Critical Sociology* (pt. 2); and Giddens's
       discussion of the hermeneutic tradition in *New Rules of Sociological Method.*

15   See Richard Bernstein, *The Restructuring of Social and Political* Theory;
       Anthony Giddens, *Studies in Social and Political Theory;* and John Rex,
       Sociology and the Demystification of the Modern World.

16   Giddens, *Studies in Social and Political Theory,* p. 15.

17   See Krishan Kumar, *Prophecy and Progress: The Sociology of Industrial and
       Post-Industrial Society;* and Giddens's discussion of this "theory" in *Studies
       in Social and Political Theory,* pp. 14-20. The relevant works of the authors
       cited here are: Raymond Aron, *The Industrial Society;* Daniel Bell, *The Coming
       of Post-industrial Society;* and Ralf Dahrendorf, *Class and Class Conflict in
       Industrial Society.*

18   I have taken these arguments from Giddens's discussion in *Studies in Social
       and Political Theory,* pp. 14-20.

19   Giddens, *Class Structure,* pp. 16-19.

20   See Ralph Miliband, *Marxism and Politics.*

21   Ibid., pp. 3-5

22   I have taken this point from Giddens, *Class Structure,* pp. 13-22; and *Studies in Social and Political Theory,* pp. 208-34.

23   John Rex, "Threatening Theories" in *Society* 15:3 (1978).

24   I am referring primarily to the following works and authors: Richard Bernstein, *The Restructuring of Social and Political Theory;* Anthony Giddens, *Capitalism and Modern Social Theory, Class Structure of the Advanced Societies,* and *Studies in Social and Political Theory;* Edward Thompson, *The Poverty of Theory and Other Essays;* Perry Anderson, *Arguments within English Marxism;* Ralph Miliband, *Marxism and Politics;* and Raymond Williams, *Marxism and Literature.* A key figure in these debates is the Marxist writer Louis Althusser. See *Lenin and Philosophy and Other Essays.*

25   In developing this strategy I have been influenced by C. Wright Mills's arguments outlined years ago in *The Sociological Imagination.* In his criticisms of "grand theory" and other formalist fetishes in sociology, Mills suggests that sociologists ought to develop "structural" analyses of societies by examining "classical" problems with attention paid to the *historical specificity* of the societies, institutions, and cultural forms one is studying. Yet this attention to history ought not to be separated from a "theory of social structure" (pp. 44-47). One can also say that Mills suggests we need to go even further than this and try to recover in such theories the unity of empirical, interpretive, and evaluative analysis, and a specific emphasis on problems of human choice and possibility in social life. A solid theoretical context for developing this emphasis, I believe, is spelled out in the writings of Bernstein, Giddens, and the other authors noted above. Also see Mills's essay on "The Classic Tradition" in social analysis in *Images of Man.*

26   Mills, *Sociological Imagination,* chap. 1.

27   See Raymond Williams, *Culture and Society, The Long Revolution,* and *Marxism and Literature;* Stuart Hall and Tony Jefferson, eds., *Resistance through Rituals;* John Clarke, Charles Critcher, and Richard Johnson, eds., *Working Class Culture: Studies in History and Theory;* and Paul Willis, *Learning to Labour.* For examples of the Canadian authors mentioned see Wallace Clement, *The Canadian Corporate Elite;* Leo Panitch, ed., *The Canadian State: Political Economy and Political Power;* Gary Teeple, ed., *Capitalism and the National Question in Canada;* and also the work of Canadian social historian Bryan Palmer, *A Culture in Conflict.* For a bibliographic overview of recent writing in Canadian political economy see D. Drache and W. Clement, *A Practical Guide to Canadian Political Economy.*

28   See, for example, John Talamini and Charles Page, *Sport and Society: An Anthology;* George Sage, *Sport in American Society;* Marie Hart, *Sport in the Sociocultural Process;* and Loy, Kenyon, and McPherson, *Sport, Culture and Society* (2d. ed.).

29   Charles Page, "The World of Sport and Its Study," in *Sport and Society: An Anthology,* ed. John Talamini and Charles Page.

30   Notable among these exceptions is Allen Guttmann, *From Ritual to Record: The Nature of Modern Sports,* a book critically discussed in later chapters. An equally important exception is the work of Alan Ingham, especially Ingham's as yet unpublished doctoral thesis *American Sport in Transition: The*

Maturation of Industrial Capitalism and Its Impact on Sport. In addition to these non-Marxist studies, see Paul Hoch, *Rip Off the Big Game,* and Cary Goodman, *Choosing Sides: Playground and Street Life on the Lower East Side,* for some neo-Marxist analyses that emphasize class, sports, and social development. As a general rule the class and development emphasis has been more strongly pronounced in European writing. See, for example, Eric Dunning and Kenneth Sheard's provocative *Barbarians, Gentlemen and Players,* and some works in British social history: Tony Mason, *Association Football and English Society, 1863-1915,* and Peter Bailey, *Leisure and Class in Victorian England.* Also see the study of sport, class forces, and third world development, C.L.R. James, *Beyond a Boundary.*

31   In formulating this argument I have been greatly influenced by Giddens, *Capitalism and Modern Social Theory,* pp. 246-47.

Chapter 1   Problems of Agency and Freedom in Play, Games, and Sport

1   See Steven Lukes, "Power and Structure," in *Essays in Social Theory,* p. 3.

2   I am not going to take the space here to conduct a detailed analysis of the literature devoted to clarifying formal definitions of play, games, and sports. I will only say that, although widespread variations exist in this literature on certain issues, there nonetheless appears to be an underlying consensus on the "formal" characteristics of each of these activities. Following Huizinga, play is usually seen to be a generic activity that is expressive, nonutilitarian, meaningful, and pursued for its own sake. Play can be seen to be spontaneous and unorganized or it can be more rule-bound, structured, and regulated. In the case of the latter, as Guttmann points out in *From Ritual to Record* (chap. 1), it is common to suggest that all forms of such organized play can be called games. There are, of course, great variations of game forms. Besides ranging in their degrees of organization and instrumentality, Roger Caillois *(Man, Play and Games)* has noted that games also emphasize characteristic elements such as mimicry, chance, vertigo, and competition. But it is the agon, the contest, that most writers in the West have been drawn to. Game-contests which involve a demonstration of physical exertion or skill have received special attention. The modern institutionalized versions of these game-contests provide the foundation for today's sports. As I suggest in the main body of this chapter, however, there is considerable debate about the degrees of overlap between play, games, and sports, especially over the degree to which sport can be *generically related* to play. I would argue strongly that much of this debate, focused as it is at the level of abstract classification, misses the point. For, ultimately, if the meanings and significations of play, games, and sports are historically and socially constituted, then wrangling over abstract definitions will only offer the broadest of ideal-typical insights at the expense of a more adequate understanding of the activities as contested and varying processes and practices. Play, games, and sports are not abstract "things" to be concretely defined; rather they are complex processes and relationships that can never be adequately encapsulated into rigid definitional schemes or formulas. However, for some of the better attempts to work out such schemes and formulas see Alan Ingham and John Loy, "The Social System of Sport: A Humanistic Perspective," *Quest* 19 (1973); John Loy, "The Cultural System of Sport," *Quest* 29 (1978); Allen Guttmann, *From Ritual to Record* (chap. 1);

and Alan Ingham, *American Sport in Transition: The Maturation of Industrial Capitalism and Its Impact on Sport.*

3   This, of course, was Marx's view—a position Huizinga labeled "a shameful misconception" *(Homo Ludens,* p. 192). It does not appear, however, that Huizinga's characterization is entirely fair. Marx's conception of praxis, seen as forms of private and social labor, clearly involves notions of creative mastery and self-expression that seem quite removed from an overly close association of the idea of necessity with economics. Yet, the exact status of play as nonpurposive action in this formulation is somewhat troubling; for however broadly one identifies Marx's conception of labor or "the labor process" there is the strong sense in which it is inevitably tied to the idea of necessity. Marx himself recognized near the end of volume 3 of *Capital* that labor, even under conditions of socialism, ". . . nonetheless remains a realm of necessity. Beyond it begins that development of human energy which is an end in itself, the true realm of freedom, which however, can blossom forth only with this realm of necessity as its basis" (p. 820).

This position, and Marx's general views on work, have been the subject of a good deal of criticism. Specifically, it has often been argued that a metaphysical anthropology of *homo faber* dominates Marxist analysis (see Paul Ricoeur, *History and Truth).* One of the few Marxist attempts to integrate a concept of play into Marxist epistemology can be found in the work of Kostas Axelos, *Vers la pensée planétaire.* More recently, James Hans in *The Play of the World* has developed an extremely provocative argument for the centrality of play in the concept of production. I think Hans's analysis is important but I disagree fundamentally with his attempt to argue that play has a primary and generative role in human social interaction.

4   For discussions of the idealist conceptions of culture and consciousness in western philosophy and literature, see Raymond Williams, *Culture and Society;* and H. Stuart Hughes, *Consciousness and Society* (especially p. 183 ff.).

5   Huizinga, *Homo Ludens,* p. 1.

6   In his essay, "Political Ritual and Social Integration" *(Essays in Social Theory,* p. 68), Steven Lukes notes how, for Durkheim, ritual plays "a cognitive creative role, rendering intelligible society and social relationships, serving to organize people's knowledge of the past and present and their capacity to imagine the future." Durkheim ties this, however, to an integrative function by arguing that rituals aid in the development of social consensus. Huizinga's analysis follows this Durkheimian integrative slant and in this way fails to note how rituals also dramatize social cleavages and conflicts in social life (cf., Lukes's discussion of "political" rituals). One final note on the relationship of rituals to play, games, and sports: it is interesting to examine the parallels Durkheim makes between the sacred "rite" and the "game" in *The Elementary Forms of Religious Life* (bk. 3). Durkheim argued that participation in a rite was something different than playing a game; however, "the game has its share of that feeling of comfort which the believer draws from the rite performed . . . [games are] . . . one of the forms of that moral remaking which is the principle object of the positive rite." See Lukes, *Emile Durkheim,* p. 470.

7   Huizinga, *Homo Ludens,* p. 25.

8   See Williams's criticisms of idealist tendencies in cultural analysis in *Culture and Society* and *Marxism and Literature.*

9   This passage has been adapted from Raymond Williams's criticisms of the argument that language is the fundamental generative process in social and cultural life. See *Marxism and Literature*, pp. 21-44.

10 See Max Weber, *Economy and Society*, 3 vols.

11 See Weber's discussion in *Economy and Society*, vol. 3, and the discussion of feudalism and patrimonialism in Reinhard Bendix, *Max Weber: An Intellectual Portrait*, pp. 361-70.

12 Michael Novak, *The Joy of Sports*, p. xi.

13 Ibid., pp. 223-26.

14 Fred Inglis, *The Name of the Game*, p. 128.

15 See John Berger, *A Painter of Our Time*.

16 Inglis, *Name of the Game*, p. 48.

17 See Frank Manning's excellent essay "Celebrating Cricket: The Symbolic Construction of Caribbean Politics," *American Ethnologist* (1981): 616-32, and Orlando Patterson's earlier discussion of "The Cricket Ritual in the West Indies," *New Society* (June 26, 1969), for demonstrations of the conflicting contextual meanings often given to the metaphoric qualities of sport. Citing Patterson's analysis of the riots that are provoked when the West Indian team loses to a visiting English team, Steven Lukes makes the following observation:

> In the West Indies, a test match is not so much a game as a collective ritual—a social drama in which almost all the basic conflicts within the society are played out symbolically. At certain moments this ritual acquires a special quality which reinforces its potency and creates a situation that can only be resolved in violence. Cricket is the Englishman's game, and yet it also gives the West Indian masses "a weapon against their current aggressors, the carriers of the dominant English culture in local society." See Lukes, "Political Ritual," p. 208.

18 On the depoliticized and ideological nature of myth in capitalist societies see Roland Barthes, *Mythologies*, and Alan Swingewood, *The Myth of Mass Culture*.

19 Lukes, *Individualism*, pp. 73-78.

20 Jean-Marie Brohm, *Sport: A Prison of Measured Time*, p. 175.

21 Ibid., p. 41.

22 See, for example, the famous "First Thesis on Feuerbach," in *The German Ideology:*

> The chief defect of all materialism up to now (including Feuerbach's) is, that the object, reality, what we apprehend through our senses, is understood only in the form of the *object of contemplation;* but not a sensuous human activity, as *practice;* not subjectively. Hence in opposition to materialism the *active* side was developed abstractly by idealism—which of course does not know real sensuous activity as such.

A detailed discussion of Marx's method is outlined in the general introduction to *Grundrisse* (1973 ed.).

23 I have been very influenced in this section by Raymond Williams's arguments in "Base and Superstructure in Marxist Cultural Theory," *New Left Review* 82:8 (1973), and in *Marxism and Literature*.

24   This final point is also made by Christopher Lasch in response to the "cultural criticism" of Paul Hoch and other writers whose work shares certain common themes with Brohm. Lasch also comments on Novak's *The Joy of Sports.* Much of what Lasch argues in the review essay where these discussions can be found is of considerable analytic importance. There is a sense, however, in which Lasch cannot free himself from an idealist frame of reference that on occasion romanticizes the "formal" qualities of play and games. Like Huizinga before him, Lasch's critique hinges on an abstract separation of play as an ideal from real social process; the "corruption of sports" that he documents is simply another version of "the debasement of play." See Lasch, "The Corruption of Sports," in *The New York Review of Books* (April 28, 1977), and Hoch, *Rip Off the Big Game.*

25   Miliband, *Marxism and Politics,* p. 52.

26   My discussion on this point has been greatly influenced by Giddens's *New Rules of Sociological Method* and by his "Notes on the Theory of Structuration," in *Studies in Social and Political Theory.*

27   See Herbert Marcuse, *One Dimensional Man* and *Eros and Civilization.*

28   See Althusser's *Lenin and Philosophy and Other Essays.*

29   For this critique of Althusser, I am heavily indebted to Edward Thompson's *The Poverty of Theory and Other Essays.*

30   Guttman, *From Ritual to Record,* p. 15.

31   Ibid., p. 157.

32   See Susan Birrell's review of Guttmann in the *International Committee for Sociology of Sport Bulletin* 15 (November 1978); Benjamin Rader, "Modern Sports: In Search of Interpretations," *Journal of Social History* (Winter 1979); and Jack Berryman's review in the *American Historical Review* 84:2 (April 1979).

33   Birrell, *International Committee,* p. 9.

34   Guttmann's philosophical emphasis on freedom from necessity as opposed to freedom defined in broader social and political terms appears to be influenced by Huizinga's argument in *Homo Ludens* that play must be understood in a way "that leaves untouched the philosophical problem of determinism" (p. 7). This has the effect of guaranteeing that play is viewed in universal terms in a voluntarist and idealist fashion. Guttmann's attempt to solve this problem by showing that the major characteristics and social tendencies of capitalist industrialism and liberal democracy are only partly determining and generally lead to "positive freedom" is an improvement on Huizinga's view but remains unsatisfactory.

35   See Giddens's discussion of Weber's views on this in *Capitalism and Modern Social Theory,* pp. 235-36.

36   Emile Durkheim, *Moral Education,* p. 54.

37   I develop this point more fully in "Conflicting Standards and Problems of Personal Action in the Sociology of Sport," *Quest* 30 (Summer 1978), and in my introduction to *Canadian Sport: Sociological Perspectives.* I should add that there is much in this latter piece (especially in the section on definitions) that I would now want to revise.

38   For Marx's own views on this see the Introduction to *Grundrisse* and Marx's "second observation" in *The Poverty of Philosophy.* It is more than a little

ironic that in Guttmann's sketch of how Marxists view the social development of sport he cites W.W. Rostow, a self-proclaimed anti-Marxist thinker.
See *From Ritual to Record,* p. 61.

39 This lack of understanding is graphically evident in Guttmann's attempt to
ridicule the neo-Marxists' designation of sport as an aspect of alienation by
ironically suggesting that the correlation between high socioeconomic
position and active sport involvement means that alienation would have to
be most felt among the dominant class. As Guttmann puts it, "if sport is an
engine of alienation, we can only conclude that the advantaged have turned
it on themselves rather than the disadvantaged" (p. 80). Because we know
this is not the case the whole idea is false. Nonsense. Alienation is a total
process. It influences the bourgeoisie (although in different ways) as much
as it influences the proletariat. See Bertell Ollman, *Alienation: Marx's
Conception of Man in Capitalist Society;* Giddens, *Capitalism and Modem
Social Theory,* pp. 10-17; and Marx's own discussion in the 1844 *Economic
and Philosophic Manuscripts.*

40 See by contrast Raymond Williams, *Marxism and Literature;* and Edward
Thompson, *The Making of the English Working Class.*

41 Guttmann, *From Ritual to Record,* p. 81.

42 Giddens, "Marx, Weber and the Development of Capitalism," *Studies in
Social and Political Theory.*

43 I want to make an additional point about one of these examples. Guttmann's
discussion of the study of Roger Boileau et al. on the underrepresentation
of Francophones on Canadian international sports teams is somewhat
misleading. It is true that the underrepresentation of Francophones can be
related to the "traditional" rural mentality of French-speaking Quebeckers
until the "Quiet Revolution" in the 1960s. However, as I note in the "Introduction" to this section of the anthology where the article by Boileau et al. is
published, it is also true that Francophones were formally (and informally)
excluded from certain activities by the Anglophone groups that were
generally responsible for organizing sport in the province. See Alan Metcalfe's
discussion, "Organized Sport and Social Stratification in Montreal: 1804-
1901," in *Canadian Sport: Sociological Perspectives,* ed. Richard S. Gruneau
and John G. Albinson.

44 For a recent and detailed history of functionalism as a theoretical frame of
reference in sociology see Giddens, "Functionalism: Aprés la lutte," in
Studies in Social and Political Theory.

45 Lukes, "Power and Structure," p. 29.

46 I think it necessary to say an additional word here about the term "structure." "Structure" generally refers to two related conditions in social scientific research. Conventionally, it refers to a set of habitual or institutionalized
social practices (relationships) that take on a systemic existence independent of any one individual's action (e.g., the social structure). It has also
been used to refer to "deeper," more abstract *relations* which guide and
shape human practices—relations expressed, for example, in the constitutive logic of language or in a particular measure of human production (e.g.,
the wage/labor or surplus value relation). As a general rule I am skeptical of
completely "structuralist" explanations, especially those which separate
abstract forces from human agency. Yet, I would argue strongly that in
acknowledging the actions of agents, one must be careful not to lose sight

of "determinations" not readily apparent in the experiences of individuals. Although particular arrangements of agents and particular sets of "rules" in social life are not completely "determining," they nonetheless define the nature of the limits within which agents act and the possibilities that are generally available to them. A recognition of these arrangements and rules, and an analysis of their structuring and restructuring through the actions of agents, is the core of any study of social development.

Chapter 2   Problems of Class Inequality and Structural Change in Play, Games, and Sports

1   I recognize, of course, that there are a great range of social relations beyond class relations which might influence people's collective powers to "structure" play, games, and sports and "finish off" the range of meanings commonly associated with them. Gender, ethnicity, and religion, for example, all might be identified as influencing resources that can be brought to bear on the structuring of sport. Gender, in particular, seems to be an important dimension of this structuring, and its significance is readily implied in such stereotypical notions as the idea of sports as "male preserves." Yet, I think it important that this issue be understood in the context of the *ensemble of social relations* that define different ways of living in modern societies. In this study I have emphasized the role of class as a central consideration in understanding this totality. It is clear, however, that far more needs to be taken into account and I hope to do this in future work on the intersections of class and patriarchy.

2   See Giddens's discussion in *New Rules of Sociological Method* and in the essay, "Hermeneutics, Ethnomethodology and Problems of Interpretive Analysis," in *Studies in Social and Political Theory.*

3   The source for this aphorism is Marx's famous beginning to the second paragraph of *The Eighteenth Brumaire of Louis Bonaparte,* trans. Ben Fowkes: "Men make their own history, but not of their own free will, not under circumstances they themselves have chosen but under the given and inherited circumstances with which they are directly confronted" (p. 146).

4   This conclusion has been influenced by some of the structuralist writing on language referred to by Giddens in *Studies in Social and Political Theory* and by some of Jean Piaget's work on the role of play in child development. I would argue, however, that the process of reproduction that I have described does not occur in any automatic or necessary way; rather it is a mediated process monitored in and through the reflexive interpretation of signification itself. It is in this sense that I would argue that these conclusions are not incompatible with certain features of symbolic interactionism. There is a general tension in the literature on play and child development between functional and structuralist models on the one hand, and "interpretive" or "dramaturgical" models on the other. Brian Sutton-Smith, for example, has typified the interpretive position by trying to show how Piaget's emphasis on the cyclical processes of "assimilation" and "accommodation" in child development does not grant a creative role to play. For Piaget, play is supposedly nothing more than the "reproduction" of social roles and structures from the "outside" world. This point is an important one but it may not be entirely fair to Piaget. For as Lucien Goldmann has emphasized, Piaget's scheme is far more dynamic and sensitive to agency than many of his critics are willing to admit. See Jean Piaget, *Play, Dreams*

and Imitation in Childhood; Brian Sutton-Smith, "Piaget on Play: A Critique," in Child's Play, ed. R. Herron and B. Sutton-Smith; and W. Mayri's "Introduction," in Lucien Goldmann, Cultural Creation.

5   See Mead, Mind, Self and Society, and his discussion in On Social Psychology, ed. Anselm Strauss, pp. 216-28.

6   Giddens notes in Studies in Social and Political Theory that symbolic interactionism "is perhaps the only leading school of thought in English-speaking sociology that comes near to assigning a central place to agency and reflexivity" (p. 168). Yet, Giddens goes on to note how, even in Mead's writing on human reflexive capacities, the "I" often

> . . . appears as a more shadowy element than the social determined self, which is elaborately discussed. In the works of most of Mead's followers, the social self displaced the "I" altogether, thus foreclosing the option that Mead took out on the possibility of incorporating reflexivity into the theory of action. Where this happens, symbolic interactionism is readily assimilated with the mainstream of sociological thought, as a sort of "sociological social psychology" concentrated upon face-to-face interaction.

7   In Marxism and Literature, Raymond Williams defines "signification" as "the social creation of meanings through the use of formal signs. . . . It is a specific form of that practical consciousness which is inseparable from all social material activity" (p. 38). Also see Roland Barthes's seminal discussion at the conclusion of Mythologies.

8   For some general discussions of institutionalization see R. MacIver and Charles Page, Society: An Introductory Analysis; Hans Gerth and C. Wright Mills, Character and Social Structure; and Peter Blau, Exchange and Power in Social Life. An extremely provocative discussion of institutionalization in sport can be found in Alan Ingham and John Loy, "The Social System of Sport: A Humanistic Perspective," Quest 19 (1973).

9   I have elaborated on this point elsewhere. See my "Sport As an Area of Sociological Study," in Canadian Sport: Sociological Perspectives.

10   In this passage I have used language similar to that of Ingham and Loy, although the perspective employed here differs from the one developed in their work. See Ingham and Loy, "The Social System of Sport."

11   I have developed my use of the notions of "limits" and "pressures" from Raymond Williams's discussion of "determination" in Marxism and Literature.

12   John Searle, Speech Acts: An Essay in the Philosophy of Language.

13   Charles Taylor, "Hermeneutics and Politics," in Critical Sociology, ed. Paul Connerton, p. 175.

14   This point is also made by Giddens. He notes that all rules have "constitutive" and "regulative" aspects, as is suggested by the common root which both "rule" and "regulate" share. See Studies in Social and Political Theory, p. 363.

15   I cannot here enter into a discussion of the vast literature on "power" in sociological analysis and political theory. Rather I shall defer to Lukes's excellent analysis of power in Power: A Radical View. I have attempted to suggest a view which is sensitive to the idea that "power" can be equated with the transformative capacities of agents acting through and within

structures. In this regard I have adopted Giddens's understanding of power as an attempt to mediate between a methodologically individualist view and a structurally determinist view. See *Studies in Social and Political Theory,* p. 347.

16   Giddens, *New Rules of Sociological Method,* p. 85.

17   See Wittgenstein, *Philosophical Investigations;* and Giddens, *Studies in Social and Political Theory,* p. 31.

18   Ibid., pp. 131-32.

19   Ibid., p. 134.

20   I have adopted this distinction between "abilities" and "opportunities" from Steven Lukes's "Power and Structure," in *Essays in Social Theory.*

21   See Frank Parkin, *Class Inequality and Political Order;* Anthony Giddens, *Class Structure of the Advanced Societies;* and Harry Braverman, *Labour and Monopoly Capital.*

22   Few concepts in sociology are as "essentially contested" as social class. I have attempted to work through some of this literature in an earlier essay, "Sport, Social Differentiation and Inequality" in *Sport and Social Order,* ed. Donald Ball and John Loy, and I shall not reproduce my arguments here except to say that I now regard this earlier discussion to be extremely inadequate in many respects, especially in the case of my analysis of Marxist writing. For present purposes I shall simply seek to clarify some key concepts. In this connection Giddens has noted in *Class Structure of the Advanced Societies* that in its most generic sense, use of the term "class" in the analysis of social life refers to "a large-scale aggregate of individuals comprised of impersonally-defined relationships and nominally 'open' in form" (p. 100). In most studies of social class these "aggregates" are defined with some reference to their *distributive* and *relational* features.

Distributive features of class refer to the variety of underlying material and symbolic factors that contribute to social ranking and inequality; that is, those factors such as income, property, or family status. Relational features of class refer to the ways in which social groupings differentiated in a consistent way by those factors are interrelated in a systematic manner. Now set in the context of these terms, classes may be understood as abstract *descriptive categories or groupings* or they may be seen as histori- cally constituted social *formations* with a specific way of life. In each of these cases one can identify class "interests" in terms of their relationships to systems of "objective social relations" (e.g., the surplus-value relation) or in terms of a subjective "class consciousness."

In this study I have emphasized the relational and historical features of class in the whole material process that constitutes society. In particular I have accepted a view of social classes as social formations whose particular shape is defined on the basis of struggles over "ways of doing things"— struggles which can only be studied as they work themselves out over a given historical period. That the issues which surround these "ways of doing things" are generally tied in some way to opposing "interests" and to the productive relations into which human beings are born I take to be self- evident. This is not an *economic* view of class; it is a *social* one. It is also not a firm commitment to a "formal" definition, for I think it can be argued successfully that the definition of the concept of class, like the definition of sport, is in itself an "object" of struggle. In coming to this particular view I have been greatly influenced by Edward Thompson. I would not go so far as Thompson, however, in downplaying the often impersonal nature of class and the degree to which particular systems of interaction and allocative rules operate "behind people's backs." See Edward Thompson, *The Making of the English Working Class;* André Béteille, *Social Inequality;* and Giddens, *Class Structure.*

23   Ibid., p. 90. Also see C. B. Macpherson's discussion in *The Real World of Democracy.*

24   Paul Willis, *Learning to Labour,* p. 174.

25   Ibid., p. 173.

26   This view is especially common in "left-functionalist" analyses of sports in capitalist societies. In left-functionalism, as noted in my earlier critique of Jean-Marie Brohm, the functional requirements of the mode of production, of capitalism, simply take the place of the functional requirements of "society," and it is assumed that sport is reproductive because it inculcates the "values" which support capitalism. Thus, in *Rip Off the Big Game,* Paul Hoch argues that sport "socializes" people for militarism, consumerism, racism, sexism, and a host of other sins that he suggests are somehow functionally related to the reproduction of capitalism. What this position overlooks, of course, is the knowledgeable and reflexive nature of human agents, the complexity of meaning systems in capitalist society, and the imperfect nature of "socialization." See my discussion of this point in "Power and Play in Canadian Society," in *Power and Change in Canada,* ed. R. J. Ossenberg. For broader criticisms of "dominant value" theories of ideology, see Michael Mann, "The Social Cohesion of Liberal Democracy," *American Sociological Review* 35 (June 1970).

27   Raymond Williams, *Marxism and Literature,* p. 110. Hegemony is a concept developed out of the writings of the Italian Marxist theorist Antonio Gramsci. It reflects to all of those processes by means of which a dominant class extends its influence in such a way that "it can transform and refashion its ways of life, its mores and conceptualization, its very form and level of culture and civilization in a direction which, while not directly paying immediate profit to the narrow interests of any particular class, favours the development and expansion of the dominant and social and productive system of life as a whole." See Stuart Hall, "The Rediscovery of Ideology: Return of the Repressed in Media Studies," in *Culture, Society and the Media,* ed. Michael Gurevitch et al., p. 85. See also Carl Boggs, *Gramsci's Marxism,* pp. 71-76. For a preliminary outline of the implications of "hegemony theory" in the study of sport see John Hargreaves, "Sport and Hegemony: Some Theoretical Problems," in *Sport, Culture and the Modern State,* ed. Hart Cantelon and Richard Gruneau.

28   Williams, *Marxism and Literature,* p. 117.

29   Ibid., p. 125.

30   See Clifford Geertz, "Deep Play: Notes on the Balinese Cockfight," *Daedalus* (Winter 1972); John Loy, "The Cultural System of Sport," *Quest* 29 (1978); and Edwin Cady, *The Big Game: College Sports and American Life.*

31   Geertz, "Deep Play."

32   It is instructive to compare this view with Gunther Luschen's mainstream liberal functionalist analysis of sport as an element of culture. In Luschen's

view it is "shared values" which give "structure" to sport as an activity and link it as a functional element to society. Sport is seen, from this perspective, to contribute to the processes of pattern maintenance, adaptation, integration, and goal attainment that are the functional imperatives of social reproduction. Thus, Luschen concludes, it is values that one may look toward in order to understand sport and culture, its essential meanings, and even its "distribution in society." The obvious questions here, unless we are prepared to accept a perfectly consensual society, are to ask whose values we are talking about, how deeply these values can be seen to penetrate people's practical consciousness, and what the relationship of these values is to the material structuring and restructuring of the world. See Gunther Luschen, "The Interdependence of Sport and Culture," in *Sport in the Sociocultural Process,* ed. Marie Hart, p. 104.

33 Geertz, "Deep Play," p. 23.

34 Ibid., p. 25.

35 When this occurs, "cultural text" theory goes well beyond Geertz's essentially hermeneutic perspective and gets very close to Michael Novak's transcendent metaphysics of sports. The concept which opens the possibility of this transition is the notion of *form* as something that is emancipated from content. The danger is that in emphasizing the autonomy of cultural productions *as forms,* the constitutive features of the forms are separated from material reality and assume a transcendent and reified nature. Thus, Georg Simmel argues that even though social forms are constituted out of "the materials of life," they develop a form of autonomy and contain their own constitutive logic. As Simmel notes in the case of play: "Actual forces, needs, impulses of life produce the forms of our behaviour that are suitable for play. These forms, however, become independent contents and stimuli within play itself rather than as play." See Kurt Wolff, *The Sociology of Georg Simmel,* p. 40. Simmel goes on to say that the expressive form of play *depends* upon its emancipation from content. Now Simmel's work falls squarely in the idealist traditions of the *Geisteswissenschaften,* and he was committed to a view which saw social development as the development of mind. In this way he sought to "preserve the freedom of the human spirit . . . form-giving creativity over against historicism in the same way that Kant did with respect to Naturalism." In other words, Simmel's sociology of social forms undertakes to grasp material history in the traditional manner of idealist philosophy. I have been critical of this view throughout this study and there is no point in raising my criticisms of idealism again. However, I think it is telling to note that Simmel is often cited as an additional source of support in many of the attempts to incorporate sport into some kind of cultural text thesis. See *Georg Simmel: On Individuality and Social Forms;* and John Loy, "The Cultural System of Sport."

36 Geertz, "Deep Play," pp. 23, 21.

37 Ibid., p. 28.

38 See, for example, the cases of violence outlined by Michael Smith, "Sport and Collective Violence," in *Sport and Social Order,* ed. John Loy and Don Ball; and Ian Taylor, "Class, Violence and Sport: The Case of Soccer Hooliganism in England," in *Sport, Culture and the Modern State,* ed. Hart Cantelon and Richard Gruneau.

39 Fred Inglis, *The Name of the Game,* pp. 72-73.

40 It is revealing, for example, how easily Edwin Cady manages in The *Big Game* to turn a form of cultural text theory into an unabashed celebration of American intercollegiate athletics.

41 Cf. Steven Lukes, *Essays in Social Theory,* p. 65; and Inglis, *Name of the Game,* p. 71.

42 Geertz, "Deep Play," p. 17.

43 I took this point from Giddens's discussion in *Studies in Social and Political Theory,* p. 176.

44 See also Veblen, *The Theory of Business Enterprise.*

45 My discussion of Veblen's theory has been greatly influenced by C. Wright Mills's "Introduction" to the Mentor edition of *The Theory of the Leisure Class.*

46 Ibid., p. xiii.

47 See Krishan Kumar's discussion of this optimism in *Prophecy and Progress,* especially the sections on Saint Simon. Veblen's work compares to Saint Simon in the sense that both writers maintain an emphasis on the "industriousness" of labor in industrial society as distinct from idleness and unproductive labor in feudalism. See Giddens's discussion of this point in *Studies in Social and Political Theory,* p. 15.

48 Mills, "Introduction."

49 Ibid., p. xvii.

50 For a brief note on how Veblen's writing fits into utilitarian philosophy, see my "Sport, Social Differentiation and Social Inequality," in *Sport and Social Order,* ed. Don Ball and John Loy.

51 Mills, "Introduction," p. xiv.

52 Gregory Stone, "American Sport: Play and Display," in *Sport and Society: An Anthology,* ed. John Talamini and Charles Page, p. 67.

53 Max Kaplan, *Leisure in America;* Harold Hodges, *Social Stratification;* John Betts, *America's Sporting Heritage, 1850-1950.*

54 See, for example, John Loy, "The Study of Sport and Social Mobility," in *Aspects of Contemporary Sport Sociology,* ed. Gerald Kenyon; and Harry Webb's "Response" to Loy's paper in the same volume. Also see Jack Berryman and John Loy, "Secondary Schools and Ivy League Letters," *British Journal of Sociology* 27 (March 1976); and Rabel Burdge, "Levels of Occupational Prestige and Leisure Activity," in *Sport and American Society,* 2d ed., ed. George Sage. For criticisms of sport as a mobility mechanism for underclass racial groups see the review of literature provided by Jay Coakley in chapter 11, *Sport in Society,* 2d ed., and in Harry Edwards, *Sociology of Sport.*

55 Betts, *America's Sporting Heritage.*

56 The notions of "external" and "internal" inequalities comes from Durkheim. I discuss their modern "cultural" and "structural" variants as forms of explanation for differential participation in sport in my essay "Class or Mass: Notes on the Democratization of Canadian Amateur Sport," in *Canadian Sport: Sociological Perspectives.*

57 Charles Page, *Class and American Sociology,* p. xvii.

58   There is a vast body of literature on the liberal pluralist analysis of power and its strengths and limitations, and I shall not enter these debates here. For some useful discussions see C. Wright Mills, *The Power Elite;* C. B. Macpherson, *The Life and Times of Liberal Democracy;* Ralph Miliband, *The State in Capitalist Society;* and Steven Lukes, *Power: A Radical View.* I discuss some of the limitations of the liberal pluralist frame of reference for analyzing sport in my essay, "Sport and the Debate on the State," in *Sport, Culture and the Modern State,* ed. Hart Cantelon and Richard Gruneau.

59   See, for example, the remarks in the preface to Peter McIntosh's *Fair Play:*

> Since ... (1801) ... there has been a great free trade of sports and pastimes throughout the world and something quite new has appeared on the scene—international sport, which is governed and organized by new social and political institutions, and through which people are sharing their cultures and taking the first tentative steps towards a common culture of sport.

But, has the "trade" of sports and pastimes throughout the world been "free"? If one examines the Olympic Games, for example, one finds little "sharing" of cultures. There are no tribal or Third World games; rather, the "sports" that are shared are the institutionalized agonistic activities that developed in the western capitalist nations and were spread through the colonial networks of these nations. Viewed historically this is an asymmetrical sharing at best, and it shows the bias of labeling the institutionalized international sports of today as the farthest point on some ludic evolutionary scale.

60   Giddens, *Studies in Social and Political Theory,* p. 15.

61   For some criticisms of this view see Ralph Miliband, *The State in Capitalist Society;* and Wallace Clement, *The Canadian Corporate Elite: An Analysis of Economic Power.*

62   Robert Heilbroner, "Economic Problems of a 'Post-Industrial' Society," *Dissent* (Spring 1973).

63   Ibid., p. 169.

64   This accounts in part for the element of "vanguardism" in Brohm's work, insofar as it is implied that the proletariat is no longer a social force in capitalism.

65   Giddens, *Studies in Social and Political Theory,* p. 18.

66   The "classic" work in the dependency literature is *Dependencia y Desarrollo en Américana Latina,* by F. Cardoso and E. Faletto. Cardoso and Faletto note how dependency theory tries to separate the political from the economic and suggests that, although imperialism sets up specific *limits* on development, the range of possible responses to a given situation depends upon internal alliances and conflicts between the classes and class fractions of a given society. Because the history of each country gives a peculiar mix of possible actions and responses, results cannot be provided by general theories but require careful study of social and historical trends and the realities of power in each society. One of the keys to understanding these trends, however, is a focus on the internal response to conditions of dependence of imperialist powers. Additional material on dependency can be found in J. Cockroft et al., *Dependency and Underdevelopment: Latin America's Political Economy;* Samir Amin, *Unequal Development;* and

K. Clements and D. Drache, eds., "Symposium on Progressive Modes of Nationalism in New Zealand, Canada and Australia," *Australia and New Zealand Journal of Sociology* 14:3 (October 1978). For a criticism of some key features of dependency theories see Ernesto Laclau, *Politics and Ideology in Marxist Theory.* A provocative discussion of the "consumption" of dependency theory in the United States is provided by Cardoso in the *Latin American Research Review* 12: 3 (1977).

67   Giddens, *Studies in Social and Political Theory,* pp. 19-20.

Chapter 3   Class, Sports, and Social Development

1   Philip Abrams, "History, Sociology, Historical Sociology," *Past and Present* 87 (May 1980); also see Michael Scriven, "Truisms as Grounds for Historical Explanations" in *Theories of History,* ed. P. Gardiner.

2   This explanation of the term "problematic" (used as a noun) comes from Abrams's essay "History, Sociology, Historical Sociology." For a more detailed discussion of the nature of such problematics see Richard Johnson, "Three Problematics: Elements of a Theory of Working Class Culture," in *Working Class Culture: Studies in History and Theory,* ed. John Clarke, Charles Critcher, and Richard Johnson.

3   To accomplish this I have had to emphasize some processes more than others and select out some "facts" at the expense of others. In this way the "history" presented is given continuity by the theoretical problematic which informs it. In some ways, of course, this kind of selective analysis is characteristic of all historical writing. In *A Culture in Conflict,* Bryan Palmer cites Lévi-Strauss's statement that,

> What is true of the constitution of historical facts is no less so of their selection. From this point of view, the historian and the agent of history choose, sever and carve them up, for a truly total history would confront them with chaos. Every corner of space conceals a multitude of individuals each of whom totalizes the trend of history in a manner which cannot be compared to the others; for any one of these individuals, each moment of time is inexhaustibly rich in physical and psychical incidents which all play their part in his totalization. Even history which claims to be universal is still only a juxtaposition of a few local histories within which (and between which) very much more is left out than is put in. And it would be vain to hope that by increasing the number of collaborators and making research more intensive one would obtain a better result. Insofar as history aspires to meaning, it is doomed to select regions, periods, groups of men and individuals in these groups and make them stand out, as discontinuous figures, against a continuity barely good enough to be used as a backdrop. [P. 2]

4   The research material for this section comes from a file I have been keeping for many years on the changing relationships between sport and social class in Canada. I began the file in 1971 with material collected in support of a national sample survey I was conducting on the social origins of Canadian amateur athletes. Some of this material was subsequently included in my essay, "Class or Mass: Notes on the Democratization of Canadian Amateur Sport," in *Canadian Sport: Sociological Perspectives.* In the mid-1970s, I extended my 1971 study to include samples of "elite" figures in Canadian sports organizations at different periods in Canadian history. Preliminary tabulations of some of the historical survey materials and

interviews were published in 1978 in an essay entitled "Elites, Class and Corporate Power in Canadian Sport," in *Sociology of Sport,* ed. W. Orban and F. Landry. While doing background reading for this study I had occasion to do archival work in the National Library of Canada and went through some of the minute books of the *Amateur Athletic Union of Canada* and the *Montreal Amateur Athletic Association.* I also managed, thanks to Jake Gaudaur, to get access to the minute books of the *Canadian Rugby Union* (1891-1916). This background reading and archival work became progressively less systematic as I became convinced of the narrowness and empiricism of the "elite group" emphasis that I was maintaining. The result was a great broadening in the range of material that I began to collect and a great decrease in its degree of detail. What this chapter represents is an attempt to make sense of the diversity of material in my file at the present time based on the problematic that I have developed in earlier chapters.

5   Eric Dunning employed a somewhat similar emphasis on *phases* in the social development of sport in his work on rugby football in England. Pierre Bourdieu also refers to "supply" and "demand" phases in his discussion of the changing relationships between sport and social class. In each of these uses of the idea of critical phases (and in my own use of the conception), it is important to recognize the degree to which the phases are not clear-cut, self-contained processes that "replace" one another; rather they often overlap and coincide with one another. See Eric Dunning, "Industrialization and the Incipient Modernization of Football," *Stadion* 1:1 (1976); and Pierre Bourdieu, "Sport and Social Class," *Social Science Information* 17:6 (1978).

6   A "staple" is a "product with a large resource content . . . which does not require elaborate processing involving large quantities of labour or rare skills . . . which will bear transport charges and is in international demand" (Caves and Holton, cited in Dan Glenday, "Unity in Diversity: The Political Economy of Subordination in Canada," in *Power and Change in Canada,* ed. R.J. Ossenberg). Examples of "staples" would be trade in furs or timber. The staples approach has dominated Canadian economic history, especially through the contributions of Harold Innis. See Harold Innis, *The Fur Trade in Canada;* W.A. Macintosh, "Economic Factors in Canadian History," *Canadian Historical Review* 4 (March 1923); Donald Creighton, *The Empire of the St. Lawrence;* and W.T. Easterbrook and M.H. Watkins, eds., *Approaches to Canadian Economic History.* All of these works provide discussions of the staples approach and its application to the analysis of Canadian social development.

7   See Creighton, *Empire of the St. Lawrence* for a view which demonstrates this point while celebrating the central role of merchants in the social development of Canada. For a more critical perspective, see H. Clare Pentland, "The Role of Capital in Canadian Economic Development before 1875," *Canadian Journal of Economics and Political Science* 16 (1950), pp. 460-61; and *Labour and Capital in Canada,* 1650-1860. Also see Tom Naylor, *The History of Canadian Business.*

8   This is a widely accepted point in Canadian historical writing. See, for example, Tom Naylor, "The Rise and Fall of the Third Commercial Empire of the St. Lawrence," in *Capitalism and the National Question in Canada,* ed. Gary Teeple, p. 6. Also see Kenneth McNaught, *The Pelican History of Canada,* chap. 5; and, for a Marxist view of the same issue, Stanley Ryerson, *Unequal Union.*

9   The *Constitutional Act of 1791* allowed the Governor General in the Canadas to appoint office holders throughout the colony. This, combined with clearly delimited colonial policies of immigration and trade, set the stage for nearly fifty years of oligarchical rule modeled on highly paternalistic lines. See Kenneth McNaught, *The Pelican History of Canada*, chap. 5, for a descriptive sketch of these developments, as well as J.M.S. Careless, *Canada: A Story of Challenge*, and the essays included in Careless's edited anthology, *Colonists and Canadians, 1760-1867*. For works that attempt to situate these developments more directly in the context of class struggle, see Stanley Ryerson, *Unequal Union;* Gustavus Myers, *A History of Canadian Wealth;* and Gary Teeple, "Land, Labour and Capital in Pre-Confederation Canada," in *Capitalism and the National Question in Canada*.

10   See, for example, Max Howell and Nancy Howell, *Sports and Games in Canadian Life*, pp. 54-56; and H. Roxborough, *One Hundred Not-Out: The Story of Nineteenth-Century Canadian Sport*.

11   I think it is fair to say that most sport historians have tended to understand the social significance of early games and pastimes of Canadian life in the context of a tacit acceptance of a "frontier thesis" of the nature of pioneer life, which equated life on the frontier with inherently democratic forms of social interaction. Borrowing from the work of Frederick Jackson Turner in the United States, this thesis, in varying forms, has had great impact on Canadian historiography. When this is merged with the powerful underlying idealist emphases to be found in most writings on the nature of sport, it is not surprising that the overriding emphasis in reference to early forms of physical recreation is on the supposedly democratic and integrative nature of the activities; that is, class differences are downplayed and class domination tends to be ignored. On the role of the frontier thesis in Canadian historiography see J.M.S. Careless, "Frontierism, Metropolitanism and Canadian History," in *Approaches to Canadian History*, ed. Carl Berger.

12   S.F. Wise and D. Fisher, *Canada's Sporting Heroes*, p. 8; also see the letters and diaries in Michael Cross, *The Workingman in the Nineteenth Century*. Between January 19 and December 25, 1837, a farmer, P.H. Gosse, did not make a single reference to physical recreation activities of any type. Similarly, the diary of David Nelson, 1864-1886 held only the scantest references to county shows, bees, or social activities beyond the family. Farm life, as Cross points out, was often dreary and was always hard. Similarly, the farmers were, for the most part, far from being completely "independent" commodity producers. They were often closely tied to money lenders and needed second incomes to supplement their farming. To be sure, Canadians took advantage of the rivers, lakes, and forests for their recreation, but it may be easy to overstate the amount of activity that actually occurred, especially by people on the frontier.

13   For this brief sketch of the nature of early colonial games I am indebted to Alan Metcalfe who shared with me a preliminary draft of his forthcoming book, *The Emergence of Modern Sport in Canada, 1867-1914*. In writing the sketch I have also drawn on material from Peter Lindsay's doctoral thesis, "A History of Sport in Canada: 1807-1867".

14   This sense is hinted at in the fragments of materials outlined in Howell and Howell, *Sports and Games in Canadian Life*, pp. 7-18, but is not taken up in their discussion. Frequent reference is made to the degree to which European traditions of hierarchy and folk culture were imported to the Canadian

scene in the late eighteenth and early nineteenth centuries. One element of folk culture that Howell and Howell mention is the "charivari." For an analysis of the class-related meanings of the nineteenth-century charivari see Bryan Palmer, "Discordant Music: Charivaris and Whitecapping in Nineteenth-Century North America," *Labour/LeTravailleur* 3 (1978).

15   For a description of the paternalistic features of the labor process of this time, see H. Clare Pentland, *Labour and Capital in Canada, 1650-1860*, pp. 54-56. A discussion of the quasi-aristocratic nature of the era is also outlined in the essays by S.F. Wise and Michael Cross in *Colonists and Canadians*, ed. J.M.S. Careless.

16   *Acadian Recorder* (Halifax), December 20, 1817, cited in Howell and Howell, *Sports and Games in Canadian Life*, p. 8.

17   I realize the speculative nature of this point, but I think there are some theoretical grounds to support it. Throughout the history of folk cultures in medieval and feudal Europe there were always "profane" rituals which mocked the dominant classes. I am suggesting that one might argue that elements of these traditions were imported into Canada. There is, I think, fragmentary evidence to support this thesis in Bryan Palmer's discussion of working-class cultural activities in nineteenth-century Hamilton. See *A Culture in Conflict*, chap. 2. For a sense of what I mean when I refer to "profane" or oppositional amusements or rituals, see Mikhail Bakhtin, "Rabelais in the History of Laughter," in *Rabelais and His World*.

18   As Michael Cross notes in his chapter in *Colonists and Canadians*, ed. J.M.S. Careless: "The eighteenth century (in Canada) was a lusty, playful old aristocrat. The reports of his death in anno domini 1800 were greatly exaggerated, for he was alive and apparently well in British North America in 1820" (p. 149). Alfred Dubuc also comments, in his essay "Problems in the Study of the Stratification of the Canadian Society from 1760 to 1840," in Michiel Horn and R. Sabourin, *Studies in Canadian Social History*, that social historians "broadly" accept the view that a social group defining itself as superior status to the other classes of society will try to maintain, by a new type of activity and a new way of living, a prestige that lower economic functions may put in jeopardy. Thus would be explained the rise of conspicuous consumption, the prolixity of social life at the royal court or elsewhere, the aversion towards commercial activities, the reliance on constant revenues and the recourse to credit. [P. 130]

19   I have drawn this point from my reading of the descriptive material in Peter Lindsay's thesis, "A History of Sport in Canada: 1807-1867". Lindsay emphasizes the role of the military garrison in the first structurings of Canadian sport. The central role played by the garrisons helped to imprint these earliest structurings (for the colonial ruling class) with a distinctly aristocratic bias.

20   For an elaboration of this point see Tom Naylor, *History of Canadian Business*.

21   Arthur Lower, "Two Ways of Life: The Primary Antithesis of Canadian History," in *Approaches to Canadian History*, ed. Carl Berger.

22   Cf. Gustavus Myers, *A History of Canadian Wealth;* Stanley Ryerson, *Unequal Union;* and Michael Cross, "The 1820's," in J.M.S. Careless, ed., *Colonists and Canadians*.

23   See John Moir, *Church and State in Canada, 1627-1867.*

24   Gary Teeple, "Land, Labour and Capital in Pre-Confederation Canada," in *Capitalism and the National Question in Canada.*

25   See Ryerson, *Unequal Union.*

26   See Teeple, "Land, Labour and Capital"; and Moir, *Church and State in Canada.*

27   See Cross, "Introduction," *The Workingman.*

28   Ibid., p. 2.

29   For one of the best examples see Jean Burnet, "The Urban Community and Changing Moral Standards," in *Urbanism and the Changing Canadian Society,* ed. S.D. Clark; also Moir, *Church and State in Canada.*

30   Christopher Lasch, "The Corruption of Sports," *New York Review of Books* (April 28, 1977); Peter Bailey, *Leisure and Class in Victorian England.*

31   See Peter Bailey's doctoral thesis, "Rational Recreation: The Social Control of Leisure and Popular Culture in Victorian England, 1830-1885," p. 22. *Leisure and Class in Victorian England* is a revised version of this thesis.

32   See Max Weber's discussion of the conflicts between aristocrats and Protestants over sport in England in *The Protestant Ethic and the Spirit of Capitalism,* pp. 177-78. This issue is also discussed in Dennis Brailsford, *Sport and Society: Elizabeth to Anne;* and Robert Malcolmson, *Popular Recreations in English Society, 1700-1850.*

33   On the question of ritual inversions and games of "order" and "disorder," see Brian Sutton-Smith, "Towards an Anthropology of Play," in *Sport in the Socio-Cultural Process,* 3rd ed., ed. Marie Hart and Susan Birrell, pp. 114-25; and "Games of Order and Disorder," in *Sport in the Modern World: Changes and Problems,* ed. O. Gruppe. Sutton-Smith's arguments in these essays are extremely important, I believe, but they require "grounding" in concrete historical processes of class and status-group interaction.

34   Edward Thompson, *The Making of the English Working Class, p.* 442.

35   Francis Hearn, "Toward a Critical Theory of Play," *Telos* 30 (Winter 1976).

36   Donald Guay, "Problèmes de l'intégration du sport dans la société Canadienne, 1830-1865: Les cas des courses de chevaux," *Canadian Journal of History of Sport and Physical Education* 4:2 (1973).

37   Eric Dunning, "Industrialization and the Incipient Modernization of Football," *Stadion* 1:1 (1976).

38   Rupert Wilkinson, *Gentlemanly Power: British Leadership and Public School Tradition;* Walter Arnstein, "The Survival of the Victorian Aristocracy," in *The Rich, the Well-Born and the Powerful,* ed. F.C. Jaher.

39   Arnstein, "Survival of the Victorian Aristocracy," p. 236.

40   J.G. Hodgins, *Schools and Colleges of Ontario, 1792-1910,* vol. 1, p. 198.

41   In "Industrialization and the Incipient Modernization of Football," Eric Dunning notes how codified rules for rugby emerged in Britain by the 1850s. Similar rules did not develop in Canada until the 1860s. See the section on football in Howell and Howell, *Sports and Games in Canadian Life.*

42   One should not be surprised that cricket, at this stage in Canadian development, was the game for young gentlemen. S.F. Wise points out, for example, the social background of participants in a well-publicized cricket match

between Upper Canada College and the "gentlemen" of Toronto in 1836: "The list of participants is like a roll-call of the colonial elite: it included two Robinsons, two Keefers, a Philipott, a Boulton, Rowsell (the government printer), William Henry Draper and the inimitable Sir Francis Bond Head himself." See S.F. Wise, "Sport and Class Values in Old Ontario and Quebec," in *His Own Man: Essays in Honour of A.R.M. Lower,* ed. W.H. Heick and R. Graham. Sir Francis Bond Head's presence in the games may lend some support to the *Toronto Patriot's* contentions about the antagonisms between cricket and democracy. For Sir Francis was no friend of democratic thinking. Commenting in his *Narratives,* Sir Francis sought to oppose criticisms of the family compact of ruling merchants and gentry by noting that

> the "family compact" of Upper Canada is composed of those members of society who, either by their abilities or character, have been honoured by the confidence of the executive government or who by their industry and intelligence have amassed wealth. The party, I own, is comparatively a small one; but to put the multitude at the top and the few at the bottom is a radical revision of the pyramid of society which every reflecting man must foresee can end only by its downfall.

This statement is cited from F. Underhill, "The Liberal Tradition in Canada," in *Approaches to Canadian History,* ed. Carl Berger.

43   On the decline of cricket in Canada see S.F. Wise and D. Fisher, *Canada's Sporting Heroes.*

44   Cf. Ryerson, *Unequal Union,* p. 133.

45   Cf. Tom Naylor, "The Rise and Fall of the Third Commercial Empire of the St. Lawrence," in *Capitalism and the National Question in Canada,* ed. G. Teeple, p. 9.

46   See Creighton, *The Empire of the St. Lawrence.*

47   For example, capital-intensive expenditures in such areas as transportation (first canals and later railroads) could not be financed within the colony and brought the commercial capitalist and politicians together in order to petition British financial houses which demanded state-guaranteed loans. The colonial mercantile connection was also maintained, as Myers has pointed out, by the continuing power of chartered mercantile companies, most notably, the Hudson's Bay Company. See Wallace Clement, *The Canadian Corporate Elite,* pp. 53-55; and Gustavus Myers, *A History of Canadian Wealth,* p. 140.

48   Cf. Cross, *The Workingman,* p. 2.

49   See Allison Prentice's discussion of this controversy in *The School Promoters.*

50   Susan Houston, "Politics, Schools and Social Change in Upper Canada," *Canadian Historical Review* 3:3 (1972), p. 251.

51   See F. Cosentino and M. Howell, *A History of Physical Education in Canada;* J. Gear, "Factors Influencing the Development of Government-Sponsored Physical Fitness Programmes in Canada From 1850-1972," *Canadian Journal of History of Sport and Physical Education* 4:2 (1973); and T. Roberts, "The Influence of the British Upper Class on the Development of the Values Claim for Sport in the Public Education System of Upper Canada," *Canadian Journal of History of Sport and Physical Education* 4:1 (1973).

52   See Alan Metcalfe's paper "Organized Sport and Social Stratification in Montreal: 1840-1901." Metcalfe notes that there were a number of clubs

founded earlier in the century. However, the major growth of clubs occurred primarily between the 1850s and the 1880s.

53 Ibid.

54 See Robert Simpson's master's thesis, "The Influence of the Montreal Curling Club on the Development of Curling in the Canada's, 1807-1857." Simpson makes an important point about the ways in which the early rules of curling in Canada were more "socially restrictive" than "procedurally explicit," p. 67.

55 See Metcalfe, "Organized Sport," pp. 80-84.

56 The "rationalization" of working time refers to the processes whereby production was no longer geared to the natural rhythms of the day and season and became subject to arbitrary measurement. With the advent of the factory system a concept of time developed whereby time became progressively delineated into recognized divisions of "employer's time" or "work-time" and "free-time." This delineation was important to the creation of "modern" sport because it gave people the basic prerequisites of regular, organized sporting competitions—free time at regular intervals.

57 See Ian Jobling's discussion of these processes in R. Gruneau and J. Albinson, eds., *Canadian Sport: Sociological Perspectives.*

58 Cf. Cross, *The Workingman,* p. 5.

59 By "liberal-toryism" I am referring to the incorporation of certain elements of liberal values into the value system of the dominant classes in nineteenth-century Canada. The values are "liberal" because they reject the rigidly ascriptive bases of aristocratic rule and partially accept the notions of "self-help" and individual advancement through enterprise. They are "tory" because they continue to emphasize continuity and tradition and elements of paternalism and hierarchy and combine this with an outright rejection of "Republicanism."

60 Eric Dunning and Kenneth Sheard, "The Bifurcation of Rugby Union and Rugby League: A Case Study of Organizational Conflict and Change," *International Review of Sport Sociology* 11:2 (1976).

61 Metcalfe, "Organized Sport."

62 Ibid., p. 81.

63 See Metcalfe, "Working Class Physical Recreation in Montreal, 1860-1895," *Working Papers in the Sociological Study of Sports and Leisure* 1:2 (1978).

64 See my discussion in "Sport, Social Differentiation and Social Inequality," pp. 130-31, in *Sport and Social Order,* ed. Don Ball and John Loy.

65 See John Mallea, "The Victorian Sporting Legacy," *McGill Journal of Education* 10:2 (1975).

66 Dunning and Sheard, "The Bifurcation of Rugby Union and Rugby League."

67 Alan Metcalfe has noted how many of the first "national" associations were national in name only. They drew their executives primarily from the business community in Ontario and Quebec. See "Organized Sport."

68 For support of this point see S.F. Wise, "Sport and Class Values in Old Ontario and Quebec"; Metcalfe, "Organized Sport"; and R. Gruneau, "Elites, Class and Corporate Power in Canadian Sport: Some Preliminary Findings."

69   T.W. Acheson, "The Social Origins of the Canadian Industrial Elite, 1880-1885," in *Canadian Business History,* ed. D.S. Macmillan.

70   There has been no attempt in current writing in Canadian sport history to delineate labor force sector differences in the backgrounds of sports organized in this key period in Canadian history. Because I believe these differences are important, I did some preliminary research on the topic. From *Lovell's Montreal Directory* (1885), Polk's *Toronto Directory* (1885), Wise and Fisher's *Canada's Sporting Heroes,* and *Athletic Life* (1896), I compiled a list (a sample based on availability) of the executives of major clubs and sporting associations (e.g., president, vice-president, and boards of directors). My sample included executives of the M.A.A. and affiliates, the A.A.U. of Canada, the Montreal and Toronto Jockey Clubs, the National Lacrosse Association, the Canadian Wheelman's Association, the Canadian Association of Amateur Oarsmen, the Canadian Rugby Union, and selected individuals who held two or more executive positions in sports clubs or who had been identified in newspaper accounts as key sports figures of the time. I ended up with over 100 executives and tried to use newspapers and city directories to discover their occupations. I was successful in 71 cases. Of the 71 executives, 48 percent were businessmen, bankers, merchants or store owners; 15 percent were managers and company executives; 17 percent were bookkeepers, clerks, and sales personnel; 11 percent were professionals; 7 percent were involved in military careers; and 2 percent were in skilled labor occupations. When I cross-classified the people in commercial occupations by economic sector, only about 10 percent of the executives were found to be involved in industry and manufacturing. By far the greatest concentration of executives was in the areas of finance (e.g., banking and retail or wholesale trade).

71   This is not to say that a certain proportion of Canada's elite fragments within the upper class was not involved. They were often present, but not in great numbers. On the issue of the Victorian focus and concerns for organization and hierarchy, consider the following notice of the Montreal Lacrosse Club on April 14, 1880, printed on its withdrawal from the (increasingly "professional") National Lacrosse Association of Canada:

> It is a well established fact that no pastime has ever been fostered by professionalism; and once the money element is introduced into a game it loses prestige, the continuance of the better and more desirable class is alienated; trickery, subterfuge and disreputable means are brought into play and all idea of legitimate sport and fair play is abandoned to the wind.

On a somewhat similar line, consider the following example of the emphasis on discipline and rank in late nineteenth-century "Victorian" club sports in the constitution by-laws of the Montreal Bicycle Club in 1883.

> Section 1: No member while riding with the club shall be allowed to pass the officer in command without his permission. Section 2: All officers shall be provided with whistles and badges denoting rank.

72   See Acheson, "Social Origins of the Canadian Industrial Elite."

73   An example of this economic "nationalism" was the National Policy, a controversial tariff designed to attract foreign capital into Canadian manufacturing as well as to stimulate domestic industrial capital accumulation. The National Policy asserted the independence of Canada from American expansionism in the West and "declared that central Canada was to rule the

western hinterland." See Wallace Clement, *The Canadian Corporate Elite,* p. 63.

74 This is not to say that all members of the "amateur" sports associations completely accepted temperance as a value (although it is quite likely that even in these cases "moderation" was the norm). Indeed, even for many of the "amateur" associations the tavern remained a place for meetings and club celebrations. On the function of the tavern in the social development of Canadian sport, see H. A. Christie's M.P.E. thesis, "The Function of the Tavern in Toronto, 1834-1875, with Special Reference to Sport."

75 Dunning and Sheard, "Bifurcation of Rugby Union and Rugby League."

76 Much more research is needed on this point. Fragmentary evidence can be found, however, in Alan Metcalfe's paper, "Working Class Physical Recreation in Montreal, 1860-1895," and Bryan Palmer's chapter, "In Street and Field and Hall," in *A Culture in Conflict.*

77 Metcalfe, "Organized Sport."

78 For discussions of the role of Mechanics' Institutes in Canadian working-class life, see Pentland, *Labour and Capital in Canada,* pp. 182-84. For a slightly different type of analysis see Palmer, *Culture in Conflict,* pp. 49-52.

79 See Metcalfe, "Working Class Physical Recreation." For a history of Canadian recreation, see Elsie McFarland, *The Development of Public Recreation in Canada.*

80 Metcalfe, "Working Class Physical Recreation," p. 22.

81 Ibid.

82 On the importance of baseball in Canadian working-class culture, see Palmer, *Culture in Conflict,* chap. 2.

83 Metcalfe, "Working Class Physical Recreation."

84 Ian Jobling, "Urbanization and Sport in Canada, 1867-1900," in *Canadian Sport: Sociological Perspectives,* ed., Richard Gruneau and John Albinson. Also see Palmer, *Culture in Conflict.*

85 See the short account of "Ned Hanlan and National Pride," in Cross, *The Workingman,* pp. 225-26. Also see Jobling, "Urbanization and Sport in Canada." Jobling notes, for example, that the railway companies knew that Ned Hanlan's popularity as a rowing champion would bring revenue from passenger traffic, "so commissions were paid to the Hanlan Club (a group of businessmen that managed Hanlan's rowing commitments), which subsequently gave Hanlan his share."

86 See John Mallea, "The Victorian Sporting Legacy," *McGill Journal of Education* 10:2 (1975).

87 For a detailed chronicle of the development of the concept of professionalism in Canadian sport, see Frank Cosentino's Ph.D. dissertation, "A History of the Concept of Professionalism in Canadian Sport".

88 While I was going through the minute books of the Canadian Rugby Union, 1891-1916, I was struck by the endless debates over "amateurism" and professionalism that occurred both within the organization and over its relationships to other organizations. At least one "issue" pertaining to amateurism was discussed at every annual meeting in the period examined.

89 Dunning and Sheard, "Bifurcation of Rugby Union and Rugby League."

90   On the concept of "scientific play" see John Weiler, "The Idea of Sport in Late Victorian Canada," a paper presented at the annual meeting of the Canadian Historical Association, Kingston (June 1974). A relevant portion of this paper is included in Cross, *The Workingman,* pp. 228-31.

91   See my discussion in "Sport, Social Differentiation and Social Inequality," in *Sport and Social Order,* ed. D. Ball and J. Loy, pp. 129-32.

92   Metcalfe, "Organized Sport."

93   Wise and Fisher note in *Canada's Sporting Heroes* how many of the first promoters and organizers of "professional" sports were originally tavern owners and small businessmen. See also Bryan Palmer's discussion of Hamilton sports clubs in *A Culture in Conflict;* and Bruce Kidd, *The Political Economy of Sport.*

94   Michael Bliss, *A Living Profit: Studies in the Social History of Canadian Business, 1883-1911.*

95   In fact, Terry Copp has argued in *The Anatomy of Poverty: The Condition of the Working Class in Montreal, 1897-1929,* that social inequalities in Montreal became more pronounced in this period.

96   Eugen Weber has argued that because the economic slumps of the latter two decades of the nineteenth century meant higher relative incomes for the upper and middle classes in Europe, the "leisured young" could devote much of their time to sporting activity before joining the labor force. This argument is only partially applicable to the Canadian scene, but there is no doubt that economic recession helped to define the generally restricted and class-based character of "amateur" sport by limiting the "participation resources" of the working class. Commercial sport, on the other hand, offered financial returns for participation that partially offset these limitations. See Eugen Weber, "Gymnastics and Sports in fin-de-siècle France: Opium of the Classes," *American Historical Review* 76:1 (1971).

97   Wallace Clement, *The Canadian Corporate Elite,* p. 104.

98   Harry Braverman, *Labour and Monopoly Capital.*

99   Canada Public Records, Division Holdings Inventory (Sport), The National Archives, Ottawa.

100   See the history of hockey presented in Wise and Fisher, *Canada's Sporting Heroes.*

101   See Bruce Kidd, *The Political Economy of Sport,* p. 34.

102   Colin Jones, "The Economics of the National Hockey League," in *Canadian Sport: Sociological Perspectives,* ed. Richard Gruneau and John Albinson.

103   On the "cartel" nature of modern professional team sports, see Roger Noll, "The U.S. Team Sports Industry: An Introduction," in *Government and the Sports Business.*

104   See Jones's discussion of these developments in "Economics of the National Hockey League." As an illustration, however, consider the following example. According to *Financial Post* records, between 1966 and 1974, the Toronto Maple Leaf Hockey Club made $4,581,715 through expansion franchise fees and the selling of a farm club. This breaks down to an extra $572,714 per season *in excess of normal operating profits.* Further examples of such profits can be found in Bruce Kidd's discussion of "cartelization" in hockey in *The Political Economy of Sport.*

105 The case of the Canadian Football League is a fascinating one and cannot be dealt with in detail here. As noted above, its development has been greatly influenced by *internal* dependency relations between bourgeois class fractions in eastern and western Canada. This East-West tension and its association to the economic organization of the league, to league rules, and to the broader cultural significance of the game itself has been noted many times but has rarely been subjected to rigorous analysis. However, for a history of the C.F.L., see Frank Cosentino, *Canadian Football: The Grey Cup Years.*

106 A comparison with John Betts's work, *America's Sporting Heritage, 1850-1950* would be valuable here. It should be noted, however, that in comparing the two countries the absence of a strong indigenous industrial bourgeoisie in Canada and the continued ties with Britain facilitated the comparatively greater strength of the Victorian legacy of the gentleman-amateur as the *dominant* definition of acceptable sporting practice in Canada.

107 One of the reasons for this was the degree to which larger numbers of the amateur clubs were so "temperance-minded." To cite an example, consider the following description of the rationale for the founding of the Toronto Athenaeum Club as noted in *Athletic Life* 3, no. 1, 1896: "in the spring of 1883, several public spirited young men recognizing that they and other young men, engaged during the day in professional and mercantile pursuits, required recreation of a healthy character, free from the objectionable associations of drinking and gambling, determined to organize a club of such a character."

108 An interesting statistical analysis of the career paths of Canadian hockey players (up to the early 1970s) can be found in M. Smith and F. Diamond, "Career Mobility in Professional Hockey," in *Canadian Sport: Sociological Perspectives,* ed. Richard Gruneau and John Albinson.

109 Charles Page, "Introduction: The World of Sport and Its Study," in *Sport and Society: An Anthology,* ed. John Talamini and Charles Page.

110 B. Okner, "Taxation and Sports Enterprises," in *Government and the Sports Business,* ed. Roger Noll.

111 Yet there is no doubt that sports promoters and team owners worked extremely hard to get their particular "message" across. John Bassett, owner of the Toronto Argonauts and chairman of the board of the Toronto Maple Leafs in the mid-1960s is quoted in a 1967 *Financial Post* article as saying: "You must educate your audience and merchandise your product (Sport), and this can be done through television" (p. 141). This awareness of the power of television should not be surprising, in that Bassett also had extensive media interests including C.T.V. See Wallace Clement's discussion of the Bassett media complex in the 1960s and 1970s in *The Canadian Corporate Elite.* On a similar point, in *Rip Off the Big Game,* Paul Hoch cites the above quote by Bassett, as well as another *Financial Post* story which featured plans by the Montreal Expos baseball team to "educate" their future fans in Quebec with a series of special half-hour television shows.

112 On the history of the media in Canada during this period, see Albert Shea, *Broadcasting the Canadian Way;* and Paul Rutherford, *The Making of the Canadian Media.* For a preliminary study of sport and the Canadian media, see G. Smith and C. Blackman, *Sport in the Mass Media.* It is certainly no accident that the growth of commercial sport in the 1960s in Canada paralleled the growth of Canadian television.

113 See, for a general discussion of this point, Ira Horowitz, "Sports Broadcasting," in *Government and the Sports Business,* ed. Roger Noll.

114 As Colin Jones notes in "The Economics of the National Hockey League," N.H.L. owners have frequently argued that they should be exempt from rules in the *Combines Act* which constrain normal business practices, because hockey provides a valuable "community service" and requires special status in order to function effectively.

115 A discussion of broader intercorporate linkages between Canadian and American companies can be found in Wallace Clement, *Continental Corporate Power.*

116 See, as an example, Bruce Kidd's discussion in *The Political Economy of Sport* (p. 42) of how the N.H.L. elected to put a new franchise in Oakland in 1967 because of their search for a national American television market. This was done despite the promise of greater box office support in Vancouver.

117 Clement, *Continental Corporate Power,* p. 20.

118 P. Kiviaho and M. Simola, "Who Leads Sport in Finland?" *Eripainos Sosiologia* N:05-6 (1974).

119 For discussions of the workers' sport movement see D. Steinberg, "The Workers' Sport Internationals, 1920-28," *Journal of Contemporary History* 13:2 (1978); and R.F. Wheeler, "Organized Sport and Organized Labour," *Journal of Contemporary History* 13:2 (1978).

120 Bruce Kidd, "Canadian Participation in the People's Olympic Games of 1936," a paper presented at the annual meeting of the North American Association for Sport History, Windsor, Ontario (1977).

121 The W.S.A. also sponsored teams in a variety of industrial and amateur leagues. See Bruce Kidd, "Canadian Opposition to the 1936 Olympics in Germany," *Canadian Journal of History of Sport and Physical Education* 9:2 (1978), p. 28.

122 The "People's Olympics" were ill-fated because the Spanish Civil War broke out on the morning of the scheduled opening ceremonies and the games were cancelled. See ibid.

123 Kidd, "Canadian Participation," p. 35.

124 The extent to which the cultural emphasis and meanings of workers' sports differed from bourgeois sports is an important question that needs to be researched. There have been some suggestions that the beginnings of an "alternative" to bourgeois sport may have been evident in the international workers' sports movement. The rationale for this argument is that the internationalist emphasis of workers' sports was closely tied to a conception of working-class solidarity and sociability which made social transformation a central goal. Certainly the early Workers' Olympics held in conjunction with the Socialist Workers' Sports International in 1921 and 1931 were extremely successful and politically important. However, workers' sports often came in contact with bourgeois sport on the basis of standards and traditions that had emerged out of bourgeois culture. These standards and traditions dramatized bourgeois rather than working-class interests and meant that workers could not compete on their own terms. Moreover, any international thrust of workers' sports as an alternative to bourgeois sport was completely undermined when the Soviet Union was accepted for membership by the International Olympic Committee.

125   See C. Lipton, *The Trade Union Movement of Canada, 1827-1959;* R. Howard and J. Scott, "International Unions and the ideology of Class Collaboration," in *Capitalism and the National Question in Canada,* ed. Gary Teeple; and I. Abella and D. Millar, eds., *The Canadian Worker in the Twentieth Century.*

126   Howard and Scott, "International Unions."

127   Interview with Bob Russell, 1958. *Public Archives of Manitoba,* cited in Abella and Millar, *The Canadian Worker in the Twentieth Century,* p. 53. Also see R.F. Wheeler, "Organized Sport and Organized Labour," *Journal of Contemporary History* 13:2 (1978). Wheeler notes, in a general discussion of the role of sport in relationships between business and labor, that sport was often used by management as a way to combat worker militancy and ensure "industrial peace."

128   Although at the cultural level this does not mean workers cannot "penetrate" the commodity form of sport and, in some cases, use this form and adapt it to their own advantages. This point, however, is an extremely crucial one and requires considerably more attention than it has received in writing on sport and ideology or sport and culture.

129   See, for some examples, Jim Curtis and Brian Milton, "Social Status and the 'Active' Society," in *Canadian Sport: Sociological Perspectives,* ed. Richard Gruneau and John Albinson; and my essay, "Class or Mass: Notes on the Democratization of Canadian Amateur Sport," in the same volume.

130   See Gruneau, "Class or Mass."

131   It is in such associations that a residual emphasis on amateurism (in modified form) remains strongest. The Canadian Olympic Association is both exclusive and closely connected as an "elite forum" to Canada's corporate elite. Consider, in this regard, the social composition of the special fund-raising arm of the C.O.A., the Olympic Trust. The Olympic Trust involves some of the most powerful people in the Canadian business community. Comparing members of the Olympic Trust to the Canadian corporate elite (as defined by Wallace Clement) it was found that the trust is an impressive assembly of representatives from Canada's dominant class and reveals a predictable association with established financial capital. Of the 43 members of the trust, 30 can be classed as members of Clement's "corporate elite." These 30 hold 85 "dominant" directorships in 113 dominant corporations in Canada, including notable interlocks with commercial sport and with 23 major corporations who have more than one director on the Olympic Trust. Among the banks alone, the Canadian Imperial Bank of Commerce is represented by eight directorships, the Royal Bank by seven, the Bank of Nova Scotia by three, and the Toronto Dominion and Bank of Montreal with two each. I want to thank Wally Clement for bringing these relationships to my attention.

132   Rob Beamish, "Socio-Economic and Demographic Characteristics of the National Executives of Selected Amateur Sports in Canada," *Working Papers in the Sociological Study of Sports and Leisure* 1:1 (1978).
      Bob Hollands and I have gone on and incorporated Beamish's data into a larger study of the *changing* social origins of these executives since 1955. Our study not only gives support to Beamish's analysis, but also shows how there has been no democratization whatsoever in recruitment to executive positions in sports organizations. In fact, our data seems to suggest an increasing crystallization of exclusivity. Over 46 percent of the executives

in 1975 had fathers who were involved in managerial, professional, or technical occupations, compared to 37 percent in 1955. Over 80 percent of the executives sampled were themselves involved in managerial, professional, or technical work compared to 66 percent in 1955. See Robert Hollands and Richard Gruneau, "Social Class and Voluntary Action in the Administration of Canadian Amateur Sport," *Working Papers in the Sociological Study of Sports and Leisure* 2:3 (1979).

133   Beamish, "Socio-Economic and Demographic Characteristics," p. 25.

134   The most thorough presentation of data documenting the growth of Canadian government involvement in sport is Bill Hallett's Ph.D. dissertation, "A History of Federal Government Involvement in the Development of Sport in Canada, 1943-1979". Also see Eric Broom and Richard Baka, *Canadian Governments and Sport.* These studies tend to be excellent descriptive analyses but lack any theoretical basis. Moreover, when causal explanations are included they tend to be directed at the level of individual agents rather than broader limits and pressures of change. In this brief sketch of state sport I want to focus upon these broader concerns.

135   And, as Bruce Kidd notes in *The Political Economy of Sport,* when there has been intervention, as in the case of the attempt to bring a World Football League team to Toronto in the early 1970s, the state acted to support the monopoly position of the C.F.L. On the other hand, the state has also put pressure on both the C.F.L. and N.H.L. on numerous occasions through the *Combines Act* and various features of Federal Budgets.

136   I do not have space here to discuss all the forces and events surrounding the Task Force report in the late 1960s (and responses to it). It will suffice, perhaps, to note that the 1960s was a time of nationalist fervor in Canada, and this spilled over into an attempt by the state to develop a more aggressive nationalist cultural policy. A unique combination of circumstances allowed sport to become increasingly drawn into this policy. But the type of sport that became emphasized in most programs was a kind of elite or high performance sport rather than some other form. This occurred in part because of the perceived need to effectively "market" the new "products" of Canadian sports policy, and elite sport is most amenable to this type of marketing.

137   The 1969 report prepared by *P. S. Ross and Partners* for the Directorate of Fitness and Amateur Sport referred to the importance of expanding the visibility and media coverage of new government programs in sport and of Canadian amateur athletes in general. The Ross Report noted that media coverage of the Canada Games, for example, did not really take off until the games were presented in a "professional" way. There was a need, then, to properly "package" and present the new amateur sports "product." In such arguments one sees the penetration of commodified conceptions of sport interweaving, through the state, with more traditional amateur conceptions.

138   For a recent collection of papers which lay out the preliminary ground work for such speculation, see Hart Cantelon and Richard Gruneau, *Sport, Culture and the Modern State.*

139   Nicos Poulantzas, "The Problem of the Capitalist State," in *Ideology in Social Science,* ed. Robin Blackburn; see also Louis Althusser, *Lenin and Philosophy and Other Essays.*

140   Willis, *Learning to Labour,* p. 176.

141   See Leo Panitch, "The Role and Nature of the Canadian State," in *The Canadian State: Political Economy and Political Power;* and Kay Herman, "The Emerging Welfare State: Changing Perspectives in Canadian Welfare Policies and Programs, 1867-1960," in *Social Space: Canadian Perspectives,* ed. D.I. Davies and K. Herman.

142   See Ronald Labonte's intriguing criticism of Canadian health and fitness programs, "Half-Truths About Health," *Policy Options* 3:1 (January/February 1982).

143   Indeed, it was in large measure a response to the "challenge" to democracy posed by the success of Soviet athletes that Canadian state programs in organized sports were initiated. See Bruce Kidd's discussion of this point in *The Political Economy of Sport.*

144   This comment refers to Iona Campagnolo, Minister of State for Sport and Fitness, whose well-publicized remarks about the federal government's medal "expectations" prompted British journalists to refer to Canada as the "East Germany of Commonwealth Sport."

Chapter 4   The Limits and Possibilities of Modern Sport

1   For example, Allen Guttmann has done this in *From Ritual to Record* with respect to the centrality of the "scientific world view."

2   Raymond Williams, *Marxism and Literature.*

3   Richard Lipsky, *How We Play the Game: Why Sports Dominate American Life.* Lipsky's discussion of the attractions of sports is excellent, but he tends to overlook the important ways in which sports occasionally become forums for *resistance* to modes of domination in social life. His "political theory" of sports symbolism, in this sense, overemphasizes the integrative features of sport and ignores the fragile nature of hegemony. Similarly, his discussions of power and integration lack "grounding" in any discussion of conflicting class interests.

4   In developing this argument I have relied heavily on Stuart Hall's discussion of ideology and media "products" in "The Rediscovery of Ideology: Return of the Repressed in Media Studies."

A Postscript, 15 Years Later

1   *Silencing the Past: Power and the Production of History* (Boston: Beacon Press, 1995), p. xix.

2   These ideas were first introduced in Giddens's books *New Rules of Sociological Method* (New York: Basic books, 1976); *Studies in Social and Political Theory* (Berkeley: University of California Press, 1979); and *Central Problems in Social Theory* (Berkeley: University of California Press, 1979). The theory of structuration is elaborated more fully in Giddens's later book *The Constitution of Society* (Cambridge: Polity Press, 1984).

3   I found the opening essay on "Power and Structure" in Lukes's book *Essays in Social Theory* (New York: Columbia University Press, 1977) to be particularly useful.

4   See, for example, Giddens's discussion of Goffman and the intersections between "discursive" and "practical" consciousness in *The Constitution of Society,* pp. 68-73.

5   My reading of Williams's treatment of these concepts was especially indebted to *Marxism and Literature* (Oxford: Oxford University Press, 1977).

6   Clifford Geertz, "Deep Play: Notes on the Balinese Cockfight", *Daedalus*, Winter 1972.

7   Useful overviews of the "Gramscian" turn in cultural studies in the late 1970s and early 1980s can be found in *Popular Culture and Social Relations*, eds. Tony Bennett, Colin Mercer, and Janet Woollacott (Milton Keynes: Open University Press, 1986). An additional overview can be found in my essay "Notes on Popular Culture and Political Practice" in *Popular Culture and Political Practices*, ed. Richard Gruneau (Toronto: Garamond Press, 1988). A provocative critical assessment of the uses of Gramsci in contemporary cultural studies can be found in David Harris, *From Class Struggle to the Politics of Pleasure* (London: Routledge, 1992). Useful histories of the Canadian political economy tradition can be found in *The New Canadian Political Economy*, eds. Wallace Clement and Glen Williams (Montreal: McGill-Queen's University Press, 1989) and *Understanding Canada: Building on the New Canadian Political Economy* (Montreal: McGill-Queen's University Press, 1997).

8   For example, see Bourdieu's discussion of social practice and the "habitus" in *Outline of a Theory of Practice* (Cambridge: Cambridge University Press, 1977, originally published in 1972). My discussion of "rules" in sport as social practices came from an attempt to synthesize some ideas from John Searle's discussion of speech acts, Giddens's discussion of structuration, and Bourdieu's arguments about social reproduction. But I paid insufficient attention to Bourdieu's key insight that rules are necessarily *embodied* practices. A useful discussion of rules as embodied practices can be found in Charles Taylor, "To Follow a Rule . . ." in *Bourdieu: Critical Perspectives*, eds. Craig Calhoun, Edward LiPuma and Moishe Postone (Chicago: University of Chicago Press, 1993), pp. 45-60.

9   This point is developed further in Richard Gruneau, "The Critique of Sport in Modernity: Theorizing Power, Culture, and the Politics of the Body" in *The Sports Process: A Comparative and Developmental Approach*, eds. Eric Dunning, Joseph Maguire, and Robert Pearton (Champaign, IL: Human Kinetics Press, 1993), pp. 85-109.

10   Jacques Derrida, *Specters of Marx: the State of the Debt, the Work of the Mourning, and the New International* (London: Routledge, 1994).

11   Examples include: Richard Gruneau, David Whitson, and Hart Cantelon, "Methods and Media: Studying the Sports/Television Discourse", *Loisir et Societé*, 11, 2, (1988), pp. 265-279; Hart Cantelon and Richard Gruneau, "The Production of Sport for Television" in *Not Just a Game*, eds. Jean Harvey and Hart Cantelon (Ottawa, University of Ottawa Press, 1988), pp. 177-193; and Richard Gruneau, "Making Spectacle: A Case Study in Television Sports Production" in *Media, Sports and Society*, ed. Larry Wenner (Newbury Park, CA: Sage, 1989), pp. 134-154.

12   Some of these themes are explored in Richard Gruneau and David Whitson, *Hockey Night in Canada: Sport, Identities, and Cultural Politics* (Toronto: Garamond Press, 1993).

13   Useful summaries of these processes, and differing explanations of them, can be found in David Harvey, *The Condition of Postmodernity* (Cambridge: Basil Blackwell, 1989); *Post-Fordism*, ed. Ash Amin (Oxford: Blackwell, 1994);

and Manuel Castells, *The Information Age: Economy, Society and Culture. Vol. 1. The Rise of the Network Society* (Oxford: Blackwell, 1997).

14   See Castells, *The Information Age. Vol. 2. The Power of Identity* (Oxford: Blackwell, 1997); and the essays in *Culture, Globalization and the World-System*, ed. A.D. King (London: Macmillan, 1991).

15   A wide range of issues associated with this point are discussed in David Rowe and Geoffrey Lawrence "Beyond National Sport: Sociology, History and Postmodernity", *Sporting Traditions* 12, 2 (May, 1996), pp. 3-16; B. Houlihan, "Homogenization, Americanization, and Creolization of Sport: Varieties of Globalization", *Sociology of Sport Journal*, 11 (1994), pp. 356-375; J. Maguire, "Sport, Identity Politics and Globalization: Diminishing Contrasts and Increasing Varieties", *Sociology of Sport Journal*, 11 (1994), pp. 398-427; and Gruneau and Whitson, *Hockey Night in Canada*, Chapters 9-12, pp. 199-283.

16   For some illustrative works by Elias see *The Civilizing Process* (Oxford: Blackwell, 1978; 2 vols.; originally published in 1939); *The Civilizing Process, vol.2: State Formation and Civilization* (Oxford: Blackwell, 1982); *What Is Sociology* (London: Hutchinson, 1978); and *Involvement and Detachment* (Oxford: Blackwell, 1987). Elias's contribution to the sociology of sport is evident in Norbert Elias and Eric Dunning, *Quest for Excitement* (Oxford: Blackwell, 1986).

17   Joseph Maguire, "Sport, Identity Politics and Globalization", *Sociology of Sport Journal*, 11 (1994); and "Globalization and Sportization: A Figurational Process/Sociological Perspective", *Avante*, 4, No. 1, (1998), pp. 67-89.

18   Eric Dunning "Industrialization and the Incipient Modernization of Football," *Stadion*, 1, 1 (1976); Eric Dunning and Kenneth Sheard, *Barbarians, Gentlemen and Players* (London: Martin Robertson, 1979).

19   See, for example, Michel Foucault, *The Order of Things* (London: Tavistock, 1970); *The Archaeology of Knowledge* (London: Tavistock, 1974); *Discipline and Punish: The Birth of the Prison* (New York: Vintage Books, 1977); *Power/Knowledge: Selected Interviews and Other Writings, 1972-1977* (Brighton: Harvester Press, 1980); and *The History of Sexuality* (Harmondsworth, Middlesex: Penguin, 1981). Useful discussions of Foucault's work in respect to the sociology of sport can be found in Jean Harvey and Robert Sparks, "The Politics of the Body in the Context of Modernity", *Quest*, 43 (1989), pp. 164-189; Cheryl Cole, "Resisting the Canon: Feminist Cultural Studies, Sport, and Technologies of the Body", *Journal of Sport and Social Issues*, 17, No. 2 (August, 1993); and David Andrews, "Desperately Seeking Michel: Foucault's Geneology, the Body, and Critical Sport Sociology", *Sociology of Sport Journal*, 10 (1995), pp. 148-167.

20   Robert Connell, "Why is Classical Theory Classical?", *American Journal of Sociology*, Vol. 102, 6 (1997), p. 1512.

21   Connell, "Why is Classical Theory Classical?", p. 1511.

22   Connell, "Why is Classical Theory Classical?", p. 1535.

23   Connell, "Why is Classical Theory Classical?", p.1546.

24   In the North American literature, both Susan Birrell and Cheryl Cole began to develop an interest in the intersections between gender and race in the late 1980s and early 1990s. See Susan Birrell, "Race Relations in Sport: Suggestions for a More Critical Analysis", *Sociology of Sport Journal*, 6 (1989), pp. 212-227; and "Women of Color, Critical Autobiography, and

Sport" in *Sport, Men and the Gender Order: Critical Feminist Perspectives,* ed. M.A. Messner and D. Sabo (Champaign, IL: Human Kinetics Publishers, 1990), pp. 185-189; and Cheryl Cole and H. Denny, "Visualizing Deviance in Post-Reagan America: Magic Johnson, Aids, and the Promiscuous World of Professional Sport", *Critical Sociology*, 20 (1995), pp. 123-147.

25   For an example, see John Bale and Joe Sang, *Kenyan Running: Movement Culture, Geography, and Global Change,* (London: Frank Cass, 1996).

26   See, for example, J.A. Mangan, "Duty Unto Death: English Masculinity and Militarism in the Age of the New Imperialism", *The International Journal of the History of Sport*, 12, no. 2, (1995), pp. 10-38; Richard Holt, "Contrasting Nationalisms: Sport, Militarism, and the Unitary State in Britain and France before 1914", *The International Journal of the History of Sport*, 12, No. 2 (1995), pp. 39-54.

27   The reasons students gave for their choices ranged from an attraction to big time U.S. sports, such as the NBA, to the comparative absence of research articles on other dimensions of "race and sport". (The lack of material on Asian athletes and Asian identities in sport was a frequently-voiced complaint.)

28   Manual Castells, *The Information Age: Economy, Society and Culture. Vol. 2. The Power of Identity* (Oxford: Blackwell, 1997), p. 199.

29   Nancy Fraser, *Unruly Practices: Power, Gender and Discourse in Contemporary Social Theory* (Minneapolis: University of Minnesota Press, 1989), p. 4.

30   Bianca Beccali, "The Modern Women's Movement in Italy", *New Left Review,* 204, March/April (1994), p. 86.

references

Abella, I., and Millar, D., eds. *The Canadian Worker in the Twentieth Century.* Toronto: Oxford University Press, 1978.

Abrams, P. "History, Sociology, Historical Sociology." *Past and Present* 87, May 1980.

Acheson, T.W. "The Social Origins of the Canadian Industrial Elite, 1880-1885." In *Canadian Business History,* edited by D.S. Macmillan. Toronto: McClelland and Stewart, 1972.

Althusser, L. *For Marx.* Middlesex: Penguin Books, 1969.

——. *Lenin and Philosophy and Other Essays.* London: New Left Books, 1971.

Amin, S. *Unequal Development.* Sussex: Harvester Press, 1976.

Anderson, P. *Arguments within English Marxism.* London: New Left Books, 1980.

Arnstein, W. "The Survival of the Victorian Aristocracy." In *The Rich, the Well-Born and the Powerful,* edited by F.C. Jaher. Urbana: University of Illinois Press, 1973.

Aron, R. *The Industrial Society.* New York: Praeger, 1967.

Axelos, K. *Vers la pensé planétaire.* Paris, 1964.

Bailey, P. *Leisure and Class in Victorian England.* London: Routledge, 1978.

——. "Rational Recreation: The Social Control of Leisure and Popular Culture in Victorian England, 1830-1885." Ph.D. dissertation, University of British Columbia, 1975.

Bakhtin, M. *Rabelais and His World.* Cambridge: M.I.T. Press, 1968.

Barthes, R. *Mythologies.* London: Paladin Books, 1973.

Beamish, R. "Socio-Economic and Demographic Characteristics of the National Executives of Selected Amateur Sports in Canada." *Working Papers in the Sociological Study of Sports and Leisure,* vol. 1 (1). Kingston: *Our Time:* Middlesex: Penguin Books, 1965.

Berlin, I. "Does Political Theory Still Exist?" In *Philosophy, Politics and Society,* edited by P. Laslett and W.G. Runciman. 2d Series. Oxford: Basil Blackwell, 1962.

Bernstein, R. *The Restructuring of Social and Political Theory.* Philadelphia: University of Pennsylvania Press, 1978.

Berryman, J. "Review of *From Ritual to Record.*" *American Historical Review* 84(2), April 1979.

Berryman, J., and Loy, J. "Secondary Schools and Ivy League Letters." *The British Journal of Sociology* 27, March 1976.

Béteille, A. *Social Inequality.* Baltimore: Penguin Books, 1969.

Betts, J. *America's Sporting Heritage, 1850-1950.* Reading: Addison Wesley, 1974.

Birnbaum, N. "An End to Sociology?" In *Crisis and Contention in Sociology,* edited by T. Bottomore. London: Sage Publications, 1975.

Birrell, S. "Review of *From Ritual to Record.*" *International Committee for Sociology of Sport Bulletin* 15, November 1978.

Blau, P. *Exchange and Power in Social Life.* New York: John Wiley, 1964.

Bliss, M. *A Living Profit: Studies in the Social History of Canadian Business, 1883-1911.* Toronto: McClelland and Stewart, 1974.

Boggs, C. *Gramsci's Marxism.* London: Pluto Press, 1976.

Boileau, R., et al. "Les Canadiens francais et les grands jeux Internationaux." In *Canadian Sport: Sociological Perspectives,* edited by R. Gruneau and J. Albinson. Toronto: Addison-Wesley, 1976.

Bottomore, T. *Sociology: A Guide to Problems and Literature.* New York: Vintage Books, 1972.

Bourdieu, P. "Sport and Social Class." *Social Science Information* 17(6), 1978.

Brailsford, D. *Sport and Society: Elizabeth to Anne.* Toronto: University of Toronto Press, 1969.

Braverman, H. *Labour and Monopoly Capital.* New York: Monthly Review Press, 1974.

Brohm, J.-M. *Sport: A Prison of Measured Time.* London: Ink Links, 1978.

Broom, E., and Baka, R. *Canadian Governments and Sport.* Ottawa: Canadian Association of Health, Physical Education and Recreation, 1978.

Burdge, R. "Levels of Occupational Prestige and Leisure Activity." In *Sport and American Society,* edited by G.H. Sage. Reading: Addison-Wesley, 1974.

Burnet, J.R. "The Urban Community and Changing Moral Standards." In *Urbanism and the Changing Canadian Society,* edited by S.D. Clark. Toronto: University of Toronto Press, 1961.

Cady, E. *The Big Game: College Sports and American Life.* Knoxville: University of Tennessee Press, 1978.

Caillois, R. *Man, Play and Games.* New York: The Free Press, 1961.

Cardoso, F. "The Consumption of Dependency Theory in the United States." *Latin American Research Review* 12(3), 1977.

Cardoso, F., and Faletto, E. *Dependencia y Desarrotio en América Latina.* Mexico: D.F. Siglo, 1971.

Careless, J.M.S., ed. *Colonists and Canadians 1760-1867.* Toronto: Macmillan, 1971.

————. *Canada: A Story of Challenge.* 3rd ed. Toronto: Macmillan, 1970.

————. "Frontierism, Metropolitanism, and Canadian History." In *Approaches to Canadian History,* edited by C. Berger. Toronto: University of Toronto Press, 1967.

Christie, H.A. "The Function of the Tavern in Toronto, 1834-1875, with Special Reference to Sport." M.P.E. thesis, University of Windsor, 1973.

Clarke, J.; Critcher, C.; and Johnson, R., eds. *Working Class Culture: Studies in History and Theory.* London: Hutchinson, 1979.

Clement, W. *The Canadian Corporate Elite.* Toronto: McClelland and Stewart, 1975.

————. *Continental Corporate Power.* Toronto: McClelland and Stewart, 1977.

Clements, K., and Drache, D., eds. "Symposium on Progressive Modes of Nationalism in New Zealand, Canada and Australia." *Australia and New Zealand Journal of Sociology* 14(3), October 1978.

Coakley, J. *Sport in Society: Issues and Controversies.* 2d ed. St. Louis: C.V. Mosby, 1982.

Cockroft, J., et al. *Dependence and Underdevelopment: Latin America's Political Economy.* New York: Anchor Books, 1972.

Connerton, P. *Critical Sociology.* Middlesex: Penguin Books, 1976.

Copp, T. *The Anatomy of Poverty: The Condition of the Working Class in Montreal, 1897-1929.* Toronto: McClelland and Stewart, 1974.

Cosentino, F. *Canadian Football: The Grey Cup Years.* Toronto: Musson, 1969.

————. "A History of the Concept of Professionalism in Canadian Sport." Ph.D. dissertation, University of Alberta, 1973.

Cosentino, F., and Howell, M. *A History of Physical Education in Canada.* Toronto General Publishing, 1971.

Creighton, D. *The Empire of the St. Lawrence.* Toronto: Macmillan, 1970.

Cross, M., ed. *The Workingman in the Nineteenth Century.* Toronto: Oxford University Press, 1974.

Curtis, J., and Milton, B. "Social Status and the 'Active' Society." In *Canadian Sport: Sociological Perspectives,* edited by R. Gruneau and J. Albinson. Toronto: Addison-Wesley, 1976.

Dahrendorf, R. *Class and Class Conflict in Industrial Society.* Stanford: Stanford University Press, 1959.

Drache, D., and Clement, W. *A Practical Guide to Canadian Political Economy.* Toronto: James Lorimer, 1978.

Dubuc, A. "Problems in the Study of Stratification of the Canadian Society from 1760 to 1840." In *Studies in Canadian Social History,* edited by M. Horn and R. Sabourin. Toronto: McClelland and Stewart, 1974.

Dunning, E. "Industrialization and the Incipient Modernization of Football." *Stadion* 1(1), 1976.

Dunning, E., and Sheard, K. "The Bifurcation of Rugby Union and Rugby League: A Case Study of Organizational Conflict and Change." *International Review of Sport Sociology* 11 (2), 1976.

————. *Barbarians, Gentlemen and Players.* London: Martin Robertson, 1979.

Durkheim, E. *Moral Education.* New York: The Free Press, 1969.

Earl, D.W. *The Family Compact: Aristocracy or Oligarchy.* Toronto: Copp Clark, 1967.

Easterbrook, W.T., and Watkins, M.H., eds. *Approaches to Canadian Economic History.* Toronto: McClelland and Stewart. 1967.

Edwards, H. *Sociology of Sport.* Homewood: Dorsey, 1973.

Gadamer, H.G. *Philosophical Hermeneutics.* Los Angeles: University of California Press, 1977.

Gear, J. "Factors Influencing the Development of Government-Sponsored Physical Fitness Programmes in Canada From 1850-1972." *Canadian Journal of History of Sport and Physical Education* 4(2), 1973.

Geertz, C. "Deep Play: Notes on the Balinese Cockfight." *Daedalus,* Winter 1972.

Gerth, H.H., and Mills, C.W. *Character and Social Structure.* New York: Harbinger Books, 1964.

Giddens, A. *Capitalism and Modern Social Theory.* Cambridge: Cambridge University Press, 1971.

————. *The Class Structure of the Advanced Societies.* London: Hutchinson Books, 1973.

————. *New Rules of Sociological Method.* New York: Basic Books, 1976.

————. *Studies in Social and Political Theory.* New York: Basic Books, 1977.

Glenday, D. "Unity in Diversity: The Political Economy of Subordination in Canada." In *Power and Change in Canada,* edited by R.J. Ossenberg. Toronto: McClelland and Stewart, 1980.

Goldthorpe, J., et al. *The Affluent Worker.* 3 vols. London: Cambridge University Press, 1968.

Goodman, C. *Choosing Sides: Playground and Street Life on the Lower East Side.* New York: Schocken Books, 1979.

Gouldner, A. *The Coming Crisis of Western Sociology.* New York: Basic Books, 1970.

Gruneau, R. "Sport, Social Differentiation and Social Inequality." In *Sport and Social Order,* edited by D. Ball and J.W. Loy. Reading: Addison-Wesley, 1975.

————. "Sport As an Area of Sociological Study." In *Canadian Sport: Sociological Perspectives,* edited by R. Gruneau and J. Albinson. Toronto: Addison-Wesley, 1976.

————. "Class or Mass? Notes on the Democratization of Canadian Amateur Sport." In *Canadian Sport: Sociological Perspectives,* edited by R. Gruneau and J. Albinson. Toronto; Addison-Wesley, 1976.

————. "Elites, Class and Corporate Power in Canadian Sport: Some Preliminary Findings." In *Sociology of Sport,* edited by F. Landry and W. Orban. Miami: Symposia Specialists, 1978.

————. "Conflicting Standards and Problems of Personal Action in the Sociology of Sport." *Quest* 30, Summer 1978.

————. "Power and Play in Canadian Society." In *Power and Change in Canada,* edited by R.J. Ossenberg. Toronto: McClelland and Stewart, 1980.

————. "Sport and the Debate on the State." In *Sport, Culture and the Modern State,* edited by H. Cantelon and R. Gruneau. Toronto: University of Toronto Press, 1982.

Guay, D. "Problèmes de l'intégration du sport dans la société Canadienne 1830-1865: Les cas des courses de chevaux." *Canadian Journal of History of Sport and Physical Education* 4(2), 1973.

Guttmann, A. *From Ritual to Record: The Nature of Modern Sports.* New York: Columbia University Press, 1978.

Habermas, J. *Toward a Rational Society.* Boston: Beacon Press, 1970.

Hall, S. "The Rediscovery of Ideology: The Return of the Repressed in Media Studies." In *Culture, Society and the Media,* edited by M. Gurevitch, T. Bennett, J. Curran, and I. Woolacott. London: Methuen, 1982.

Hall, S., and Jefferson, T., eds. *Resistance through Rituals.* London: Hutchinson, 1976.

Hallett, W. "A History of Federal Government Involvement in the Development of Sport in Canada, 1943-1979." Ph.D. dissertation, University of Alberta, 1981.

Hans, J. *The Play of the World.* Amherst: University of Massachusetts Press, 1981.

Hargreaves, J. "Sport and Hegemony: Some Theoretical Problems." In *Sport, Culture and the Modern State,* edited by H. Cantelon and R. Gruneau. Toronto: University of Toronto Press, 1982.

Hart, M. *Sport in the Sociocultural Process.* 2d ed. Dubuque: William C. Brown, 1976.

Hearn, F. "Toward a Critical Theory of Play." *Telos* 30, Winter 1976.

Heilbroner, R. "Economic Problems of a 'Post-Industrial' Society." *Dissent,* Spring 1973.

Helmes, R. "Canadian Sport as an Ideological Institution." M.A. Thesis, Queen's University, 1977.

————. "Ideology and Social Control in Canadian Sport: A Theoretical Review." *Working Papers in the Sociological Study of Sports and Leisure,* vol. 1(4). Kingston: Sport Studies Research Group, Queen's University, 1978.

Henricks, T. "Review of *From Ritual to Record.*" *American Journal of Sociology* 85(5), March 1980.

Herman, K. "The Emerging Welfare State: Changing Perspectives in Canadian Welfare Policies and Programs, 1867-1960." In *Social Space:Canadian Perspectives,* edited by D.I. Davies and K. Herman. Toronto: New Press, 1971.

Hoch, P. *Rip Off the Big Game.* New York: Doubleday, 1972.

Hodges, H.M. *Social Stratification.* Cambridge: Schenkman Publishing, 1964.

Hodgins, J.G. *Schools and Colleges of Ontario, 1792-1910,* vol. 1. Toronto: K.K. Cameron, 1910.

Hofstadter, R. *Social Darwinism in American Thought, 1860-1915.* London: Oxford University Press, 1944.

Hollands, R., and Gruneau, R. "Social Class and Voluntary Action in the Administration of Canadian Amateur Sport." *Working Papers in the Sociological Study of Sports and Leisure,* vol. 2(3). Kingston: Sport Studies Research Group, Queen's University, 1979.

Horowitz, I.L. *The New Sociology.* New York: Oxford Press, 1969.

Horowitz, I. "Sports Broadcasting." In *Government and the Sports Business,* edited by R. Noll. The Brookings Institution, 1974.

Houston, S.E. "Politics, Schools and Social Change in Upper Canada." *Canadian Historical Review* 3(3), 1972.

Howard, R., and Scott, J. "International Unions and the Ideology of Class Collaboration." In *Capitalism and the National Question in Canada,* edited by G. Teeple. Toronto: University of Toronto Press, 1972.

Howell, N., and Howell, M. *Sports and Games in Canadian Life.* Toronto: Macmillan, 1969.

Hughes, H.S. *Consciousness and Society.* New York: Vintage Books, 1977.

Huizinga, J. *Homo Ludens.* Boston: Beacon Press, 1955.

Ingham, A.G. "American Sport in Transition: The Maturation of Industrial Capitalism and Its Impact on Sport." Ph.D. dissertation, University of Massachusetts, 1978.

Ingham, A.G., and Loy, J.W. "The Social System of Sport: A Humanistic Perspective." *Quest* 19, 1973.

Inglis, F. *The Name of the Game.* London: Heinemann Books, 1977.

Innis, H. *The Fur Trade in Canada.* Toronto: University of Toronto Press, 1956.

James, C.L.R. *Beyond a Boundary.* London: Hutchinson, 1963.

Jobling, I. "Urbanization and Sport in Canada, 1867-1900." In *Canadian Sport: Sociological Perspectives,* edited by R. Gruneau and J. Albinson. Toronto: Addison-Wesley, 1976.

Johnson, R. "Three Problematics: Elements of a Theory of Working-Class Culture." In *Working Class Culture,* edited by J. Clarke et al. London, 1979.

————. "Histories of Culture/Theories of Ideology: Notes on an Impasse." In *Ideology and Cultural Production,* edited by M. Barrett et al. London: Croom Helm, 1979.

Jones, J.C.H. "The Economics of the National Hockey League." In *Canadian Sport: Sociological Perspectives,* edited by R. Gruneau and J. Albinson. Toronto: Addison-Wesley, 1976.

Kaplan, M. *Leisure in America.* New York: Wiley, 1960.

Kenyon, G. "A Sociology of Sport: On Becoming a Sub-Discipline." In *Sport in American Society,* edited by G.H. Sage. 2d ed. Reading: Addison-Wesley, 1974.

Kenyon, G., and Loy, J.W. "Toward a Sociology of Sport." *Journal of Health, Physical Education and Recreation* 36, 1965.

Kidd, B. "Canadian Participation in the Peoples' Olympic Games of 1936." A paper presented at the annual meeting of the North American Association for Sport History, Windsor, Ontario, 1977.

————. *The Political Economy of Sport.* Ottawa: Canadian Association of Health, Physical Education and Recreation, 1979.

Kiviaho, P., and Simola, M. "Who Leads Sport in Finland?" *Eripainos Sosiologia* N:05-6, 1974.

Kornhauser, P. *The Politics of Mass Society.* Glencoe: The Free Press, 1959.

Kumar, K. *Prophesy and Progress: The Sociology of Industrial and Post-Industrial Society.* Middlesex: Penguin Books, 1978.

Labonte, R. "Half-truths about Health." *Policy Options* 3(1), January/February, 1982.

Laclau, E. *Politics and Ideology in Marxist Theory.* London: New Left Books, 1977.

Larrabee, E., and Meyersohn, R., eds. *Mass Leisure.* Glencoe: The Free Press, 1958.

Lasch, C. "The Corruption of Sports." *The New York Review of Books,* April 28, 1977.

Laxer, R., ed. *Canada Ltd.: The Political Economy of Dependency.* Toronto: McClelland and Stewart, 1973.

Lindsay, P. "A History of Sport in Canada: 1807-1867." Ph.D. dissertation, University of Alberta, 1969.

Lipsky, R. *How We Play the Game: Why Sports Dominate American Life.* Boston: Beacon Press, 1981.

Lipton, C. *The Trade Union Movement of Canada, 1827-1959.* Toronto: New Canada Press, 1967.

Lower, A. "Two Ways of Life: The Primary Antithesis of Canadian History." In *Approaches to Canadian History,* edited by C. Berger. Toronto: University of Toronto Press, 1967.

Loy, J.W. "The Study of Sport and Social Mobility." In *Aspects of Contemporary Sport Sociology,* edited by G.S. Kenyon. Chicago: The Athletic Institute, 1969.

————. "The Cultural System of Sport." *Quest* 29, 1978.

Loy, J.W., and Kenyon, G.S., eds. *Sport, Culture and Society.* Toronto: Macmillan, 1969.

Loy, J.; Kenyon, G.; and McPherson, B. Preface to *Sport, Culture and Society,* 2d ed. Philadelphia: Lea and Febiger, 1981.

Loy, J.; McPherson, B.; and Kenyon, G. *The Sociology of Sport As an Academic Specialty: An Episodic Essay on the Development of an Hybrid Sub-field in North America.* Ottawa: Canadian Association of Health, Physical Education and Recreation, 1978.

Lukes, S. *Individualism.* Oxford: Basil Blackwell, 1973.

————. *Power: A Radical View.* London: Macmillan, 1974.

————. *Emile Durkheim: His Life and Work.* New York: Harper and Row, 1975.

————. *Essays in Social Theory.* New York: Columbia University Press, 1977.

Luschen, G. "The Interdependence of Sport and Culture." In *Sport in the Socio-cultural Process,* edited by Marie Hart. 2d ed. Dubuque: William C. Brown, 1976.

MacIver, R., and Page, C. *Society: An Introductory Analysis.* New York: Rinehart, 1949.

Macintosh, W.A. "Economic Factors in Canadian History." *Canadian Historical Review* 4, March 1923.

Macpherson, C.B. *The Real World of Democracy.* Toronto: Canadian Broadcasting Corporation, 1965.

Macpherson, C.B. *The Life and Times of Liberal Democracy.* London: Oxford, 1977.

Malcolmson, R. *Popular Recreations in English Society, 1700-1850.* London: Cambridge University Press, 1973.

Mallea, J. "The Victorian Sporting Legacy." *McGill Journal of Education* 10(2), 1975.

Mann, M. "The Social Cohesion of Liberal Democracy." *American Sociological Review* 35, June 1970.

Manning, F. "Celebrating Cricket: The Symbolic Construction of Caribbean Politics." *American Ethnologist,* 1981.

Marcuse, H. *Eros and Civilization.* New York: Vintage Books, 1962.

———. *One Dimensional Man.* Boston: Beacon Press, 1964.

Marshall, T.H. *Citizenship and Social Class.* London: Cambridge University Press, 1950.

———. *Class, Citizenship and Social Development.* Chicago: University of Chicago Press, 1977.

Marx, K. *Capital: A Critique of Political Economy,* 3 vols. Moscow: Progress Publishers, 1971.

———. *Grundrisse.* Middlesex: Pelican Books, 1973.

———. "The Eighteenth Brumaire of Louis Bonaparte." In *Karl Marx, Surveys from Exile,* edited by D. Fernbach. Middlesex: Penguin Books, 1973.

———. "The Poverty of Philosophy." In *Collected Works,* by K. Marx and F. Engels. London: Lawrence and Wishart, 1975.

Marx, K., and Engels, F. *The German Ideology.* London: Lawrence and Wishart, 1964.

Mason, T. *Association Football and English Society: 1863-1915.* Highlands, New Jersey: Humanities Press, 1980.

Mayrl, W. Introduction to *Cultural Creation,* by L. Goldmann. St. Louis: Telos Press, 1976.

McFarland, E. *The Development of Public Recreation in Canada.* Ottawa, 1970.

McIntosh, P. *Fair Play: Ethics in Sport and Education.* London: Heinemann Books, 1979.

McNaught, K. *The Pelican History of Canada.* London: Penguin Books, 1969.

Mead, G.H. *Mind, Sell and Society.* Chicago: University of Chicago Press, 1934.

———. *On Social Psychology.* Chicago: University of Chicago Press, 1964.

Metcalfe, A. "Organized Sport and Social Stratification in Montreal: 1840-1901." In *Canadian Sport: Sociological Perspectives,* edited by R. Gruneau and J. Albinson. Toronto: Addison-Wesley, 1976.

———. "Working Class Physical Recreation in Montreal, 1860-1895." *Working Papers in the Sociological Study of Sports and Leisure,* vol. 1(2). Kingston: Sport Studies Research Group, Queen's University, 1978.

———. *The Emergence of Modern Sport in Canada, 1867-1914.* Toronto: McClelland and Stewart, 1983.

Miliband, R. *The State in Capitalist Society.* London: Quartet Books, 1969.

————. *Marxism and Politics.* Oxford: Oxford University Press, 1977.

Mills, C.W. Introduction to *The Theory of the Leisure Class,* by Thorstein Veblen. New York: Mentor Books, 1953.

————. *The Power Elite.* Oxford: Oxford University Press, 1956.

————. "The Classic Tradition." In *Images of Man,* edited by C.W. Mills. New York: George Braziller, 1960.

————. *The Sociological Imagination.* Middlesex: Penguin Books, 1970.

Moir, J.S. *Church and State in Canada, 1627-1867.* Toronto: McClelland and Stewart, 1967.

Myers, G. *A History of Canadian Wealth.* Toronto: James Lewis and Samuel, 1972.

Naylor, R.T. "The Rise and Fall of the Third Commercial Empire of the St. Lawrence." In *Capitalism and the National Question in Canada,* edited by G. Teeple. Toronto: University of Toronto Press, 1972.

————. *The History of Canadian Business.* 2 vols. Toronto: James Lorimer, 1975.

Novak, M. *The Joy of Sports.* New York: Basic Books, 1976.

Okner, B. "Taxation and Sports Enterprises." In *Government and the Sports Business,* edited by R. Noll. Washington: The Brookings Institution, 1974.

Oliman, B. *Alienation: Marx's Conception of Man in Capitalist Society.* Cambridge: Cambridge University Press, 1971.

Page, C.H. "An Introduction Thirty Years Later." In *Class and American Sociology.* New York: Schocken Books, 1969.

————. "The World of Sport and Its Study." In *Sport and Society,* edited by J. Talamini and C.H. Page. Boston: Little Brown, 1973.

Palmer, B. "Discordant Music: Charivaris and Whitecapping in Nineteenth-Century North America." *Labour/Le Travailleur* 3 (1978).

Palmer, B. *A Culture in Conflict: Skilled Workers and Industrial Capitalism in Hamilton Ontario, 1860-1914.* Montreal: McGill-Queen's University Press, 1979.

Panitch, L. "The Role and Nature of the Canadian State." In *The Canadian State: Political Economy and Political Power,* edited by L. Panitch. Toronto: University of Toronto Press, 1977.

Parkin, F. *Class Inequality and Political Order.* London: Paladin Books, 1972.

————. "Strategies of Social Closure in Class Formation." In *The Social Analysis of Class Structure,* edited by Frank Parkin. London: Tavistock, 1974.

Parsons, T. *The Structure of Social Action.* Glencoe: The Free Press, 1949.

Patterson, O. "The Cricket Ritual in the West Indies." *New Society* 352, June 26, 1969.

Pentland, H.C. "The Role of Capital in Canadian Economic Development before 1875." *Canadian Journal of Economics and Political Science* 16 (1950).

————. *Labour and Capital in Canada, 1650-1860.* Toronto: James Lorimer, 1981.

Piaget, J. *Play, Dreams and Imitation in Childhood.* New York: Norton and Company, 1962.

Porter, J. *The Vertical Mosaic.* Toronto: University of Toronto Press, 1966.

Poulantzas, N. "The Problem of the Capitalist State." In *Ideology in Social Science,* edited by R. Blackburn. New York: Vintage Books, 1973.

Prentice, A. *The School Promoters.* Toronto: McClelland and Stewart, 1977.

Rader, B. "Modern Sports: In Search of Interpretations." *Journal of Social History,* Winter 1979.

Rex, J. *Sociology and the Demystification of the Modern World.* London: Routledge and Kegan, 1974.

————. "Threatening Theories." *Society* 15(3), 1978.

Ricoeur, P. *History and Truth.* Evanston, Illinois, 1965.

Roberts, T. "The Influence of the British Upper Class on the Development of the Values Claim for Sport in the Public Education System of Upper Canada." *Canadian Journal of History of Sport and Physical Education* 4(1), 1973.

Rosenberg, B., and White, D.M., eds. *Mass Culture: The Popular Arts of America.* New York: The Free Press, 1957.

Ross, P.S., and Partners. *A Report on Physical Recreation, Fitness and Amateur Sport in Canada.* Ottawa: Health and Welfare: Directorate of Fitness and Amateur Sport, 1969.

Roxborough, H. *One Hundred-Not Out: The Story of Nineteenth Century Canadian Sport.* Toronto: Ryerson Press, 1966.

Rutherford, P. *The Making of the Canadian Media.* Toronto: McGraw-Hill Ryerson, 1978.

Ryerson, S. *Unequal Union.* Toronto: Progress Books, 1973.

Sage, G., ed. *Sport in American Society.* Reading: Addison-Wesley, 1974.

Scriven, M. "Truisms As Grounds for Historical Explanations." In *Theories of History,* edited by P. Gardiner. New York, 1959.

Searle, J. *Speech Acts: An Essay in the Philosophy of Language.* Cambridge: Cambridge University Press, 1969.

Shea, A. *Broadcasting the Canadian Way.* Montreal: Harvest House, 1963.

Shotter, J. "Prolegomena to an Understanding of Play." *Journal for the Theory of Social Behaviour* 3(1), 1973.

Simmel, G. *Georg Simmel: On Individuality and Social Forms.* Chicago: University of Chicago Press, 1971.

Simpson, R. "The Influence of the Montreal Curling Club on the Development of Curling in the Canada's, 1807-1857." M.A. thesis, University of Western Ontario, 1980.

Smith, G., and Blackman, C. *Sport in the Mass Media.* Ottawa: Canadian Association of Health, Physical Education and Recreation, 1979.

Smith, M.D. "Sport and Collective Violence." In *Sport and Social Order,* edited by J. Loy and D. Ball. Reading: Addison-Wesley, 1975.

Smith, M.D., and Diamond, F. "Career Mobility in Professional Hockey." *In Canadian Sport: Sociological Perspectives,* edited by R. Gruneau and J. Albinson. Toronto: Addison-Wesley, 1976.

Steinberg, D. "The Workers' Sport Internationals, 1920-28." *Journal of Contemporary History* 13(2), April 1978.

Stone, G. "American Sport: Play and Display." In *Sport and Society,* edited by J. Talamini and C.H. Page. Boston: Little Brown, 1973.

Sutton-Smith, B. "Piaget on Play: A Critique." In *Child's Play,* edited by R. Herron and B. Sutton-Smith. New York: John Wiley, 1971.

———. "Games of Order and Disorder." In *Sport in the Modern World: Changes and Problems,* edited by O. Gruppe. Berlin: Verlag, 1974.

———. "Toward an Anthropology of Play." In *Sport in the Socio-Cultural Process,* 3rd ed., edited by Marie Hart and Susan Birrell. Dubuque: William C. Brown, 1981.

Swingewood, A. *The Myth of Mass Culture.* New Jersey: Humanities Press, 1977.

Talamini, J., and Page, C.H., eds. *Sport and Society.* Boston: Little Brown, 1977.

Taylor, C. "Hermeneutics and Politics." In *Critical Sociology,* edited by P. Connerton. Middlesex: Penguin Books, 1976.

Taylor, I. "Class Violence and Sport: The Case of Soccer Hooliganism in England." In *Sport, Culture and the Modern State,* edited by H. Cantelon and R. Gruneau. Toronto: University of Toronto Press, 1982.

Teeple, G., ed. *Capitalism and the National Question in Canada.* Toronto: University of Toronto Press, 1972.

———. "Land, Labour and Capital in Pre-Confederation Canada." In *Capitalism and the National Question in Canada,* edited by G. Teeple. Toronto: University of Toronto Press, 1972.

Thompson, E.P. "Time, Work-Discipline and Industrial Capitalism." *Past and Present* 38, December 1967.

———. *The Making of the English Working Class.* Harmondsworth: Pelican Books, 1968.

———. *The Poverty of Theory and Other Essays.* New York: Monthly Review Press, 1978.

Touraine, A. *La société post-industrielle.* Paris: Denoël, 1969.

Tulchinsky, G. "The Montreal Business Community, 1837-1853." In *Canadian Business History,* edited by D.S. Macmillan. Toronto: McClelland and Stewart, 1972.

Underhill, F. "The Liberal Tradition in Canada." In *Approaches to Canadian History,* edited by C. Berger. Toronto: University of Toronto Press, 1967.

Veblen, T. *The Theory of the Leisure Class.* New York: Mentor Books, 1953.

Vinnai, G. *Football Mania.* London: Ocean Books, 1973.

Watkins, G. "Professional Team Sports and Competition Policy: A Case Study of the Canadian Football League." Ph.D. dissertation, University of Alberta, 1972.

Webb, H. "Reaction to Loy's Paper." In *Aspects of Contemporary Sport Sociology,* edited by G.S. Kenyon. Chicago: The Athletic Institute, 1969.

Weber, E. "Gymnastics and Sports in fin-de-siècle France: Opium of the Classes." *American Historical Review* 76 (1), 1971.

Weber, M. *The Protestant Ethic and the Spirit of Capitalism.* New York: Charles Scribner, 1958.

———. *Economy and Society.* New York: Bedminster Press, 1968.

Weiler, J. "The Idea of Sport in Late Victorian Canada." A paper presented at the Canadian Historical Association Annual Meeting, Kingston, June 1974.

West, T. "Physical Fitness, Sport and the Federal Government 1909 to 1954." *Canadian Journal of History of Sport and Physical Education* 4 (2), December 1973.

Wheeler, R.F. "Organized Sport and Organized Labour." *Journal of Contemporary History* 13(2), April 1978.

White, M. *Social Thought in America: The Revolt against Formalism.* Boston: Beacon Press, 1957.

Wilkinson, R. *Gentlemanly Power: British Leadership and Public School Tradition.* New York: Oxford University Press, 1964.

Williams, R. *Culture and Society.* London: Chatto and Windus, 1958.

———. *The Long Revolution.* Middlesex: Penguin Books, 1965.

———. "Base and Superstructure in Marxist Cultural Theory." *New Left Review* 82(8), November-December 1973.

———. *Marxism and Literature.* Oxford: Oxford University Press, 1977.

Willis, P. *Learning to Labour: How Working Class Kids Get Working Class Jobs.* Westmead: Saxon House, 1977.

Wise, S.F. "Sport and Class Values in Old Ontario and Quebec." In *His Own Man: Essays in Honour of A.R.M. Lower,* edited by W.H. Heick and R. Graham. Montreal: McGill-Queen's Press, 1974.

Wise, S.F., and Fisher, D. *Canada's Sporting Heroes.* Toronto: General Publishing, 1974.

Wolff, K. *The Sociology of C. Simmel.* New York: The Free Press, 1950.

index

credits

Parts of chapter 1 were originally published in the *Journal of Sport History* 7, no. 3 (1980), and are reprinted by permission of the North American Society for Sport History. Much of the material included in chapter 3 was originally published in *Working Papers in the Sociological Study of Sports and Leisure* 2, no. 1 (1979) and is reprinted here with permission of the Queen's University Centre for Sport and Leisure Studies. Quotations from frequently cited works appear with permission: Anthony Giddens, *Class Structure of the Advanced Societies,* Hutchinson Books, © 1973, and *Studies in Social and Political Theory* Basic Books, © 1977; Fred Inglis, *The Name of the Game,* Heinemann Books, © 1977; Paul Willis, *Learning to Labour: How Working Class Kids Get Working Class Jobs,* © Saxon House (1977) and Columbia University Press (1981). Clifford Geertz, "Deep Play: Notes on the Balinese Cockfight" reprinted by permission of *Daedalus,* Journal of the American Academy of Arts and Sciences, from the issue titled "Myth, Symbol, and Culture," Winter 1972, vol. 101, no. 1.

about the author

Richard Gruneau is Professor of Communication at Simon Fraser University in Burnaby, British Columbia, where he teaches in the areas of mass media and popular culture, cultural studies, and the political economy of communication. He received a PhD in sociology from the University of Massachusetts.

Professor Gruneau is the coauthor of *The Missing News: Filters and Blindspots in Canada's News Media*. He is also the co-author, with David Whitson, of *Hockey Night in Canada: Sport, Identities, and Cultural Politics*. In addition, he has edited or coedited four other books and is the author of more than forty book chapters, scholarly articles, and research papers.

Professor Gruneau has been principal researcher, coresearcher, or consultant to several nationally funded research projects in Canada. These studies include examining and exposing neglected issues in the Canadian news media, a study of television sports production in Canada, and government sport policy in Canada. He is also the originator and academic editor of a recent book series entitled *Culture and Communication in Canada*.

The author currently serves on the editorial boards of three scholarly journals: *Body and Society*, *The Canadian Journal of Sociology*, and *The Canadian Journal of Communication*.

Related Books From Human Kinetics

Power and Ideology in American Sport
A Critical Perspective, Second Edition
George H. Sage

1998 • Paper • 344 pp • Item BSAG0660
ISBN 0-88011-660-9 • $29.00 ($43.50 Canadian)

This popular, widely acclaimed analysis of sport in America is now completely updated, with expanded treatment of contemporary issues. Clear, accessible, and passionately argued, *Power and Ideology in American Sport* challenges the status quo of big-time sport and points the way toward a more humane, equitable sporting culture.

Feminism and Sporting Bodies
Essays on Theory and Practice
M. Ann Hall

1996 • Paper • 144 pp • Item BHAL0969
ISBN 0-87322-969-X • $22.00 ($27.95 Canadian)

Examine the history, current trends, and future of gender relations in sport through the eyes of one of the field's most recognized authorities. *Feminism and Sporting Bodies* traces Ann Hall's 30-year journey across the feminist terrain—from liberal, radical, Marxist, and socialist feminism to more recent trends in contemporary cultural theory in sport.

Strong Women, Deep Closets
Lesbians and Homophobia in Sport
Pat Griffin

1998 • Paper • 264 pp • Item BGRI0729
ISBN 0-88011-729-X • $19.95 ($29.95 Canadian)

In *Strong Women, Deep Closets*, former athlete and coach Pat Griffin provides a critical analysis of discrimination and prejudice against lesbians in sport. The author lists obstacles lesbian athletes face in transforming sports and details numerous personal and political strategies for leveling the playing field.

To request more information or to order, U.S. customers call 1-800-747-4457, e-mail us at humank@hkusa.com, or visit our Web site at http://www.humankinetics.com/. Persons outside the U.S. can contact us via our Web site or use the appropriate telephone number, postal address, or e-mail address shown in the front of this book.

HUMAN KINETICS
The Information Leader in Physical Activity
P.O. Box 5076, Champaign, IL 61825-5076
2335